# Fully Instructed and Vehemently Influenced

## Catholic Preaching in Anglo-Colonial America

# Fully Instructed and Vehemently Influenced

## Catholic Preaching in Anglo-Colonial America

BY

JOSEPH C. LINCK

SAINT JOSEPH'S UNIVERSITY PRESS

PHILADELPHIA

Linck, Joseph C., 1964-
   "Fully instructed and vehemently influenced": Catholic preaching in
Anglo-Colonial America / by Joseph C. Linck
      p. cm.
Includes bibliographical references and index.
   ISBN 0-916101-40-1
   1. Catholic preaching--Maryland--History--18th century. 2. Catholic
preaching--Pennsylvania--History--18th century. I. Title.
BV4208.U6 L56 2001
251'.0088'22--dc21

                                                         2001005135

Published by:
Saint Joseph's University Press
5600 City Avenue
Philadelphia, Pennsylvania 19131-1395


Saint Joseph's University Press is a member
of the Association of Jesuit University Presses

# Table of Contents

# LIST OF ILLUSTRATIONS

# FOREWORD

Catholics in British America, John Adams once remarked, were as
rare as earthquakes. In much of Anglo-Colonial America, Adams's
hyperbole had a point. But in an area of the mid-Atlantic region, from
southeastern Pennsylvania to both shores of Maryland, there was a
small but significant Catholic community that stretched back, in
Maryland, to the first third of the seventeenth century. For much of its
history, this community of Roman Catholic laymen and Jesuit priests
and brothers lived in an outcast, if not outlaw status. From 1689, when
the Catholic Calverts were overthrown as proprietors of the Maryland
colony, to the American Revolution, Catholics in Maryland, who
constituted the vast majority of their faith in British America, lived
under the same penal laws that their ancestors had fled England to
escape: unable to vote, to worship publicly, to hold public office; taxed
to support an Anglican clergy; fined for educating their children in
Catholic schools abroad; and forbidden to inherit property unless they
swore the oath of allegiance to their monarch as head of the Church of
England. Catholic priests were virtually barred from the colony under
the threat of life imprisonment. The fact that the laws involving
education, property, and the admission of priests went largely un-
enforced still left no doubt about the status of Catholics. Periodically
there were threats to invoke all of the penal laws, such as in the 1750s
during the French and Indian War, when Catholics in Maryland were

accused, or at least suspected, of conspiring with the Catholic imperial enemy. Priests were arrested on a few occasions on charges that ranged from saying Mass to being French agents, but they were never convicted or imprisoned. Several attempts were made to seize the extensive property of the Society of Jesus, but Protestant gentry, with many ties by marriage to their Catholic counterparts, invariably stopped the efforts in the legislature. In general, the Catholic community not only survived this "penal age," but also in some respects could be said to have flourished in the late colonial period. Despite the political and religious disabilities, there were apparently few defections from the faith, at least among the Catholic gentry; indeed the community grew, bolstered not only by the influx of Irish indentured servants, but also by conversions among Maryland natives as well. A number of prominent Protestant families by the middle of the eighteenth century had Catholic branches, at least in part due to the preaching and influence of the Catholic clergy, if complaining Anglicans can be believed. In the same period there was a great traffic of Catholic children crossing the Atlantic to secure education in one of the schools English Catholics had established in Flanders. Leading Catholic families in Maryland—the Boones, Boarmans, Brookes, Carrolls, Digges, Neales, Semmes, and Sewalls—all sent several sons and daughters abroad. Out of this group came scores of religious vocations to the Jesuits, Carmelites, and other religious orders.

By the American Revolution Catholics numbered some 35,000 in British America, yet, except for some of the leading gentry, like Charles Carroll or Richard Bennett, all too little is known of these Catholics, including the priests. Hence the immense value of the more than 460 sermons, virtually all from the eighteenth century, that have survived in the American Catholic Sermon Collection at Georgetown University. Among the Catholic clergy in America, the tradition of the written sermon prevailed, amid an American evangelical culture that was increasingly prizing the reliance on inspiration rather than preparation in preaching the Word, and fortunately a great number of sermons have come down to us. Father Joseph Linck is the first historian to plumb them as an entry into the life of that largely hidden community. As he shows so well, despite the highly derivative character of most of the sermons, the clergy who adopted them from various sources also, in many if not most cases, adapted them extensively to the context in which they were being preached so that they "provide an intriguing glimpse into the life and teaching of a group of men who left behind little else to describe their work and ministry," as well as "offer us a window into the religious life and practice of the Catholic "pioneers" of Anglo-colonial America." For such knowledge and understanding of this little known community, this volume is welcome indeed.

These were not the brief homilies modern Catholics are accustomed to hearing. The typical sermon, he concludes, took more than a half hour to deliver. It was the centerpiece in the ongoing education and formation of congregations by the itinerant priests who served them. The clergy in Anglo-America, he notes, took very seriously their obligation to serve as moral and religious guides to their hearers living in a hostile, challenging world. And the pulpit was the major forum they had for such guidance. "Theirs was a very practical homiletics," to ensure that their flocks, as Father Richard Molyneux put it in the second quarter of the eighteenth century, were "fully instructed and vehemently influenced." This was a preaching that largely focused on behavior and not belief, conduct and not dogma. It was a preaching that was very situation-oriented, in the sense that the preachers were attempting to address the actual conditions in which their hearers lived. Their larger purpose was to sustain a community amid a larger society that both contemned Catholics and disabled them civilly and politically. Through the sermons one catches glimpses of the moral shortcomings and challenges of the Catholic community in America, ranging from the dangers of mixed marriages, in a society in which it was customary to raise the child in the religion of his or her parent, to the material and spiritual care of the slaves who constituted a fifth of the Catholics in Maryland.

Under Father Linck's scrutiny the sermons reveal a traditional but unique Catholic culture in which devotion to the saints, particularly to Mary and Ignatius Loyola, was seen as a distinctive witness to the authenticity of Catholic Christianity in a largely Protestant world. The rosary was an integral part of the community's prayer life; spiritual reading and the sacraments (particularly the Eucharist and Reconciliation) were at the core of Anglo-American Catholic public practice. As Father Linck points out, the reception, indeed frequent reception, of Holy Communion was regarded as the key to the experience of *metanoia* in the life of individual Catholics. The concrete practice of charity, mini-retreats, and a certain amount of penance, such as fasting, were seen as staples of a devout life. During the course of the eighteenth century, there was a growth in devotion to the Blessed Sacrament, with the introduction of Benediction and Eucharistic exposition into the spiritual culture of the Catholic community.

Highly conscious of their minority status within an, at least nominally, Protestant world, Catholic preachers focused on the distinctions that made Catholicism the true Church within Christendom. In the early part of the century, there was a rather hard-edged attitude toward Protestants as heretics. By the end of the century, a John Carroll was regarding them, not as heretics, but as brethren, who, for all their erring ways, were part of the Church.

If Catholics were outspoken about their Protestant neighbors, they were, unlike their Protestant counterparts, extremely reticent about political matters. Given their precarious standing in American society, this was entirely natural. One searches in vain during the colonial period for a sermon such as Carroll delivered sometime after the Revolution in which he praised the American rebellion as the precise instrument through which "Divine providence has so directed the course of human affairs; the Holy Ghost has so worked upon & tutored the minds of men, that now . . . we [Catholics] may sing canticles of praise to the Lord, in a country no longer foreign or unfriendly to us [as British America had been] but in a country now become our own, & taking us into her protection" (undated Carroll sermon, American Catholic Sermon Collection, Georgetown

University Special Collections). By that time Catholics had already proven their right to full citizenship through their war record, including that of Carroll. By that time the Catholic colonial community was a memory. Thanks to Father Linck's work, we now have a better purchase on that memory.

Robert Emmett Curran
Georgetown University

# Acknowledgements

The Jesuit George Hunter, one of the homilists whose work makes up this study, is credited with penning a "Birthday Soliloquy," dated 14 April 1749. In this poetical examination of conscience, he asks: "Have I been faithful in the important trust / Both to my God, myself, and neighbor just?" I would be less than faithful if I failed to offer my thanks to those "neighbors just" who assisted me in this undertaking.

First, to George Berringer and his staff at the Georgetown University Special Collections, who were good enough to put up with my endless daily requests for files and boxes over a period of five months, my thanks for their never-failing assistance, support and encouragement.

Thanks also go to Garner Raney of the Archives of the Episcopal Diocese of Maryland, who met my requests for information on colonial Anglican sermons with exceptional kindness and courtesy, and made the time I spent working in the archives a distinct pleasure.

I am indebted as well to Susan Ramaswamy and Robert Sette for the invaluable assistance they offered in the translation of numerous French sermons.

Two sons of St. Ignatius aided me in my research. Rev. William Clancy, S.J., was kind enough to share with me his insights into published English Catholic homiletic material, and Rev. Charles Edwards O'Neill, S.J., earned my gratitude and admiration for not only introducing me to colonial Catholic spirituality and the sermons themselves in a fateful seminar in the spring of 1989, but also for the support he has continued to offer over the years.

Rev. Bede Peay provided me with invaluable guidance as I investigated the state of research into American homiletics, both Protestant and Catholic. My thanks to him too for his constant encouragement during the dark days of putting pen to paper; like his namesake, he was always willing "to learn, to teach, and to write."

There will always be a special place in my heart for my dear friends Ruth O'Halloran and Raymond Kupke, with whom I have shared the highs and lows of my scholastic journey (as well as many other "rambles"), and also the members of the Oratory of Saint Philip Neri in Pittsburgh, who suffered with me (and from me) during the long years of research and writing. I am grateful as well to Rev. Leo Stajkowski, pastor of St. Mary's Church in Reading, Pa., and its parishioners, for their kind hospitality during the revision of this manuscript.

I am deeply indebted to my director and readers, without whose constant guidance, support and encouragement this work—which began life as a dissertation at The Catholic University of America— would never have been completed. Rev. Msgr. Robert Trisco and Dr. Christopher Kauffman gave generously of their time and talents. Each of them has offered not only direction and advice, but also the impressive and compelling witness of their own scholarly dedication to furthering the historical understanding of Christ's Church.

This book would never have seen the light of day without the enthusiastic support of Rev. Joseph Chorpenning, O.S.F.S., and the staff at Saint Joseph's University Press. They have my thanks and gratitude for making a dream come true.

Finally, I must thank my mother and father for their constant love and support. Truly, they have inspired and nourished my own love for the Church from my youth, and have been a continual source of inspiration and encouragement throughout my seemingly endless scholarly pursuits. It is to them, with my deepest love, affection and gratitude, that I dedicate this work.

# List of Abbreviations

ACSC    American Catholic Sermon Collection

AEDM    Archives of the Episcopal Diocese of Maryland

JCP     The John Carroll Papers

MPA     Archives of the Maryland Province of the Society of Jesus

# Introduction

From the earliest days of the Church, preaching has always occupied an honored place in Christian life and worship. St. Justin Martyr, setting forth the teachings and practices of those who followed "the Way" in the middle of the second century, wrote the following: "On the day which is called Sunday we have a common assembly of all who live in the cities or in the outlying districts, and the memoirs of the Apostles or the writings of the Prophets are read, as long as there is time. Then, when the reader has finished, the president of the assembly verbally admonishes and invites all to imitate such examples of virtue."[1] From the time of the Apostles to the present day, homilists have been inviting and admonishing their congregations to ponder the Gospel more deeply, and model their lives on its teachings.

The style and substance of what is preached has of course varied down through the centuries. The faithful have been charmed by the simplicity of a Francis of Assisi, transfixed by the denunciations of a Savanarola, enthralled by the quiet eloquence of a John Henry Newman—and, we must not hesitate to add, bored to distraction by countless preachers far less eloquent! Yet, as St. Paul, the exemplar of preachers, has declared, "faith comes through what is heard" (Rom 10:17); regardless of the style of preaching, "how can they believe in him of whom they have not heard?" (Rom 10:14)

The inhabitants of the thirteen British colonies of colonial America, though they dwelt on the frontiers of a new world, were not deprived of the comforts and challenges offered by the preached word, for preaching held an important place in their lives. Indeed, the eighteenth century in colonial America has been called an era marked by "great preaching."[2] Although the quality of the sermons seems to have varied with the denomination under consideration,[3] there was no doubt that most ministers were zealous in their dedication to spreading the Gospel—even traveling as "circuit-riders" to reach up to twenty-four different pulpits a month—a devotion which "drove them forth into every nook and corner of a needy land."[4] Colonists who were unable to attend church on a regular basis, and who were wealthy enough to afford a library at home, often read from a book of sermons "to comfort or strengthen [their] faith."[5]

When we read such comments about the colonial churches, however, we need to remind ourselves that they most often refer to Protestant preachers and their flocks. Were we to inquire about the homiletic activity of the marginalized but energetic Catholic missionaries of Maryland and Pennsylvania, most authors fall silent, and note there is little material on which to base any evaluation. Typical in this regard is Donald Smith, who in his comprehensive treatment of eighteenth-century American preaching, in the few pages devoted to the Roman Catholic church, writes: "It is difficult to evaluate Catholic preaching, since so little has been written on the movement from the preaching standpoint."[6] He does remark: "The Catholic Church was not a preaching church. Much like the Anglican, the Catholic Church was strong on ritual. Though not a preaching pulpit, it was definitely an aggressive pulpit."[7]

Indeed, it must be said that until fairly recently the study of Catholic preaching in the United States was a *terra incognita.* "Compared with Protestant preaching," writes Jay Dolan, "very little is known about Catholic preaching in the United States."[8] The best source, in a technical sense, for information concerning standards for preaching in American Catholicism is Robert F. McNamara's *Catholic Sunday Preaching: The American Guidelines, 1791-1975,* though this only summarizes official precepts.[9] A number of studies have been written on twentieth-century developments in American Catholic homiletics,[10] but nothing has yet appeared which analyzes in a thematic way the history and development of this preaching from colonial times.[11] Colonial Catholic homiletics has attracted little attention, perhaps because of the assumption that little relevant material survives from the eighteenth century (after all, Catholics constituted only 1 percent of the population in 1785).

The mostly Jesuit clergy who cared for the colonial Catholics were hardly careless with the texts of the sermons they delivered, however, and so an archive of their homiletic efforts does indeed survive, consisting of 462 separate texts, all of them composed prior to the year 1801.[12] Almost all of the sermons in this collection were preached in Maryland and Pennsylvania, where the vast majority of the Catholic population in the English-speaking colonies was concentrated until the turn of the century. They represent the homiletic labors of forty-four Catholic priests, all but four of whom were at one time members of the Society of Jesus.[13] Of course there are a number of preachers whose sermons are not contained in the collection,[14] as well as a large number of Jesuit sermons that will forever remain unknown.

Reading through these homilies is a fascinating experience. Taken in their entirety, they provide an intriguing glimpse into the life and teaching of a group of men who left behind little else to describe their work and ministry. Though the sermons contain within them no great surprises (e.g., no hitherto unknown information relating to the attitude of Catholics toward the War for Independence), they do disclose fascinating information relating to their originality, the sources used in their composition, their presentation of Catholic doctrine and behavior, and the attitude of their authors toward society at large.

Harold A. Bosley, in his essay "The Role of Preaching in American History," has identified a number of themes in Protestant preaching that are, with certain adaptations, helpful in analyzing this body of colonial Catholic preaching. The six aspects he highlights are: (1) a fundamental concern with the Word of God as found in Scripture, (2) an emphasis on a personal experience of salvation, (3) the great weight given to the explication of correct doctrine, (4) a hostile and critical stance with regard to Roman Catholicism, (5) a strong regard for personal morality and public order, and (6) a level of involvement in issues of contemporary concern.[15] These categories can be briefly summarized as a preacher's concern for: sources, experience, doctrine, relations with other churches, morality, and society. If these broad characterizations of Bosley's schema are accurate, then his thematic summary remains, *mutatis mutandis*, a valuable aid in interpreting colonial Catholic sermons.

For example, while the homilists were reliant on Scripture to a lesser degree than their Protestant brothers, they did make ample use of Scriptural citations and allusions throughout their sermons, and indeed almost always headed their manuscripts with a scriptural text. In addition, they made use of a broad range of other sources for their homilies, including (but not limited to): teachings of church councils, writings of the Fathers of the church, and moralistic examples from classical antiquity.

While Catholic preaching was not aimed as squarely at a personal experience of salvation as was Protestant preaching, the missioners did seek to encourage their listeners to commit themselves as individuals to the Catholic faith in light of the challenging conditions in which they lived. Like their Protestant counterparts, the Catholic missioners stressed both the nature of correct doctrine and the necessity of its being professed, and though their sectarian rhetoric was perhaps not as fiery as that being preached against them, they definitely adopted a critical stance towards their "separated brethren." Morality was also a primary concern in their preaching, though, unlike the Protestant preachers, they almost never commented on current events or political developments (as one would expect considering the precarious nature of their social position). Using the above six criteria as a framework for a discussion of the sermons is thus quite helpful, for it serves to highlight the various aspects of colonial Catholic preaching, weaving together elements of history, theology, spirituality and rhetoric.

I would argue the sermons are best understood as catechesis, as an attempt—and a highly successful one at that—by their authors to nurture and sustain the faith of a scattered flock. The diaspora condition in which the colonial Catholics lived, as well as the proselytizing influence of the denominations surrounding them and the general inertia of an often hostile culture, gave rise to many strains that threatened their ability to live out their faith and hand it on to their children.[16]

In this regard there is some basis for seeing the colonial Catholic homilists as following in the tradition of the "mission" priests of seventeenth and eighteenth century Europe, and as forerunners of the parish mission preachers of mid-nineteenth century America. While for the majority of his flock the visit of the colonial missioner was not an event that occurred only once every few years (like that of a typical "mission priest"), their aims were very much the same. One author has described the components of a seventeenth century mission as "preaching, catechizing, reminding the people of the great truths of their faith, moving hearts and souls, and...hearing confessions,"[17] while a historian of the Catholic missions of nineteenth-century America has noted that the mission "whatever its duration...provided a period of intense preaching, the possibility of receiving the sacraments of Penance and the Eucharist, and the opportunity of getting religion and setting one's self straight with God...."[18] Similarly, the routine of the colonial homilists also consisted of sporadic visits to outlying communities which would include Mass, preaching, confession, and catechetical instruction. The sermons formed an integral part of this experience.[19]

Our first chapter will sketch the historical background of the Catholic community in Maryland and Pennsylvania—in particular the life of the Jesuit missionaries, drawn in part from some personal "asides" contained in the homilies. The second chapter will offer an introduction to the sermons from a literary standpoint as well as an examination of their structure and the sources used in their composition. This literary analysis, while not exhaustive, will provide some tentative conclusions about the originality of the sermons. The third and fourth chapters present the spiritual and moral teaching presented in the sermons, arranged around the themes of the Christian's struggle against the "world" and the cultivation of the spiritual life. The fifth chapter then discusses the way in which the homilists regarded the culture (both religious and political) in which they lived.

The sermons offer us a window into the religious life and practice of the Catholic "pioneers" of Anglo-colonial America, whose quiet existence, both by choice and by necessity, leaves so few avenues of access. The Maryland and Pennsylvania Catholics found themselves very much on the "frontier" of the New World, isolated in varying degrees both physically and spiritually from the culture around them.[20] The circuit-riding priests of colonial America ministered to this dispersed flock as best they could, with dedication and commitment. Though their preaching was but one of many ways in which they supported and nurtured this community throughout the difficult eighteenth century, it was certainly one through which their hearers could claim to be "fully instructed and vehemently influenced."[21]

## NOTES

1   *The First Apology*, trans. Thomas B. Falls (New York: Christian Heritage, 1948), 67.

2   Donald George Smith, "Eighteenth Century American Preaching — A Historical Survey" (Ph.D. diss., Northern Baptist Theological Seminary, 1956), 29.

3   Smith judges Congregational "New Light" preaching to have been "straightforward and down to earth and yet more doctrinal and scholarly than that of other Eighteenth Century preaching." On the other hand, Presbyterian sermons "consisted of much polemics against the practice of others," Baptist preaching "was marked by sobriety and simplicity," and Anglican sermons were judged "ineffective with little spark or fire." Ibid., 88, 105, 225, 324.

4    Harold A. Bosley, "The Role of Preaching in American History," in *Preaching in American History*, ed. Dewitte Holland (Nashville: Abingdon Press, 1969), 29.

5    Richard Beale Davis, *Intellectual Life in the Colonial South. 1585-1763*, 2 vols. (Knoxville: University of Tennessee Press, 1978), 2:581. Davis notes that "Those less likely to read for themselves were likely to hear at a service on an average Sunday (for then the clergyman was likely to be at another place) some one of the sermons of a great English preacher read by a layman (lay reader) in charge of the service...." Idem.

6    Smith, 337. Richard Davis likewise overlooks the subject of Catholic preaching in his treatment of sermons in the context of Southern Colonial intellectual life, while not omitting the activities of Anglican preachers in Maryland. *Intellectual Life*, 2:585, 705-24.

7    Smith, 346.

8    Jay Dolan, *The Immigrant Church* (Baltimore: Johns Hopkins University Press, 1975), 141.

9    (Washington, D.C.: Word of God Institute, 1975).

10   See, for example, Bede S. Peay, O.S.B., "Change in the Theology and Practice of Preaching in the Roman Catholic Church in the United States, 1935-1983" (Ph.D. diss., St. Louis University, 1990); Harold Edgar Scott, "The Renewal of Preaching in the Roman Catholic Church in America" (Th.D. diss., Princeton Theological Seminary, 1966); and William Henry Levering, "The Development of the Field of Homiletics in America from 1960-1983" (Ph.D. diss., Temple University, 1986).

11   A model for such a study might be Joseph Connors' excellent "Catholic Homiletic Theory in Historical Perspective" (Ph.D. diss., Northwestern University, 1962).

12   These sermons, once dispersed among the collections of Georgetown University, Woodstock College, and the Maryland Province of the Society of Jesus, are now preserved in the Special Collections of Georgetown University as the "American Catholic Sermon Collection", where they were identified, arranged and catalogued by George Berringer, the Director. Robert Emmett Curran, S.J., has made use of the collection as part of his study of Jesuit spirituality, resulting in an admirable introduction to the Jesuit homilists and their themes, which has been used as a foundation for my research: *American Jesuit Spirituality. The Maryland Tradition, 1634-1900* (New York: Paulist Press, 1988).

13   The four non-Jesuits are: Germain Barnabas Bitouzey, Francis Fleming, Simon Francis Gallagher, and Ambrose Maréchal. Though it is true that after the suppression of the Jesuits in 1773 those priests ministering in the colonies (all of whom remained in their particular ministry) were no longer members of the Society of Jesus (which would not be restored until the beginning of the nineteenth century), in this study terms like "Jesuit homilists" will often be used to refer to the homilists as a whole.

14   One could point, for example, to the sermons delivered by the chaplain of the

French legation in Philadelphia, Fr. Seraphim Bandol, on 4 July 1779, and 4 November 1781, to a distinguished ecumenical audience at St. Mary's Church, which are reprinted in Peter Guilday, *The Life and Times of John Carroll,* 2 vols. (New York: The Encyclopedia Press, 1922), 1:107-110.

15  Bosley, 29-30.

16  McNamara has pointed out that the decrees of Trent, which would have regulated preaching throughout the colonial era, insisted that sermons should teach "those things necessary for all to know in order to be saved...." emphasizing plainly "the vices they must avoid and the virtues they must cultivate...." This indicates a catechetical thrust for all preaching, but even more so for the Catholics of Maryland and Pennsylvania. *Catholic Sunday Preaching,* 10.

17  Henri Daniel-Rops, *The Church in the Seventeenth Century* (New York: E.P. Dutton, 1963): 86-87.

18  Jay P. Dolan, *Catholic Revivalism: The American Experience 1830-1900* (Notre Dame: University of Notre Dame Press, 1978): 15-16.

19  No doubt "missions," because of their intensity and specialization differed somewhat from the usual pastoral care offered by the colonial clergy. Thus it is likely that what are called "missions" in the strict sense more properly correspond to what the colonial priests called "retreats." Cf. Dolan, *Catholic Revivalism,* 16ff. on Jean-Baptist David's "retreats" in Maryland at the beginning of the nineteenth century.

20  See Thomas Spalding's comments in "Frontier Catholicism," *Catholic Historical Review* 77 (July, 1991): 477-78.

21  American Catholic Sermon Collection (ACSC), Special Collections, Lauinger Library, Georgetown University, Washington, DC, Mo-1. All quotations from the sermons have been altered to reflect contemporary punctuation, spelling, and capitalization.

# CHAPTER ONE

# "Pastors Learned and Eloquent"

## THE COLONIAL CATHOLICS AND THEIR CLERGY

No one knows with any certainty when a Catholic sermon was first preached in English in Anglo-colonial America. One was no doubt delivered by Andrew White, S.J., on 25 March 1634, accompanying a celebration of the Mass, the circumstances of which he recounted in his famous *Relation*:

On the day of the Annunciation of the Most Holy Virgin Mary in the year 1634, we celebrated the Mass for the first time, on this island [St. Clement's Island]. This had never been done before in this part of the world. After we had completed the sacrifice, we took upon our shoulders a great cross, which we had hewn out of a tree, and advancing in order to the appointed place . . . we erected a trophy to Christ the Saviour, humbly reciting, on our bended knees, the Litanies of the Sacred Cross, with great emotion.[1]

This was the beginning of a sustained Jesuit missionary presence in the English-speaking colonies, a mission that continues to the present day, surviving countless vagaries of history, while reflecting that history and shaping it as well. Our present study is concerned only with the eighteenth century, but before examining the life of the Jesuits in that era, it will be necessary to briefly outline the growth of their mission, and the circumstances of Catholic life in Maryland and Pennsylvania.[2]

## The Maryland Experience

There has been endless debate on the motives surrounding George Calvert's desire for a colony in the New World in the early seventeenth-century. Was he driven by a philosophical spirit of toleration to provide a refuge, a "Land of Sanctuary" for his Catholic co-religionists, or was his advocacy of religious toleration based on sheer opportunism?[3] Perhaps the best way to respond to such a question is to remove the necessity of choosing only one extreme, and answering, as Michael Graham does, by noting: "Toleration was both a means and an end. As the centerpiece of Lord Baltimore's Maryland Design, toleration constituted the primary goal he sought to secure in his provincial program, but under the pressure of province needs in Maryland and through the vicissitudes of English politics, toleration became as well the chief avenue by which he could approach that goal."[4] This perspective does not deny that the Lords Baltimore (George Calvert, ca. 1580-1632, and his son Cecil, 1606-1675) had a desire "to open for all dissenters, and most especially for . . . fellow Roman Catholic countrymen, civil freedoms not available to them in England."[5] Rather, it recognizes that a colony founded exclusively as a "Catholic refuge" could never have progressed beyond the drawing board in early seventeenth-century England, not only as a result of governmental opposition, but also because such an enterprise would never have been financially profitable.[6]

It is fundamental for an understanding of later developments in the colony that Cecil Calvert (who inherited the charter on his father's death in 1632) be seen, not as a religious idealist, but as an astute "governor" who realized that what was best for the peaceful and prosperous survival of his colony was also most beneficial for his fellow Catholics. As John Krugler has commented: "Baltimore's policy toward religion was conditioned by three realities. The first was that he and his fellow Catholics were a distinct minority within Maryland, albeit a dominant one in the beginning. The second reality was that the majority of the settlers reflected traditional hostilities toward

Catholicism. The last was his relative weakness as an "absolute" proprietor who had to labor within the confines of a militant Protestant country."[7]

This resulted in a rather unusual arrangement for the first Jesuit missionaries on board the Ark and the Dove, and those who succeeded them. Allotted no financial subsidy from the Calverts, they had to accept the "Conditions of Plantation" like any other settler, receiving 2,000 acres of land for every five men brought to the colony. Under these guidelines, "Thomas Copley, who came over as superior in 1637, therefore petitioned for land for [Fathers] White and Altham who had brought over thirty men in 1633 and for himself and Father John Knolles, who brought nineteen more in 1637."[8] Thus began the system of Jesuit plantations, which would grow to include eight sizable farms by 1765,[9] and which continued to provide the means of subsistence for the missioners until the late eighteenth century.

Sadly, the early years of the colony were stormy ones. The Jesuits became embroiled in a controversy with Cecil Calvert that threatened to end their ministry altogether,[10] and the vulnerable colony was twice attacked resulting in a disruption of Calvert rule. The first incident occurred between 1644 and 1646, triggered by the incursions of a Parliamentarian "pirate" named Richard Ingle and exacerbated by an ongoing land dispute between the Calverts and William Claiborne.[11] During this "Plundering Time" two of the Jesuits (White and Copley) were taken back to England in chains, the chapel at Saint Mary's City was burned, the government of the colony was thrown into chaos, and many of the manors were looted. Governor Leonard Calvert (Cecil's brother) regained control of the colony in 1646, but died the following year.[12]

Cecil Calvert, aware of Protestant discontent in the colony, appointed one of their co-religionists, William Stone, to succeed his brother as governor. He also sent the legislature an "Act Concerning Religion" for passage, which has entered history as Maryland's "Toleration Act."[13] It enacted fines for blasphemy and insulting speech (e.g.: "Jesuited papist" and "Antinomian"), and promised: "No person or persons...professing to believe in Jesus Christ shall from henceforth be any ways troubled, molested or discountenanced for or in respect of his or her religion...."[14] Graham, commenting on the Act, writes, "Begun as a pious hope, toleration grew under the pressure of events;"[15] but it failed to head off the crisis that Calvert feared.

Less than ten years later, Claiborne once again reappeared on the scene, this time availing himself of the pretext of a Cromwellian commission and the support of many of the Maryland Puritans (who had been given asylum in 1649) to wage a successful civil war against the Calvert administration, headed by Stone. The resulting Puritan ascendancy lasted from 1655 to 1657, during which time the new government rescinded the 1649 "Act Concerning Religion," and prohibited Catholics from exercising the franchise.[16] Cecil Calvert continued to fight for the rights granted to him under his royal charter and in 1657 his rule in Maryland was re-established. With the return of the Stuarts to the throne in 1660 his colony became secure for the foreseeable future.

Thus began a brief "golden age" for both Catholics and for the colony as a whole. Krugler writes: "For about the next twenty-seven years, religious toleration formed the basis of a flourishing society."[17] The two groups who benefited most from this tranquillity were those whom Krugler calls the "most despised groups in the English-speaking world," the Catholics and the Quakers.[18] Despite their small size and the serious setbacks they had suffered in previous years, the Catholics, according to David Jordan, "nonetheless had the oldest and strongest religious institutions."[19] This was due in large part to the ministrations of the Jesuit missionaries, who enjoyed an incredible degree of freedom. Graham writes: "Liberated from the penal laws, they proselytized throughout the province, administered the sacraments openly, and organized the Catholic laity into local congregations. In Maryland, the Jesuits were not only free of the burdensome penal laws, they were likewise relieved of the restrictions imposed on them in the English mission necessitated by their close association with the English Catholic gentry."[20] Their activities would not come without a price, however. The latter half of the seventeenth century had seen a great influx of immigrants to Maryland, and as Lois Carr points out, "The very population growth that spelled success for Lord Baltimore's colony helped create conditions that contributed to the downfall of the proprietor and his policies."[21] One important factor was that the newcomers were almost entirely of the Protestant religion; as a result they were unfamiliar with, and hostile to, the freedoms enjoyed by the Mayland Catholics. In addition, many of the Protestant groups—especially the Church of England—had difficulty in supporting their own ministers in the absence of state aid, a problem which did not arise for the dissenting Quakers (who did not have ministers to support) and the Catholics (whose priests largely supported themselves).[22]

A more contentious problem than religion was the rule of the third Lord Baltimore, Charles Calvert, who had become the proprietor on his father's death in 1675. Not as able a leader as his father, Charles unwisely concentrated power in the hands of an elite strata of the colony's wealthy and privileged, including a disproportionate number of Catholics.[23] Calvert was attempting to "render the government more responsive to his own wishes and desires. [Thus he]...came to be considered as more imperious, more arbitrary, more monarchical, and less concerned about the rights and welfare of his subjects than his father had been."[24] Matters only worsened when Calvert left the colony in 1684 to return to England on business. His council, as Jordan comments, "proved even less astute than he in governing. They made many mistakes after the proprietor's departure which denied them the widespread confidence of the public. Finally, another new-comer . . . assumed the reins of government in 1688 as head of the Council. William Joseph gloried in his Catholic religion and in his divine right theories of government."[25] In the end, the Glorious Revolution in England provided the discontented smaller planters with a pretext for rebellion when Governor Joseph delayed in acknowledging the succession of William and Mary. In July 1689, these self-styled "Protestant Associators" seized the government at

Saint Mary's City in a bloodless coup. Though they claimed the motivation for their action was "to defend the Protestant religion among us,"[26] in reality religion was only the pretext that allowed them to act. As Richard Gleissner explains: "Whatever else motivated Protestant planters in 1689, religion was not among the causes of Baltimore's overthrow. Religious considerations as an excuse for the revolt, on the other hand, were used by the Associators to great effect: to add credence to the many charges of misadministration leveled at the proprietary government and to prevent any popular display of support for Baltimore."[27] Graham describes the role of religion in the coup in a similar fashion: "Anti-Catholicism formed for these small planters a powerful ideology by which they integrated their fears over such diverse problems in Maryland as economic contraction, Indian threats, and the political ambitions and policies of Charles Calvert...under the general explanatory rubric of the tyrannic ambitions predicated of a Catholic prince...."[28] Regardless of their real complaints, their "official motive" was the ever-increasing power of the "popish" religion, and the lack of an established church. The legislation approved during the succeeding twenty-eight years would address both of these issues. During the period from 1692 to 1717—Maryland's tenure as a royal colony—the Calverts were stripped of their political power, and various laws were passed to establish the Church of England and to restrict the life of the Catholic community.[29] After a decade of skirmishing with both London and the Quaker elements in their own legislature, the Maryland Assembly passed "An Act for the Establishment of Religious Worship in this Province According to the Church of England" in 1702, which adopted the Book of Common Prayer for worship and continued the annual poll tax of forty pounds of tobacco for the maintenance of each local church and minister.[30]

In 1704, the legislature passed an "Act to Prevent the Growth of Popery within this Province," which affected almost every area of Catholic life: "It prohibited any 'Popish Priest of Jesuits' to baptize any child 'other than such who have Popish parents' or to say Mass or exercise the functions of a Popish Bishop or Priest within Maryland. Also prohibited was any endeavor to persuade 'any of her Majesty's liege people of this Province to embrace and be reconciled to the Church of Rome.' In addition, it was made unlawful for any person 'making profession of the Popish religion' to keep a school...."[31] The most drastic part of this law, however—that which forbade the saying of Mass in a private home—was regularly suspended until it was permanently supplanted by a new act passed on the urging of Queen Anne in 1707. This law, though, allowed all the other restrictions against the Catholics to remain in force, as did the English laws substituted for the provincial ones in 1718.[32]

The move against the Catholics was not limited to a single series of laws. Other various and sundry measures were taken to restrict and control that part of the population which professed the "popish religion." Acts restricting the immigration of Irish Catholic servants were passed with regularity in 1699, 1704, 1708, 1716, and 1717.[33] An ordinance was approved in 1715 mandating the placement of Roman Catholic orphans in Protestant families. In 1716 oaths of allegiance were prescribed for all "places of trust" in the colony, and in 1718 Roman Catholics were disenfranchised.[34]

It must be noted at the same time, however, that the various legal strictures enacted against the Catholic community were only sporadically enforced. Beatriz Hardy has pointed out that there were decades during which the relations between Catholics and the colonial government were relatively tranquil, including 1720-50 and 1763-66. She observes that two factors affected this relationship: "existence of a crisis involving Catholics, such as war with France . . . and the presence of at least one strong politician in Maryland itself who was willing to push for discrimination against Catholics."[35]

One such politician was Governor John Hart, who was highly annoyed by the support given by a few outspoken Catholics to the "Fifteen," who backed the rebellion of the son of James II.[36] He was also angered by the attempts of Charles Carroll ("the Immigrant"), proprietary agent for the Fourth Lord Baltimore, to control political patronage in the colony. Supported by allies in the Maryland Assembly, Hart was responsible for much of the severe anti-Catholic legislation of the years 1710-20.[37]

Yet this era of hostility was followed by one of relative calm: "peaceful cooperation in virtually all areas of life characterized Catholic—Protestant relations from 1720 until the 1740's."[38] Hardy explains: "The third generation of Catholic gentry, reaching maturity between 1720 and 1750, had never known a time when Catholics could sit in the Assembly or hold provincial office; since early childhood, these Catholics had only worshipped at private chapels. [They] took a much more defensive position, not challenging the existing laws but simply trying to maintain the status quo by preventing the passage of any new laws discriminating against Catholics. During the years from 1720 to 1750, Catholics practiced their religion, raised their children, and sought their fortunes with very little interference from the government."[39] The community was supported in its existence by the activity of the priests of the Society of Jesus, who continued to go about their work despite the new restrictions under which they were forced to labor. "Priests," comments Gerald Fogarty, "were arrested, but never imprisoned."[40] With the closure of public churches, however,[41] "Catholics were forced to depend for worship either on a wealthy Catholic neighbor who could maintain a chapel which Jesuits visited on circuits, or on private Masses celebrated in their own homes by Jesuit itinerants."[42] Before long, the travels of the "itinerant" Jesuits would bring the sacraments, and the preached word, to the Catholics of neighboring Pennsylvania, where their ministrations would meet with remarkable success.

## The Pennsylvania Missions

John Tracy Ellis has called the story of Catholics in Pennsylvania "the most pleasant and positive of any of the original thirteen colonies."[43] Pennsylvania in the early eighteenth century was a prosperous and rapidly growing colony, fostered "by a liberal land policy, toleration of religious and ethnic diversity, as well as placid relations with the Indians. . . ."[44] The Jesuits had founded a mission in 1704 at Bohemia, on the Eastern Shore of Maryland, quite near the Pennsylvania border. Though it seems a remote location today,[45] in the early eighteenth century Bohemia Manor afforded the missionaries a convenient base for travels into Pennsylvania, and there were soon reports of Mass being celebrated in Philadelphia.[46] Joseph Greaton established a permanent church there in 1734, though it was little more than a "mass house" measuring an unimpressive eighteen by twenty-eight feet. This chapel was the missionaries' first urban foundation, as well as the site of the first public Catholic worship in the colonies since the chapel at Saint Mary's City was closed in 1704.[47] Soon other missions were established at Conewago and Goshenhoppen (from which substations at Reading and Lebanon were administered). The Jesuits were aided in their work in Penn's colony by the revenues from the James Fund, a trust in the amount of £4,000 set up in England, the income from which was earmarked for the Pennsylvania missions.[48]

The Pennsylvania missions were populated by large numbers of German immigrants from the Rhine valley, so the Jesuits began to beseech their German confreres to join them in Pennsylvania and minister to the people in their native tongue.[49] One of the most famous of all the German missionaries in Pennsylvania was Ferdinand Farmer (Steinmeyer), whose ministry was based in both Lancaster and Philadelphia, but whose travels into the surrounding countryside (and as far away as New York City) in search of Catholics became legendary.[50] At his death in 1786 he would be lauded by the *Pennsylvania Gazette* as one who was "charitable and benevolent and was loved and regarded as the Father of his people and the friend of civilized humanity."[51]

Yet the Catholic community was comprised of more than Germans. A census taken in 1757 showed a Catholic population in Pennsylvania of 1,365, "about equally divided between 692 men and 673 women" of whom 949 were Germans, while 416 were classed as

English or Irish.[52] By 1785, John Carroll would report that the number had grown to 7,000, though he provides no breakdown by ethnicity.[53]

There were intermittent threats to the peace of the Catholic settlers, especially at the time of the French and Indian War. In one incident a mob, quelled by peaceable Quakers, threatened to destroy St. Joseph's Church following the defeat of General Braddock in 1755. A year later, a Corpus Christi procession at Goshenhoppen was mistaken by anti-Catholic patriots for a military drill, with the result that a law was passed in 1757 forbidding Catholics to bear arms.[54] Despite these occasional threats the Jesuits and their flock enjoyed a wide degree of liberty in Pennsylvania.[55] So much so that Henry Neale was led to remark: "We have at present all liberty imaginable in the exercise of our business, and are not only esteemed, but reverenced, as I may say, by the better sort of people."[56]

In what did this "exercise of business" consist? An answer can be found by briefly examining the life of the Jesuit missionaries, drawn from their own writings: sermons, letters, and journals.

## The Life of a Missionary

The missionaries of Maryland and Pennsylvania had much in common, apart from their membership in the Society of Jesus. The vast majority of them were Anglo-Saxon; hailing either from England, or—as became more unexceptional as the century progressed—from the colonies.[57] If the homilists in the collection are at all representative, their posting to America came at an early stage of their missionary career, as their average age on arrival was a mere 30.8 years. Most had received their education at the Jesuit colleges of Saint Omers and Liège,[58] and although it is impossible to know the level of scholarship they attained,[59] a clue to their overall capabilities might be found in noting that a little less than a fifth of the missioners in the sermon collection (eight) were professed as spiritual co-adjutors, with the three evangelical vows, as opposed to those who took the fourth solemn vow.[60]

Regardless of their talents or aptitudes, the missioners of Maryland and Pennsylvania acquitted themselves uniformly well in their duties, achieving a near spotless record in terms of fidelity to their tasks and a Christian manner of life, a fact that is all the more conspicuous when compared with the deportment of some of their Anglican counterparts.[61] Had there been any flagrant misbehavior on the part of the Jesuits, it would surely not have gone unnoticed, considering the religiously charged atmosphere of the day.

One certainly would not want to pretend that the Catholic clergy were perfect, that irregularities were unknown, or that the clergy did not need occasional reminders as to their proper behavior. Quite the contrary. In 1713 Thomas Mansell, the superior of the colonial missions, was told by the English provincial that there were a number of irregularities in his houses, including the employment of a maid servant, card-playing, and a dangerous degree of familiarity with seculars, "all of which," the provincial observed, "can't be done without expense and perhaps scandal."[62]

Drinking to excess seems to have been a special concern, for in 1722 Mansell, in his last injunctions to his brethren, recommends that all the residences have "a place separate from the common cellar, for wine, rum and other strong liquors. They [the Superior] must keep them locked up, and keep the key themselves."[63] He further urges: "Wherefore I beg of all to take great care of drinking, and by what authority is communicated to one I do as much as in me lies order all masters of our residences to see these instructions complied with as punctually as possible, and in particular to be cautious not to allow strong liquor without necessity. And when strangers come to their houses not to be too forward in giving too much strong liquor...."[64] In fact we do know of one Jesuit, John Lucas, who drank heavily, caroused, and finally abandoned the priestly life, marrying the recently widowed Ann Hill.[65]

The priests were also encouraged to be on guard against

uncharitable words or deeds directed toward those outside their community, but "if anything of this nature may happen out of human frailty, let it be made up as soon as possible."[66] By April 1759, though, attention seems to have turned elsewhere, as the "Ordinations and Regulations" dated that year show a greater preoccupation with the disposition of Jesuit property and funds, as well as with an ordered prayer life, than with specific moral faults and failures.[67]

Regrettably, there is practically no information available on the Catholic community's estimation of its clergy and their abilities, apart from the views expressed during the Trustee controversies of the last fifteen years of the century.[68] For example, the complaint in New York surrounding the Irish Capuchin Father Charles Whelan centered on his qualifications as a preacher, and the faithful were, in this case, certainly not reticent about making their dissatisfaction known to John Carroll.[69] Yet this protest in New York, and others like it, did not deal directly with any of the congregations founded by the Jesuit missioners,[70] and give us no real insight into the faithful's perception of their ministry. In 1775 a letter sent to John Lewis (then superior of the missions) by a group of Catholics in Philadelphia expressed their gratitude for his care of the Philadelphia church. In particular, they laud: "The particular care you have always taken to provide for her, pastors not only learned and eloquent, but also singularly pious and edifying in their lives and conversations, and in every other respect most endearing to us all."[71]

On the one hand, the mid-eighteenth century saw ties between laity and clergy strengthened. For example, the numbers of young colonial Catholic gentlemen entrusted to religious schools on the Continent numbered 51.4 percent (up from 6 percent in the third generation of Maryland gentry), and in 1759 a group of wealthy Catholic gentry banded together to assist the Jesuits in financing the redemption of debts owed to the English Province of the Society, which threatened to bankrupt the mission.[72] Yet one must also take into account an angry outburst from Charles Carroll of Carrollton (future signer of the Declaration of Independence and the Constitution) in 1769, occasioned by a priest's rebuke of his lax response to an adulterous affair between one of his overseers and a slave. He wished, he wrote his father, "we had never sent for a priest: they are troublesome animals in a family and occasion many chops and changes."[73]

However, even if their conversations (and perhaps their sermons) had not been "pious and edifying," and their moral advice more "troublesome," the rigorous nature of their daily routine could scarcely have failed to impress their flocks. On Sundays, the missioner would have to travel to a designated location for Mass, according to a schedule that attempted to provide an opportunity for all the faithful to attend at least once every month.[74] Once he arrived at his destination, the priest would hear confessions from early in the morning until eleven o'clock. Then Mass would be celebrated and holy communion distributed, followed by a sermon and explanation of points of doctrine.[75] William Wappeler (who cared for Pennsylvania Catholics at Lancaster, Conewago, and Cordorus Creek (York)) described his schedule—which included ministering to congregations of mixed ethnicity—as follows:

As soon as I arrive at my mission place I enclose myself in my little wooden church where my lambs are either awaiting my arrival or gradually gathering. Usually I preface all activities with the Holy Sacrifice of the Mass. After that I read the Gospel from an English book, until I know the language more thoroughly, for the English members, who often mingle with the German. Then I address an allocution to my compatriots in their mother tongue. Lastly I take a catechism question and discuss it fully for the necessary instruction of both old and young.[76]

During the week, the priests were usually kept busy by the duty of visiting the sick and dying, which necessitated long rides on horseback to outlying farms. Joseph Mosley reported: "I am daily on horseback, visiting the sick, comforting the infirm, strengthening the pusillanimous, etc."[77] Writing to his sister, he gave a full report of the demanding extent of these ministrations: "I often ride about 300 miles a week, and never a week but I ride 150 or 200." Nor was Mosley reluctant in describing what these journeys were like:

And in our way of living, we ride almost as much by night as by day, in all weathers, in heats, cold, rain, frost or snow. Several may think the cold, rains, etc., to be the worst to ride in; but I think to ride in the heats far surpasses all, both for man and horse.[78]

Working in conditions such as these often led to serious health problems. Mosley lamented that "a ride of 52 miles in the rain, and another of the same length in a warm day all in the sun, cast me into violent fevers attended with constant vomitings...."[79]

If the example of their actions alone were not sufficient to edify their congregations, some of the Jesuits were more than ready to point to their own sufferings as a model to be imitated and respected. Matthias Manners observes that while the priest is the "vice-regent of Jesus Christ," he is often treated like a servant, which leads him to exclaim:

O how many tedious long rides must he take upon himself for their sake? How often is he exposed to heat and cold, rain and wind, snow and all other injuries of the weather day and night? How often, if abroad, has he not enough to eat and drink? What inconveniences wait on him in a poor lodging?[80]

John Lewis points to another hardship of missionary life, when he reminds his people how blessed they are to have been provided with

Zealous missionaries and teachers, who after sacrificing everything that was dear to them in this world, their own native country, parents and kindred, have traversed the vast Atlantic ocean without fee or reward or even the bare expectation of it to serve you night and day in all extremities of heat and cold.[81]

Separation from relatives must have been one of the most trying hardships of service in the colonies, especially for the English Jesuits, many of whom, after being posted to the colonies, never saw their families again. James Beadnall speaks of the powerful witness that the missioners give in this regard, and asks his flock:

How can you see men, delicately born and elegantly bred, quitting their houses and their homes, their pleasure and their ease, their kingdoms ... their relations and friends, and sacrificing all that's dear to them to save your souls, and you quit nothing?[82]

There is ample evidence that the Jesuits embraced this cross of theirs with good grace and much trust in God, as is witnessed by Mosley's letter to his sister, which he wrote from London before departing:

I set off for America the 10th of next month; not to be banished from my own country for only 16 years [the length of his schooling on the Continent?], but, for the love of God and the conversion of souls, to abandon it and you for always. For, if I consider the call of my state of life with which God has blessed me, I am not in all things to follow what is even innocently delightful, but to seek what tends more to the honor and glory of God. I think that seeing one another is of little satisfaction, unless our lives are such that we may see one another in a happy eternity. When there we meet, we meet forever.[83]

In fact, missionary life itself had many pleasant aspects, apart from the spiritual reward that the priests received from ministering to their fellow Catholics. Arnold Livers, if his Note Book is any indication, took great delight in the running of his farm (including the raising of horses and the cultivation of flowers).[84] Even the grinding journeys on horse-back could be enjoyable at times, as one can glimpse in a poem written by Livers entitled, "Mr. Lewis, his Journey from Patapsko to Annapolis":

> In this soft season, ere up dawn of day,
> I mount my horse, and lonely take my way,
> From woody hills that shade *Patapsko's* head,
> (In whose deep vales he makes his stony bed
> From whence he rushes with resistless force
> Though huge rough rocks retard his rapid course,) ...
>
> Through sylvan scenes my journey I pursue,
> Ten thousand beauties rising to my view;
> Which kindle in my breast poetic flame
> And bid me my *Creator's* praise proclaim.[85]

Perhaps the most difficult hardship the colonial Jesuit clergy had to face was the suppression of their community by Pope Clement XIV on 8 June 1773, in the brief *Dominus ac Redemptor*.[86] This verdict was communicated to them by Bishop Richard Challoner, who requested that they sign "a form of declaration of your obedience and submissions" which would then be forwarded to Rome.[87] Mosley's reaction to this news was most likely representative of his confreres when he wrote to his sister that he could not speak of the suppression "without tears in my eyes." He continued:

I know of no fault we are guilty of. I am convinced that our labors are pure, upright and sincere, for God's honor and our neighbor's good. Ah, I can say now, what I never before thought of: I am willing now to retire and quit my post, as I believe most of my brethren are. Labor for our neighbor is a Jesuit's pleasure; destroy the Jesuit, and labor is painful and disagreeable.[88]

John Carroll expressed his reaction to the suppression in a letter to his mother:

Our so long persecuted, and I must add, holy society is no more. God's holy will be done, and may his name be blessed forever and ever! I am not, and perhaps never shall be, fully recovered from the shock of this dreadful intelligence. The greatest blessing which in my estimation I could receive from God, would be immediate death....[89]

Carroll had asked in the same letter: "What will become of our flourishing congregations with you, and those cultivated by the German fathers?" Yet though he and the priests of the mission were thoroughly dispirited, they remained at their posts, and continued to serve the needs of their flocks until a new form of governance was arrived at ten years later, as a result of the meetings of the First General Chapter of the Clergy, at Whitemarsh, Maryland.[90] This transformation would ultimately find its completion in the appointment of John Carroll as the first Bishop of Baltimore on 14 September 1789.

## NOTES

1   Quoted in *Documents of American Catholic History*, ed. John Tracy Ellis (Milwaukee: Bruce Publishing Co., 1962), 104. Though Father White was unaware of it, missionaries had almost certainly celebrated Mass in the Chesapeake region sixty years earlier, when five Jesuits made an ill-fated attempt to found a mission in Virginia. See Clifford M. Lewis, S.J., and Albert J. Loomie, S.J., *The Spanish Jesuit Mission in Virginia, 1570-72* (Chapel Hill: University of North Carolina Press, 1953).

2   Readers seeking a fuller picture of the life of colonial Catholics should consult John Tracy Ellis, *Catholics in Colonial America* (Baltimore: Helicon, 1965); Michael James Graham, S.J., "Lord Baltimore's Pious Enterprise: Toleration and Community in Colonial Maryland" (Ph.D. diss., University of Michigan, 1983); and Beatriz Betancourt Hardy, "Papists in a Protestant Age: The Catholic Gentry and Community in Colonial Maryland, 1689-1776" (Ph.D. diss., University of Maryland, 1993).

3   For the former view see William T. Russell, *Maryland: The Land of Sanctuary, A History of Religious Toleration from the First Settlement until the American Revolution* (Baltimore: J. H. Furst, 1907); for the latter Charles E. Smith's *Religion Under the Barons Baltimore...* (Baltimore: E. Allen Lycett, 1899). Graham, 64.

4   Graham, 64.

5   Graham, 28.

6   Cf. John Bossy, "Reluctant Colonists," in *Early Maryland in a Wider World*, ed. David B. Quinn (Detroit: Wayne State University Press, 1982).

7   John D. Krugler, "Lord Baltimore, Roman Catholics, and Toleration: Religious Policy in Maryland During the Early Catholic Years, 1634-1649," *Catholic Historical Review* 65 (January, 1979): 59.

8   Gerald P. Fogarty, S.J., "The Origins of the Mission, 1634-1773," in *The Maryland Jesuits, 1634-1833*, ed. R. Emmett Curran, S.J. (Baltimore: Corporation of Roman Catholic Clergymen, 1976), 14.

9   St. Inigoe's (1634), St. Thomas Manor (1641), Whitemarsh (1642), Newtown (1668), Bohemia (1704), Goshenhoppen, Pa. (1741), Conewago, Pa. (1741), Deer Creek (1744) and St. Joseph's, Tuckahoe (1765); all with numerous sub-stations for Mass—not including the churches in Philadelphia, Pa. (St. Joseph's, 1732, and St. Mary's, 1763), and Lancaster, Pa. (1742). Cf. Fogarty, 25-26).

10  The Jesuits were protesting the introduction of secular clergy, the payment of taxes, the obligation of their servants to enlist in the militia, and restrictions on their acceptance of lands from native peoples; cf. Russell, 149. The interpretation of this feud has altered somewhat over the years. In the opinion of Thomas Hughes, S.J., the author of the monumental *History of the Society of Jesus in North America* (London: Longmans, Green and Company, 1917), Calvert was attempting to repress the Church with measures he described as

"rank feudalism" and of a "socialistic character," cf. *Text*, 1: 348-446, here 399, 401. John Krugler evaluates Hughes' reaction as coming "largely from misunderstanding the purpose of the colony. If Baltimore's purpose had been to found a Catholic refuge in which English law had no meaning, and where Jesuits were to enjoy all the privileges and immunities of Catholic countries, then Hughes' interpretation would have some validity." But Krugler believes that "To have acquiesced to the Society of Jesus would have been suicidal and Baltimore had no desire to destroy his little colony before it had been given a fair chance to succeed" (73). For his evaluation of the dispute, see above, 66-73. See also Graham, 53-57, who comments "Baltimore stated his case simply but strongly; Maryland was no more a Catholic nation than England itself, and Maryland's 'court Catholics' would have to adjust themselves to that hard fact" (57).

11    J. Moss Ives, *The Ark and the Dove* (New York: Longmans, Green and Co., 1936), 201ff. Cf. also Lois Green Carr, "Sources of Political Stability and Upheaval in Seventeenth-Century Maryland," *Maryland Historical Magazine* 79 (Spring, 1984): 44-70, esp. 54.

12    Ives, 221.

13    Carl N. Everstine, "Maryland's Toleration Act: An Appraisal," *Maryland Historical Magazine* 79 (Summer, 1984): 99-115. There is no evidence to suggest that religious intolerance had caused any problems in the young colony prior to Ingle's invasion; quite the contrary, in fact. Calvert had instructed his settlers on the voyage from England "to preserve unity and peace amongst all the passengers on shipboard and that they suffer no scandal nor any offense to be given to any of the Protestants...and that for that end they cause all acts of the Roman Catholic religion to be done privately as may be.... And this is to be observed at land as well as at sea." *Ives*, 106. That the injunctions were followed can be seen from the cases of two Catholics who were prosecuted in the decade after the founding of the colony for violating the rights of Protestants: William Lewis (a Jesuit overseer), and Thomas Gerard (a prominent Catholic physician). Krugler, 62-64.

14    Quoted in Everstine, 100.

15    Graham, 60.

16    Carr, 56; Krugler, "'With Promise of Liberty in Religion': The Catholic Lords Baltimore and Toleration in Seventeenth-Century Maryland, 1634-1692," *Maryland Historical Magazine* 79 (January, 1984): 33-35; Ellis, 337.

17    Krugler, "With Promise of Liberty in Religion," 36.

18    Ibid.

19    David W. Jordan, "'The Miracle of This Age': Maryland's Experiment in Religious Toleration, 1649-1689" *The Historian* 47 (May, 1985): 343.

20    Graham, 75-76. Jordan notes that the Jesuits reported converting 260 people between 1667 and 1674.

21    Carr, 59.

22    Idem. Father John Mattingly would remark in 1773 in a Relation to Propaganda Fidei: "Ministeria omnia gratis exercent, ita ut ne dona quidem

sponte oblata ullo pacto admittant." In "Documents," *Catholic Historical Review* 2 (October, 1916): 317.

23   Jordan, 355.

24   Graham, 236-37.

25   Jordan, 357

26   Richard A. Gleissner, "Religious Causes of the Glorious Revolution in Maryland," *Maryland Historical Magazine* 64 (Winter, 1969): 328.

27   Ibid., 341.

28   Graham, 207. See also his "Popish Plots: Protestant Fears in Early Colonial Maryland, 1676-1689," *Catholic Historical Review* 79 (April, 1993): 197-216.

29   Everstine, 108. The Calverts would regain the control of their colony only on the apostasy of Charles' son Benedict, who converted to the Church of England in 1713. Ellis, 348.

30   Everstine, 108-109. For a treatment of the establishment of the Church of England, see Graham, 259-310.

31   Everstine, 109-110.

32   Everstine, 110. He notes that the substitution of the English laws were without "any real substantive effect...."

33   Graham, 341.

34   Graham, 352.

35   Hardy, 25-26.

36   Hardy, 143.

37   Hardy, 162-71.

38   Hardy, 181.

39   Hardy, 182, 253.

40   Fogarty, 22. There were at least five clerical arrests in the years following the Glorious Revolution. Thomas Harvey was arrested in Maryland after fleeing there from New York (ca. 1689), but later released. Thomas Barton was arrested for saying Mass in the home of Colonel Sayer in 1693, along with the colonel himself. Cf. Edward Carley, *The Origins and History of Saint Peter's Church, Queenstown, Maryland, 1637-1976* (Baltimore, 1976), 23. In 1704, Robert Brooke and William Hunter were arrested, and the former charged with saying Mass, the latter with consecrating an altar. Though Hunter answered his charge by pointing out that only bishops can consecrate altars, both admitted saying Mass. Fogarty notes the outcome: "Severely reprimanding them, the governor dismissed the charges since it was their 'first offense'" (22). In 1745 Richard Molyneaux was arrested due to his presence in Lancaster at the time of a negotiation between the English and the Indians, but was discharged through the good offices of Charles Carroll. In Ellis, 354. Finally, James Beadnall was arrested in 1756 for saying Mass (in private homes) and for attempting a conversion, but ably defended himself by reference to Queen Anne's permission for Mass in private. Carley, 23.

41   The church at Saint Mary's City was demolished, and its bricks transported by river to the plantation at Saint Inigoe's, where they were employed to build a

new manor house with a private chapel used for the worship of the Catholic community. Cf. Edwin W. Beitzell, *The Jesuit Missions of Saint Mary's County, Maryland* (Abel, Md.: p.p., 1976); and John Krugler and Timothy Riordan, "'Scandalous and Offensive to the Government'; The 'Popish chappel' at St. Mary's City, Maryland and the Society of Jesus, 1634 to 1705" *Mid-America* 73 (October, 1991): 187-208, here 199-201.

42    Graham, 378.

43    Ellis, 370.

44    Robert E. Quigley, "Catholic Beginnings in the Delaware Valley," in *A History of the Archdiocese of Philadelphia* (Philadelphia: Archdiocese of Philadelphia, 1976), 8.

45    Edward Devitt, S.J., makes an insightful comment when he remarks concerning Bohemia, "These rural sites were chosen because there were no large towns, no large centers of population, at the time when these missions were founded; probably, the desire to escape observation had some influence in the matter, since at any time, intolerance might become vigilant, and the priest might be harassed by the application of the penal statutes...." "History of the Maryland - New York Province: IX. Bohemia," *Woodstock Letters* 63 (January, 1934): 3. These comments would apply to most of the other Jesuit missions as well.

46    Ellis notes that "Although there was no record of the priest's name nor of the place, Mass was said to have been offered at Christmas, 1707...." which was later relayed to Penn, causing him to order James Logan, his deputy in the colony, to look into it. Ellis, 373-374. Cf. Quigley, 12, who gives 1708 as the date of the first Mass.

47    Ellis, 374. Edward Devitt, S.J., "History of the Maryland - New York Province: X. Saint Joseph's Church, Willing's Alley," *Woodstock Letters* 63 (April, 1934): 216. Though some Philadelphians were alarmed by the appearance of a "popish" chapel in their midst, no matter how modest, the Governor and his council opted to leave it undisturbed. Sally Schwartz, *"A Mixed Multitude": The Struggle for Toleration in Colonial Pennsylvania* (New York: New York University Press, 1987), 104.

48    Ellis, 375. In 1765 George Hunter reported the amount of the yearly income to be £80, although there was some dissatisfaction among the Jesuits with the way the funds were administered for them by Bishop Challoner, cf. Hughes, 2:496-97.

49    Paul G. Gleis, "German Jesuit Missionaries in 18th Century Maryland," *Woodstock Letters* 75 (October, 1946):199-206. The first two, Theodore Schneider (former Rector Magnificus of the University of Heidelberg) and Wilhelm Wappeler arrived in 1741; Schneider going to Goshenhoppen (where he spent his winters transcribing copies of the Roman Missal, Fogarty, 24), and Wappeler to Conewago. Cf. Also Quigley, 18-22.

50    Cf. John M. Daley, S.J., "Pioneer Missionary, Ferdinand Farmer, S.J.: 1720-1786," *Woodstock Letters* 75 (June, October, December, 1946): 103-15, 207-31, 311-21.

51  Daley, 320.

52  Ellis, 376.

53  Ellis, *Documents*, 148.

54  Schwartz, 240; Fogarty, 24. See also Joseph J. Casino, "Anti-Popery in Colonial Pennsylvania," *Pennsylvania Magazine of History and Biography* 105 (October, 1981): 279-309, and Edward H. Quinter and Charles L. Allwein, *Most Blessed Sacrament Church, Bally, Pennsylvania* (Bally, Pa.: by the authors, 1976), 4.

55  Tensions did run high, however. Farmer wrote to his brother in 1755, "In these warlike circumstances we priests and the German Catholics suffer the most, and the opponents of our faith attribute all the evil which they experience or fear—I don't know for what reason—to us priests. The ruler regards our missionaries as French spies, and we all are under false suspicion of wanting to betray Pennsylvania to the enemy. Ridiculous! But our honor is damaged by these reports which are circulated among the people of opposing religions and are believed by many, not without bitterness, to the detriment of our holy precepts, and they are believed without any foundation as unquestioned truths." MPA, 25,5. See also Quinter and Allwein, 4; and Schwartz, 242.

56  Ellis, *Catholics in Colonial America*, 374. Henry Neale (1702-1748), a member of the prodigious Neale family of Maryland, who gave eleven of their sons to the Jesuits, was a talented priest skilled in mathematics and philosophy, but he died in Philadelphia only eight years after returning to the colonies. Hughes, II, 690.

57  Robert Emmett Curran notes: "The large majority were Englishmen who came to British America fully expecting to serve in that mission for the rest of their lives." *American Jesuit Spirituality. The Maryland Tradition, 1634-1900* (New York: Paulist Press, 1988), 13. In the sermon collection, while at least nineteen out of the forty-four priests hail from England, twelve are from the colonies, and six from the Continent. For a treatment of the colonial-born clergy, see James Hennesey, S.J., "Several Youth Sent from Here: Native-Born Priests and Religious of English America, 1634-1776," in *Studies in Catholic History in Honor of John Tracy Ellis*, edited by Nelson H. Minnich, Robert B. Eno, S.S., and Robert F. Trisco (Wilmington, De.: Michael Glazier, 1985), 1-26.

58  For information on the College of Saint Omers, and the life and education of its students, see Hubert Chadwick, S.J., *St. Omers to Stonyhurst* (London: Burns and Oates, 1962).

59  They most likely ranged the full spectrum of ability, from the former "Rector-Magnificus" Schneider, to the "ingenium non promptum" Digges.

60  The Jesuits who had completed their studies and training were assigned to one of two states: "Those outstanding in virtue and learning pronounce solemn vows, to which they add a fourth, to go anywhere in the world the pope might send them. These are known as the professed. The others pronounce simple vows and are known as spiritual co-adjutors." William V. Bangert, S.J., *A History of the Society of Jesus* (St. Louis: Institute of Jesuit Sources, 1972): 42. During the eighteenth century the number of those judged to be suitable for

admission only as spirtual co-adjutors declined from 20.9% under the Jesuit General González (1687-1705) to 5.1% under Ricci (1758-1773). It should be pointed out, however, that statistics for the English Province could have differed from those of the Society as a whole. George E. Ganss, S.J., "The Diversity of Grades among Priests," in *The Constitutions of the Society of Jesus*, trans. George E. Ganss, S.J. (Chicago: Institute of Jesuit Sources, 1970), 353.

61    Though recent scholarship has tended to modify the older presentation of the venal character of the Maryland Anglican clergy, Protestant contemporaries of the Jesuits were quick to point out both the failings of their confreres, and the success achieved by the Catholics as a result. For example, the Reverend Henderson wrote that the Catholics had gained ground, and while "there is a great deal owing to the diligence and ingenuity of the Romish priests," he admits that "the ill lives of many [C. of E. clergy]...have made more converts to that Church [Catholic] than their priests could have done, notwithstanding their extraordinary abilities" in *Historical Collections Relating to the American Colonial Church*, William S. Perry, ed., vol. IV (New York: AMS Press, 1969), 83. For a study rehabilitating the image of the Anglican clergy, see David C. Skaggs and Gerald E. Hartdagen, "Sinners and Saints: Anglican Clerical Conduct in Colonial Maryland," *Historical Magazine of the Protestant Episcopal Church* 47 (Summer, 1978): 177-95.

62    Archives of the Maryland Province of the Society of Jesus (MPA), 3,8. The letter is recorded in a pig-skin record book, a valuable trove of early documents.

63    MPA, 57,1.

64    Ibid. That public perception is of great concern here is evident not only in the reference to "strangers," but also when Mansell later urges that when a Jesuit visits one of his confreres' residences, "the master must break up company at, or before, eleven o'clock at night, and take great care that too much strong liquor do not be offered which may give occasion to drinking, perchance too much bring too great a charge on his house and *give scandal.*" (emphasis mine)

65    Cf. Hardy, 329.

66    Ibid.

67    Ibid. The missioners are told to be diligent in their morning prayers, their evening examens and litanies (the latter performed in the presence of the Blessed Sacrament, if possible), and their making of a yearly retreat.

68    As Jay Dolan has noted with respect to nineteenth century mission preaching: "the eyewitness accounts of the person in the pew are meagre, while the volume of the sermons is extensive." *Catholic Revivalism: The American Experience 1830-1900* (Notre Dame: University of Notre Dame Press, 1978), 113.

69    Carroll wrote to his friend Charles Plowden that Whelan was not "so learned or so good a preacher, as I could wish, which mortifies his congregation..." in Annabelle M. Melville, *John Carroll of Baltimore* (New York: Charles Scribner's Sons, 1955), 79. Carroll continued "as at N. York, and most other places of America, the different sectaries have scarce any other test to judge of a Clergyman than his talents for preaching: and our Irish Congregations, such as

70   N. York, follow the same rule." *The John Carroll Papers* (JCP), ed. Thomas
     O'Brien Hanley, S.J., vol. 1 (Notre Dame: University of Notre Dame Press,
     1976), 196-97.

70   Except Holy Trinity, which broke away from Saint Mary's in Philadelphia.

71   MPA, 57,3 Their only request is that Lewis find them another priest to assist
     Farmer and Molyneaux. It must be noted that Hughes interprets this request
     for another priest as an implicit criticism of the preaching of the two incum-
     bants, remarking, "The ardent Celtic nature, so prompt in speaking, would
     never tolerate sleepy reading." Hughes, 2:514, fn. 3.

72   Hardy, 315, 300.

73   Quoted in Hardy, 325.

74   Some regions were even more difficult to attend. For example, Joseph Mosley
     described to his sister his newly founded mission at Tuckahoe as ideally
     situated to attend the six congregations that he visited once every two months.
     The first was a distance of ten miles; the second, twenty; the third, twenty-
     four; the fourth, twenty-two; the fifth was centered at his farm; and the sixth,
     also a distance of twenty-two miles. He noted "I have two others which I visit
     but twice a year—the first thirty-nine, the other ninety mile off. This, you'll
     say, is still hard. It's easy, dear sister, to what it was." MPA, *Mosley Letters*, 7, 14
     October, 1766. Joseph Mosley (1731-1787) is one of the best known colonial
     missioners, due to the fact that a collection of his letters to his sister in England
     has survived to the present day, and has been reprinted numerous times, most
     recently in Robert Emmett Curran's *American Jesuit Spirituality*, 100-125.
     From 1764 until his death Mosley worked to build up his mission of
     St. Joseph's on Maryland's Eastern Shore, living, as John Carroll noted, in a cell
     the size of that inhabited by the prophet Elisha, "containing just enough space
     for a bed, a table, and a stool." Quoted in Curran, 100.

75   Mattingly, "Documents," 317.

76   Quoted in Quigley, 20.

77   MPA, *Mosley Letters*, 3, 8 September 1758; also Mattingly, 317.

78   MPA, *Mosley Letters*, 4, 1 September, 1759.

79   MPA, *Mosley Letters*, 5, 5 October 1760. By the latter years of their career,
     many misioners suffered from more chronic complaints. For example, twelve
     years later Mosley would tell his sister of "an ailment I shall never get clear of.
     I mean violent paroxysms, or fits of the gravel and stone." MPA, *Mosley Letters*,
     9, 5 June 1772.

80   ACSC, Ma-1. Manners' (1719-1775) real name was Sittensperger, and he had
     come to America to care for the spiritual needs of the German Catholic
     immigrants. He was the first priest to reside permanently at the Conewago
     mission in Pennsylvania (1753-1763), after which he became the superior at
     Bohemia (1764-1775). Hughes, 2:694. Charles Sewall exclaims in a similar
     vein, "And I in my profession, how many sacrifices have I to make, sacrifices of
     my will, of my liberty, of my ease, of the commodities of life?" ACSC, Se-7.
     Sewall (1744-1805) was a member of one of the wealthiest Catholic families in

Maryland. He arrived in the colonies in the celebrated year 1776, where he would remain until his death. Hughes, 2:700. For a brief description of his life see Clarence Joerndt, *St. Ignatius, Hickory, and Its Missions* (Baltimore: Publication Press, 1972), 362-70.

81    ACSC, Le-11. Born in Northamptonshire, Lewis (1721-1788) was the last superior of the Jesuits of the Maryland-Pennsylvania mission before their suppression in 1773. He was a conscientious missioner, but Carroll criticized his "irresolution" in administrative matters. Hughes, 2:694, and JCP, 1:66. Sylvester Boarman, a Marylander, altered this sermon when he preached it, changing the second person "you" to the first person "us," reflecting perhaps his own indebtedness to the English fathers.

82    ACSC, Be-7. Born in Northumberland, Beadnall (1718-1772) worked on the Maryland mission from 1749 until his death. He was arrested in 1756 and charged with saying Mass in private houses and with the attempted conversion of a Protestant, though he was later acquitted. Geoffrey Holt, S.J., *St. Omers and Bruges Colleges, 1539-1773. A Biographical Dictionary* (London: Catholic record Society, 1979), 30; and Fogarty, 22.

83    MPA, *Mosley Letters*, 2, 25 February 1758.

84    MPA, 6, 2 1/2. Livers (1705-1767), a Marylander, returned to the colony in 1734, and served in Maryland until his death. Hughes, 2:690. His "Note Book" includes such diverse topics as the proper manner of dressing skins, cures for the ailments of both man and beast (including applying the halves of a split pigeon to the feet of "mole-fallen" children)—indicating that the priest often functioned as both doctor and veterinary—recipes for "cayan butter" and canned "poke mellons," a poem written to a bird, and a list of flowers and herbs that he had grown.

85    MPA, 2,10. The poem is dated 4 April, 1730.

86    For the events surrounding the suppression of the Jesuits, see Bangert, *A History of the Society of Jesus*, 363-430.

87    In Joseph T. Durkin, S.J., "The Mission and the New Nation—1773-1800," in Curran, *Maryland Jesuits*, 35.

88    MPA, *Mosley Letters*, 13, 3 October 1774.

89    JCP, 1:32.

90    Peter Guilday, *The Life and Times of John Carroll, Archbishop of Baltimore (1735-1815)* 2 vols. (New York: The Encyclopedia Press, 1922), 1:163-77; Durkin, 39-40.

CHAPTER TWO

# "*It is to* ✒*Me*
# *the* ✒*Preacher is* ✒*Speaking*"

## THE BACKGROUND TO THE SERMONS

Before beginning a discussion of the themes found in the homilies, it might be helpful to examine first their style and composition, starting with a brief historical background to Jesuit preaching in eighteenth-century Anglo-colonial America. This will be followed by a description of the appearance, length and style of the sermons and an inquiry into both the sources used in their composition and the manner in which they were utilized.

### *Jesuit Homiletic Tradition*

The Council of Trent meeting in its first session (1545-47) found time, among other pressing matters, to examine the reform of preaching. The need was surely urgent, as Catholic homiletics— which two centuries earlier had seen promising development both in theoretical and practical spheres—had degenerated into pedantry, bombast, and legend. Joseph Connors, in his as yet unsurpassed historical survey of Catholic preaching, notes: "The abstruse themes, the extravagant legends, the doomsday predictions and the claims to private revelations, which some preachers delivered from the pulpit, were poor substitutes for a pastoral message. To these abuses, moreover, had been added a pursuit of felicity in expression which was the peculiar product of the Renaissance revival of the pagan classics."[1] To be sure, the picture was not utterly bleak, but it was serious enough to spur the Council to action. After more than three months of discussion in committee, a succinct yet incisive statement was read to the fathers that presented a much more "pastoral" view in which preachers were urged to offer to their people: "wholesome words in proportion to their own and their people's capacity, by teaching them the things that are necessary for all to know in order to be saved, and by impressing upon them with briefness and plainness of speech the vices they must avoid and the virtues that they must cultivate, in order that they may escape eternal punishment and obtain the glory of heaven."[2] This statement was complemented soon after the close of the Council by the *Cathechism of the Council of Trent*, which was (as Connors notes) not a "question-and-answer presentation of basic doctrine," but rather a handbook "written specifically for priests, to be their manual of preaching and source book of sermon material."[3] Its importance lay in the wealth of material that it put in the hands of priests charged with the preparation of a homily: "The thorough but simple presentation of the whole range of Catholic doctrine, with references to the Bible passages which supported it, and with advice on how to explain it to the people step by step, showed the preachers just what was really important for their listeners to know, and drew them away from...moot points of theology."[4]

It was fortuitous for the church in general, and the reform of preaching in particular, that the Jesuits began their apostolic endeavors (which included as primary components preaching and education) just as the Council was encouraging what Connors delineates as the "two-fold homiletic movement in the sixteenth century— to strengthen apostolic ideals of preaching and to develop a full homiletic theory...."[5] The early leaders of the order offered a number of guidelines on preaching, from the founder, Ignatius of Loyola, his successors Jacopo Laínez and Francis Borgia, to Jerome Nadal who was charged with the creation of guidelines for the education of Jesuit seminarians. What emerges from these recommendations is the necessity that the preacher be a man of prayer, who recognizes that successful homiletics is a gift from God. Nevertheless, he should not fail to prepare his sermons by studying the Scriptures and the Fathers, drawing on a knowledge of the techniques of rhetoric, always with the aim of making plain to his flock the way to live a just and moral life. Though all of the Jesuits mentioned above recognized the importance of the study of formal rhetoric, Nadal was particularly forceful in his advocacy of the development of a homiletic rhetoric rooted in the Christian tradition.

His call did not go unheeded; by the seventeenth century numerous members of the Society had produced sizable tomes on the Christian use of rhetoric. Notable examples include Charles Regius' *Orator Christianus*, Nicolas Caussin's *Eloquentiae sacrae et humanae parallela libri xvi*, and René Rapin's *Réflexions sur l'usage de l'éloquence*. All of these would have been recommended to young Jesuits preparing for ordination.

This brings us to a pertinent question: what training in preaching or homiletics might those Jesuits on the Maryland mission have received? With the exception of William Hunter (who was educated in the early 1690s),[7] all of the priests whose sermons survive to the present day were educated in the eighteenth century, the large majority of them at the Jesuit house of studies at Liège.[8] Unfortunately, there is little evidence of the specifics of their homiletic preparation from 1700 to 1773, apart from the fact that they would have been studying various texts on preaching, and practicing within the walls of their house.[9] It is almost certain, though, that at the Jesuit preparatory school of St. Omers—which many of the priests of the English province had attended as boys— the students would have been immersed in the study of classical rhetoric, including Aristotle, Cicero and Quintilian. Cypriano Soarez's *De arte rhetorica* would most likely have been their textbook, and it provides a comprehensive treatment of argumentation (the student is urged to avoid hair-splitting), division (into *exordium, narratio, confirmatio* and *peroratio*) and style (including the effective, if restrained, use of verbal patterns such as *repetitio, gradatio, geminatio,* and *paronomasia*). Peter Bayley, after detailing this course of study, notes: "Not only did the schoolboy study the art of speaking and writing through the medium of texts, but he was expected to be able to compose and declaim an oration of his own, frequently in public."[10] He summarizes his discussion by commenting: "This analysis shows how detailed and complex was the sixteenth century schoolboy's introduction to literary criticism and practice, and gives us an idea of the wealth of stylistic resources likely to appear in these sermons."[11]

Some of those schoolboys later became Jesuit novices and scholastics. It is then we might wonder what authors they studied to learn the art of crafting of a homily. Connors notes that Regius' *Orator Christianus* was the standard textbook of the Society, but since it never went through more than one edition—it was displaced by Caussin's work, at least in popularity—it would be unwise to assume that it was a standard text in the eighteenth century.[12] A solution has been to turn to the work of a Jesuit, Blaise Gisbert, entitled *L'éloquence chrétienne dans l'idée et dans la pratique*, published in 1715. It was a work influential not only at the time it was published, but also for many decades to come.[13] Furthermore, it was translated anonymously into English as early as 1718, and though the evidence would suggest that it was little known among English-speaking Catholics, this does not rule out the possibility that it was accessible to seminarians on the Continent. Based on these factors of the work's contemporaneity, its influence, and its availability in English, to say nothing of its solid foundation in Jesuit writings on preaching, a brief exposition of its contents might be helpful in determining the homiletic preparation of the scholastics of the English Jesuit province.[14]

Gisbert begins his treatise by advising his reader:

If you would please, study to do so by the Excellency and Importance of the Truths you treat of; by solid and convincing Arguments; by a proper Application and clear Exposition of the Passages in Scripture; by well chosen citations from the Fathers, and when the Subject requires it, from the Councils and the Constitutions of the Church . . . by the Elevation and Propriety of Expression; by a Sobriety, Exactness and Novelty of Thoughts . . . ."[15]

He makes it clear that preaching is meant to have a moral impact on the hearer; compared to this its stylistic qualities are relatively unimportant. Its aim should be to "Send him [the listener] away with a contrite Heart, with weeping Eyes, a troubled Conscience, and dejected Looks, beating his Breast, as a mark of his sincere Sorrow, and silently retiring."[16] In order to achieve this end, Gisbert writes that the preacher must make use of the "greatest" secret in the "art of Eloquence," which is to "manage so, that at every Proposition he [the Hearer] may say to himself, it is to me the Preacher is speaking...."[17] The sermon must be addressed, then, to the individual needs of the listener, if it is to have the requisite impact. It also follows that a sermon must be comprehensible, hence the importance Gisbert places on unadorned language: "Let your Elocution be pure and simple, such as is fit to represent clearly what you have to say. Be accurate, but natural in your Language, never curious or affected."[18] In keeping with this he advises that divisions in the text be unobtrusive, and that long sermons be avoided.[19] Of paramount importance is the imparting of practical advice: "Accustom yourself to give a practical turn to everything you shall say...."[20] Examples from the lives of the saints are a prime instance where the practical ought to triumph over the extraordinary:

The Christian Orator should endeavour much more to recommend what is imitable in the Saints, than what is wonderful, for this great reason, that what is wonderful, conduces only to the glory of the Saints, but that which is imitable to the Salvation of the Hearers.[21]

This last concern, for the "salvation of the hearers," is the thrust of Gisbert's whole work, and Connors notes that "everything he expects the preacher to be and to do...should be derived from the preacher's purpose of converting his listeners to a better life."[22]

Whether Gisbert directly influenced the preaching of the Jesuits on the mission in Anlgo-colonial America or not, his concept of preaching—with its emphasis on the delivery of practical moral truths, uncomplicated construction, and simple and direct language —is strikingly comparable to the reality of colonial homiletics as exemplified in the sermons. Yet there is one contemporary source of information on preaching in colonial Anglo-America that should be considered before we turn to an examination of the sermons themselves.

While it is true that it is extremely difficult to prove a link between a particular homiletic work or theory and a particular Jesuit on the Maryland and Pennsylvania mission, in one case there is a fairly clear connection. Among the manuscript books found in the John Digges, Jr., papers at Georgetown University is one entitled *Spiritual Dialogues*.[23] This booklet is further divided into two sections, one headed "On the Principal Points of Christian Perfection," the second left untitled. It is in this second section, which deals with the means to achieve a "recollected" heart, a "peaceful" heart, etc., that a disquisition on preaching is found within a discussion on the "free" heart. The author—almost certainly not Digges, as the manuscript exhibits every sign of being copied from another, regrettably unknown, source—notes that there are three things which intrude on the freedom of the heart: "human respects," "weakness," and "degeneracy of mind." Choosing the preacher as an example, he proceeds:

A preacher, who renounces his own interest without concerning himself with what men will say or think of him, supporting his ministry by the practice of solid virtues, will become perfectly free, and with much less labour, than the other takes, in the tenth part of his time which he employs in composing and learning his sermons....[24]

He continues by elaborating on the way in which the faithful homilist will be used by God in the course of his preaching:

When a man has good natural talents, judgment, knowledge, and moreover liberty of heart, God choosing him for his minister will put words into his mouth not perhaps that will charm empty minds, but such as will touch the hearts of sinners and convert them.[25]

It soon becomes clear that the author is advocating that the preacher should rely more on God's grace, and less on his own preparation, if he desires both to touch the hearts of his listeners, and gain a "free heart." The homilist

Who retrenches part of that Sollicitude with which he was customed to prepare and compose his sermons to leave himself to the direction of God, becomes a fitter instrument in the hands of God, and able to bear with greater dignity the ministry of his word whilst he depends entirely on him. He who confines himself to what he has written in his paper, without daring to say anything more, is shut up in his paper, like a criminal in gaol. It is better to accustom ourselves by degrees to omit part of what we have composed, e.g. having written the beginning in indulgence to human nature, to leave the middle to God, following his direction, and the guidance of his divine Spirit.[26]

The directions given in this rather limited, tangential treatment of preaching do not, therefore, consist of rules or guidelines for the composition of a sermon, but rather encourage the homilist to limit the time spent in preparation, and, by cultivating a free heart, to trust in God to provide the most effective discourse. It is unclear to what extent this manuscript (or its original source) was known by the colonial clergy, or even, granting its recognition, the degree to which its advice was heeded. Only three sermons by Digges are extant, and of the three, two are complete sermons.[27] It should be noted, though, that a number of sermons in the collection, especially funeral sermons, and those dating from the latter part of the century, do consist solely of notes.[28]

Had the priests of the Anglo-Colonial mission been aware of and accepted the method of homiletics described above, it is unlikely that they would have left behind as many complete sermon manuscripts as they did. Such a spirituality of cultivating a "free heart" would have been quite appropriate to the needs of the circuit-riders of the eighteenth century, but, perhaps precisely because of their grueling schedule, it seems they preferred to rely on their own carefully prepared, if somewhat formal, manuscripts.

## The Appearance and Nature of the Sermons

If one were to study the "typical" colonial Catholic sermon, it would be found to be a handwritten manuscript, measuring roughly six inches by seven-and-a-half inches, and of eight pages in length.[29] At the top of the first page would be found a Scripture text, written in both Latin and English, and perhaps a motto such as *Ad majorem Dei gloriam*. Also noted in the upper right and/or left-hand margins would very likely be a list of the places where the sermon was preached, and the dates on which it was delivered.[30] The discourse was usually separated into four main parts, consisting of an introduction that divided the topic into two parts (ending with a Hail Mary), the two main sections of the body of the sermon, and a conclusion. While it is not uncommon for there to be explicit notations on the manuscript marking the divisions (usually "1 Pt.", etc.), it is more unusual for all the sections of the sermon to be so labeled.[31] As the homilies were handed on from priest to priest, emendations were made to the text, sometimes of so radical a nature that the former words were rendered illegible.[32] Apart from these later alterations, the texts do not exhibit extensive correction by their original authors, although it is not unusual to see whole sections crossed out. The vast majority of the sermons were written out in full, from the opening sentence, to a generic concluding line (e.g., "which God of his goodness grant you, in the name of the Father, Son and Holy Ghost, Amen.") which was invariably abbreviated.

The sermons are best described as being in what was called in perennial rhetoric the "plain style," that is, they employ unadorned and intelligible language with the aim of educating the hearers in the truths of the faith.[33] The divisions in the sermons are simple and not overly stressed, and rarely are there more than two main points upon which the homilists enlarge. Arguments are supported not only by references to the Fathers of the Church and conciliar texts, but also to moralistic stories from classical and ecclesiastical history.[34] The overarching thrust of the sermons is to move the hearers to practice their religion and inculcate the virtues in their lives, offering practical examples of the way to achieve this.[35] As with the simplified style of the Vincentian "Little Method," though, this does not mean that the homilies are entirely without rhetorical sophistication. Just as in that approach—which grew out of the preaching of St. Francis de Sales and St. Vincent de Paul—devices of classical rhetoric were not excluded but found a ready home,[36] so too in the preaching of the colonial Jesuits, one finds numerous examples of such techniques. These include: rhetorical interrogation, rhetorical exclamation, *communicatio* (taking the audience into partnership, and asking for their opinion on some matter), *prosopopeia* (taking on the thoughts and feelings of some real or imagined person), and *occupatio* (voicing an objection someone in the congregation might make). These stylistic techniques rarely appear cumbersome or ponderous, though, but rather are used in moderation to illuminate an argument or drive home a particular point.

It is interesting to note that in many of the areas discussed above the sermons of the colonial Catholic clergy are remarkably similar to those preached by their Anglican counterparts—in style if not necessarily in theology. They too were written out on similarly sized paper, and were of a comparable, if slightly longer length, and were headed by a scriptural text (though usually quoted only in English), and also a lengthy list of locations and dates.[37] Simple divisions into two or three parts were used in ordering the text, and the argument, bolstered by quotes from the Scriptures and eminent ecclesiastics, catechized the listener on the truths of the faith and urged the adoption of a more virtuous and regular lifestyle.[38]

One interesting similarity can be found in the number of times that the sermons were preached: Carol Van Voorst remarks that the Reverend Chase "read some of his sermons over a period of thirty years," a time span that rivals and surpasses many of the Maryland Jesuit missioners.[39] Yet besides maintaining a library of manuscript sermons (both their own and those of missionary companions) and preaching from them repeatedly, how did these ministers of the

Gospel deal wih the homiletic burden under which they labored? Samuel D'Oyley, the Anglican translator of Gisbert's work lamented:

> For here our People expect from us once at least, if not twice every week a regular and well composed Discourse, which alone is sufficient Employment for all our time. And a Man must have an uncommon Genius, and a peculiar Happiness of Memory, who can prepare a new Sermon, and repeat it too at the return of every Sunday: Nor is it possible for Persons of the most accomplished Talents to perform this without neglecting other Duties of their Ministry, which require a good part of their Care....[40]

Despite D'Oyley's claim that Roman Catholic preachers are not "sensible" of the difficulty of having to balance a demanding pastoral ministry with the duty of preaching frequently,[41] the grinding schedule of the colonial Jesuit missionaries, and the number and variety of sermons they were accustomed to deliver, is sufficient to call this assumption into question. Many Anglican ministers solved the problem by borrowing in full or in part from printed sermons, and Van Voorst notes: "Reading published sermons was not an unusual practice in the English Church. Many Maryland clergy avidly collected published lectures, and Johnathan Boucher...specifically notes that he thought his curate copied a sermon by Benjamin Hoadly."[42] If such was the practice among the Anglican colonial clergy, then one might surmise that their Catholic compatriots were familiar with such methods, and it is to the thorny issue of the originality and sources of the sermons that we now turn.

## The Sources of the Sermons

In his study of the spirituality of the Maryland Jesuits, Robert Emmett Curran writes: "The sermons of the Maryland Jesuits in the eighteenth century were highly derivative, freely utilizing the published works of Bourdaloue, Colombière and others."[43] That the extant sermons are not all original to the colonial missioners is obvious, given the references in some of them to specific collections of sermons and works of spirituality; yet these references number no more than twenty, out of a total of over four hundred manuscripts. This fact, taken alone and assuming that all borrowing had been attributed, would indicate that less than five percent of the sermons are based on the works of other authors. However, the homiletic practice of the times and the specific situation of the colonial clergy—overworked, and lacking the leisure for reflection—suggest that the frequency of utilization of other sources is much higher than the level of written attribution would indicate. Assuming this, though, still presents two major questions if the question of originality is to be addressed. The first is, how pervasive was the borrowing from other sources?; the second, when the missioners drew material from published works, how extensive was their use of the material?

Since the number of surviving sermons renders the meticulous examination of each individual manuscript impossible, it was decided to pick one specific liturgical feast for which a number of manuscript sermons were extant, and then compare these with a selection of printed sermon sources which were known to be available to the colonial priests. The results of such a comparison should offer some insights into the extent of adaptation of printed sources in the sermons, especially when supplemented with random discoveries made while studying the body of manuscripts as a whole.

Christmas was chosen as the sample feast day, since its prominence in the liturgical year guaranteed that a number of both manuscript and printed sermons would be available for comparison. Thirteen sermons in the Georgetown collection were composed for Christmas,[44] the largest number for any one feast-day or Sunday, representing eleven homilists. They were compared against fourteen printed sources known to have been available to the eighteenth-century clergy in colonial Maryland and Pennsylvania.[45] Four of these are by Louis Bourdaloue, S.J.,[46] two by St. Claude la Colombière, S.J.,[47] one by Timoléon Cheminais, S.J.,[48] two by William Darrell, S.J.,[49] one by John Gother,[50] two by Jacques Bossuet,[51] one by Jean-Baptiste Massillon,[52] and the sermon outline given by the *Catechism of the Council of Trent*.[53]

The results of this comparison reveal that, of the thirteen sermons in the Georgetown collection, five can definitely be traced to one of the printed sources mentioned above. Four of these sermons, those by Joseph Mosley, Sylvester Boarman, Charles Sewall and Joseph Greaton[54] are based on the first part of Louis Bourdaloue's "*Sermon sur la Nativité de Jésus Christ.*"[55] That of Robert Molyneaux[56] is drawn from Cheminais' "*Sermon sur la Nativité.*"[57] As for the others, both John Lewis' and Matthias Manners' sermons are very similar— both announce the division in their sermons by noting that they will discuss "What Jesus did to be Savior to men, what men must do to be saved by Jesus"[58]—indicating that both homilies are drawn from another, as yet unknown, source. The remaining six sermons do not resemble the themes or structures elaborated in the printed homilies examined, yet it is neither warranted nor prudent to assume that all these were original to the colonial clergy. However, since seven out of thirteen have been established to be borrowed in part or in full, this would suggest that a majority of the sermons are derived from other sources.

This hypothesis is only strengthened when the number of unattributed borrowings—discovered at random while researching works of spirituality available to the colonial clergy—is considered. Robert Manning's *Moral Entertainments on the Most Important Practical Truths of the Christian Religion*, for example—helpfully arranged as discourses on scriptural texts—was utilized no less than seventeen times in the composition of sermons for both the Sundays of the year and funerals.[59]

The Reverend John Lewis was no stranger to Manning's work, and the opening sentence of the latter's sermon on "The Certainty of Death": "Man's greatest weakness consists in receiving too easily impressions from sensible objects,"[60] found an echo in Lewis' homily for the funeral of Joseph Greaton.[61] Lewis borrowed the first few paragraphs of his sermon from Manning, but where the latter went on to speak of the certainty of death, Lewis declares that he will treat of the effects of death.[62] This link between Manning and Lewis proved quite fruitful, and research showed that eight other sermons attributed to Lewis were based on Manning's *Moral Entertainments* either in whole or in part. Lewis' homily on the text in Luke 3:8, "Bring forth therefore worthy fruits of penance,"[63] is an example of the former, while his discourse for the feast of the Purification, wherein he utilizes Manning's treatment of recommended devotions to the Virgin Mary as the last point he covers, exemplifies his method of partial use.[64] Altogether nine sermons are drawn in varying degrees from the writings of just one author, out of a total of twenty-two surviving Lewis homilies.

Lewis, however, was not the only colonial missioner who felt the attraction of Manning's work. Missioners Ashby, Livers, and Bolton also borrowed from him,[65] and Manning's is just *one* among many works of spirituality available to the clergy through libraries which were maintained at the various mission stations.[66]

Another popular source of homiletic content was Joseph Hornyhold's *The Decalogue Explained. In 32 Discourses on the Ten Commandments.*[67] Two missioners made use of this work in their preparation of sermons on the Ten Commandments. Augustine Jenkins has two sermons that treat the Decalogue, and both of them are clearly drawn from Hornyhold's work.[68] Also, John Bolton's sermon on the veneration due the saints deals with the proper interpretation of the first commandment, some of which is drawn from Hornyhold's "Third Discourse upon the First Commandment."[69]

Finally, considering the fundamental role which the writings of Richard Challoner played in the devotional life of eighteenth-century English Catholics, it would not be surprising to discover that thoughts and images from his work found their way into the sermons of the Maryland and Pennsylvania clergy.[70] In speaking of Challoner it is essential that one bear in mind Richard Luckett's caveat: "It is never safe to assume that any passage . . . is original."[71] Still, the similarity between passages in Challoner and passages in the colonial sermons suggests they were borrowed, if not from the English Vicar-Apostolic, then from one of the authors that he himself turned to for "inspiration." These included St. Francis de Sales, Boudon, Kellison, Woodhead, and Gother,[72] many of whose works were meditated on in their own right by colonial Catholics.

Three instances could be offered where an image from Challoner resonates in a colonial sermon. For example, in Bernard Diderich's sermon on Hell, he asks: "where is the man, that would even venture to hold his finger in the flame of a candle for half a quarter of an hour, for any reward this world can give?"[73] Challoner put it almost exactly the same: "where is the man that would even venture to hold his finger in the flames of a candle, for a quarter of an hour, for any reward this world can give?"[74] Likewise, compare the following passage from a sermon of George Hunter, with a similar one from Challoner:

| Hunter | Challoner |
|---|---|
| If thou lookest up thou shalt see an infinite omnipotent judge exasperated with thy crimes; if thou casts an eye downwards, thou shalt see hell open and that cruel furnace ready glowing prepared to receive thee to torment. On thy right shall be thy Sins accusing thee, on thy left the Devils ready....[75] | Beneath his feet he sees hell open, ready to swallow him up; above his head, an angry judge preparing to thunder out, against him, the irrevocable sentence of eternal damnation. On his right, he sees his guardian angel, now abandoning him; on his left, the devils, his merciless enemies, just ready to seize upon him....[76] |

Though not identical, they are close enough to establish that borrowing has occurred, if not from Challoner, then from a third source that both have in common.

Finally, consider a similar example from a funeral sermon of Robert Harding, in which he describes the meeting of the body and soul of one who has lived a wicked life, and compare with another passage from Challoner:

| Harding | Challoner |
|---|---|
| Who can alas express the horror which ought to possess the sinners mind, when he reflects on what will become of the body he has clothed so richly, feeds so delicately, in fine makes it his choicest and only care.... "Oh! thou accursed partner of my life," will it say, "for thee have I forfeited eternal joy, and to please thee, to gratify thy senses, to indulge thy passions have I been plunged in an ocean of torments, and tumbled into the abyss of hell...."[77] | But oh! what dreadful curses shall pass between the meeting of the reprobate! "Accursed carcase!" will the soul say, "was it to please thee, to indulge thy brutal inclinations, that I have forfeited the immortal joys of heaven! Ah wretch! to give thee a filthy pleasure for a moment, I have damned both myself and thee, to all eternity!"[78] |

Again, the disparity in language between the two examples suggests that perhaps a third author is the source of both quotations; nonetheless, it indicates that borrowing from sources of spirituality was not uncommon.

What we have seen indicates that on a given Sunday or feast day, the sermon delivered to the assembled congregation was in all likelihood derived either in full or in part from a published series of sermons or work of spirituality. It now remains to investigate the second question posed above, which is the degree of adaptation of outside sources in individual homilies delivered by the colonial clergy.

As we noted in the comparisons made earlier with the works of Bishop Challoner, the use of such texts by the Jesuit homilists was rarely verbatim. They worked with the printed sources creatively, and it will be the purpose of what follows to illustrate briefly the various ways they accomplished this. Examples will be drawn primarily, but not exclusively, from the sermons where attributions were made by their author to other sources, as well as from some of those authors who were discovered to have silently engaged in borrowing.

While it would seem that the practice of copying a sermon verbatim—with no additions, changes or deletions—was not common, at least four examples can be cited that come very close. All are by Arnold Livers, who based his extant sermons on Manning's *Moral Entertainments*.[79] For example, his sermon on Luke 3:8, "Bring forth therefore fruits worthy of penance," omits Manning's first sentence concerning venial sin, and offers instead a paraphrase on the necessity of repentance, before picking up with Manning's second sentence and then faithfully following it through to the end.[80] In a similar fashion, Liver's homily for Sexagesima Sunday, on the text "The sower went out to sow his seed," begins with the first sentence of Manning's sermon on the same text, numbered the "Fifty-Fifth Entertainment," and follows it faithfully through to the last line, except for a change in the regimen he recommends for spiritual growth.[81]

Often times, as in the latter example, the reason behind a minor change can be deduced (e.g., Livers was reluctant to add a half-hour of spiritual reading to the schedule of prayer he was setting out for his audience), as is the case with modifications in the other two sermons of Livers that have been preserved for posterity. In his sermon on the dangers of the world, which follows Manning's "Thirty-Fifth Entertainment" very closely, there is at least one divergence. Whereas Manning writes:

The world may be grown too hard for our duty; and it happens but too often in the unfortunate examples of those who renounce their religion to save their estates, or to attain some preferment at court: for it is plain that the love of the world prevails in their hearts, and determines to that unhappy choice with the utter ruin of their souls."[82]

Livers renders the passage in the following way:

The world may be grown too hard for our duty; as it happens but too often in the unfortunate examples of those who renounce their religion to save their estates; or marry out of the Church, only to gratify their lust, or for some paultry temporal addition to their fortunes.[83]

Here we see that Livers is not so dull as to make use of an example that would have little meaning for his listeners—the gaining of a preferment at court—but rather substitutes one that he must have believed was both more pressing and more intelligible, that of marriage outside of the church.[84] In a like manner he adds an aside in his sermon on lukewarmness; reproducing Manning's judgment that "the tepid Christian holds on his middle way between these two [the zealous and the lax]; and therefore hears Mass indeed, if he can do it with ease...."[85] but adding on his own: "but will take care not to be at the chapel before it is just going to begin, or rather something later, for fear of being seen upon his knees some time sooner than what the positive precept requires...."[86] Again Livers contextualizes by means of an example a statement that he takes from Manning's work, this time by means of addition only, without removing any of Manning's own illustrations.

These techniques of Livers only serve as an introduction to the manifold ways in which the colonial clergy emended the material that they borrowed from other sources. Their main methods in altering a printed source for use in a sermon consisted of either additions or deletions to a text, or changes in the phrasing employed by the original author. The following examples should illuminate some of the ways in which they did this.

When additions were made to a source text, it was most often to better contextualize its message. Livers' addition of comments on Mass-going behavior was one instance of this, but others may be cited. James Beadnall, for example, one of the most creative of the colonial homilists, skipped whole sections of the sermons from which he borrowed, quoted paragraphs from the source text in reverse order, dropped numerous examples, and added some of his own. In his sermon for the Feast of the Circumcision, Beadnall makes use of Colombière's sermon for the same day, but only begins his adaptation of it halfway through his discourse. In the first part, commenting on poor use that people make of the time they are given in life, he observes:

Behold the old planter grown pale and wane. See his yellow eyes, sunken cheeks and shriveled visage. Ask him how this has come, how it has happened? He'll tell you, by heats, and by labors and toils, by troubles and afflictions.

Nor is Beadnall content with just one example drawn from life in colonial Maryland.

See that poor slave both decrepit and old, maimed in his limbs and shattered in his body. Demand how these accidents came? How these woeful disasters and evils befell him? He'll tell you by hunger and thirst, by labors and toils, by laying on the [illeg.] ground and exposing himself for his master.[87]

Certainly the images of the aged planter and the careworn slave would have had a certain resonance for the Catholics of colonial Maryland, images which one does not, nor could not, expect to find in Colombière's *"Deuxième Sermon pour le Jour de la Circoncision."*[88]

In other instances sensitivity to local conditions can be discerned even amidst an otherwise close translation of a sermon text. In Robert Harding's sermon for the Fifteenth Sunday after Pentecost on preparation for death, which follows Bourdaloue's sermon for the same day rather closely—though with many omissions—he adds a small, but interesting phrase. Bourdaloue says

God, it is true, according to the apostle, hath appointed pastors to watch over and direct us; pastors responsible to him for our souls. But, after all, we ourselves must watch; and the vigilance of the pastors of the Church would be insufficient to stay the perils of death, if not accompanied and supported by our own.[89]

Harding, however, renders this as follows:

God has given us pastors, says St. Paul, who watch over us, and who are responsible for our souls. But after all, we are our own strict pastors, *and in many cases are our only pastors*, nor will all the vigilance of the pastors of the Church defend us from the dangers of death, unless it be accompanied and backed by our own.[90]

Here Harding adds an insertion that is small, no doubt, but none the less germane to a scattered community that rarely saw their priests, and lacked ready access to them for advice and direction.

Many times the additions are more substantive, and though they are not, like Beadnall's use of planter and slave, readily recognizable as additions to the text, they are none the less telling when discovered. Take Joseph Mosley's homily "On the Ascension" which he adapted from Bourdaloue's sermon for the feast. Bourdaloue, after speaking of the sufferings that Christians experience in the world, and the way that God rewards them in his kingdom, comments:

*Mais ma douleur est, chrétiens, que les vôtres ne sont pas communément de ce caractère; ma douleur est, qu'au lieu que les saints disaient en s'adressant à Dieu, Propter te mortificamur tota die....*[91]

Mosley follows only half this thought, and then continues with his own example:

I am afraid, that I've reason to apprehend, that your sufferings are not of this stamp or character. How many are the sufferings of Christians in this life? In their families, some from your wives, some from your husbands, some from your children? How many suffer from poverty, by want, by their ill-natured neighbour? How many again by accidents, by unpleasant seasons, as heat, cold, rain? And how are these sufferings born with? The husband answers the contradictions of a wife by oaths and bitter imprecations, and perhaps with blows. The wife bears the ill-temper of her husband by foul language or revenges herself on him by opening his failings to the whole neighbourhood. The children are treated with bitter curses, or unhumanely and barbarously corrected by kicks and blows.[8]

This passage has been quoted at length, not from any desire to highlight the lurid side of colonial domestic life, but rather to illustrate the detailed quality of the additions that were often made to otherwise second-hand material. Such emendations were certainly made for a reason, and it is certainly plausible to assume that they reflected the lived experience of the colonial clergy.

Often times the appended information is of a positive, prescriptive quality, as in this insertion by Augustine Jenkins, made in the midst of commenting what little return Christians make to God for all his goodness: "Of the whole day what does God exact of us as his right? Nothing but to spend 14 or 15 minutes of it morning and evening in prayer to honor him as our Creator and Redeemer...."[93] Here Jenkins inserts his own thoughts on the amount of time that ought to be devoted to prayer, where Darrell's text is silent on the question.[94]

The homilists were just as prepared to eliminate material from the sermons they utilized as they were to add to them; perhaps even more so. One factor was that the printed sermons were often much too long for a colonial audience; this was especially true of sermons by the great French preachers Bourdaloue and Colombière. Internal evidence suggests that, on average, sermons preached to Catholic congregations in colonial Maryland and Pennsylvania lasted at least half an hour,[95] while the time involved in reading a typical French court sermon would take almost twice that. A common solution to this difficulty was to use only one of the divisions in a printed sermon as the basis for an entire sermon to be delivered in the colonies.[96]

Sentences or paragraphs were often deleted for reasons other than space or time constraints. Sometimes the motivation is obvious, as when James Ashby makes the following change in William Darrell's "Moral Reflection" for the First Sunday of Advent. Darrell comments, in regard to worldly men, that if one were to

Talk to them of the other world, they understand not the language; they are as great strangers to the dialect, as Joseph was to that of the Egyptians. One would take them for men dropped from the sphere of the moon, or lately come from the *wilds of America*; without instruction, and almost without reason.[97]

Understandably, Ashby sees fit to recast this thought in a manner less offensive to those currently residing in the "wilds of America:"

To speak to people nowadays of the next life and their duty they owe to their Creator they seem as regardless of what one said as if they were entirely ignorant of the language one speaks.[98]

One should note that in the process of refashioning the text, Ashby also eliminates the reference to Joseph in the land of Egypt, and this excising of what the colonial homilists deemed excess examples was by no means uncommon.[99]

Their deletions were often times more substantive and theological, however. James Ashby, in the same sermon noted above, removes much more than just an inappropriate reference to America. William Darrell spends almost the last half of his sermon railing against sins of lust and impurity, warming to his subject by declaring:

Although God by the mouth of his prophets has thundered out a thousand curses against this detestable sin; although he has drowned once the world, together with its impure inhabitants, and consumed five cities with fire and brimstone, and threatens the luxurious with everlasting flames; yet, in spite of preaching and punishment, it dares appear, though not without shame, yet without remorse, and even almost without reproof, in Christendom.[100]

Ashby prefers to speak rather of the dangers inherent in the misuse of the things of this world:

Take off your hearts from worldly allurements which cannot make you happy here, and probably will make you miserable hereafter. God does not condemn a reasonable care of temporal concerns, nay he absolutely commands it, but the care of our souls must be the principal.[101]

Whether Ashby declined to speak on the sins of the flesh due to a reluctance to treat of such a topic,[102] or because he simply desired to talk of a different matter, the fact remains that he felt a freedom to depart in a substantial way from the text he was using as a source.[103]

Often material was omitted because it simply did not apply to life in the colonies. James Beadnall excises from his homily on frequent communion a number of sections of the Bourdaloue sermon from which it is drawn; for example, one addressed to ministers which calls on them to make the eucharist more accessible to Christians:

*Vous, ministres de Jésus-Christ, n'oubliez jamais que vous êtes envoyés pour rassembler les fidèles à sa table, et non pour les en éloigner. Ne vous faites pas un principle de leur rendre l'accès si difficile, qu'ils désespèrent de pouvoir être admis au banquet. Ouvrez-leur la porte de la salle, ou du moins ne la leur fermez pas.*[104]

These comments of Bourdaloue, made in the midst of the controversy over Jansenism, were inapplicable to the colonial situation, which was far removed both in time and space from the context in which Bourdaloue preached.

Along with additions and subtractions, the Jesuit homilists of Anglo-colonial America were also adept at condensing paragraphs of printed text into just a few sentences, a practice necssitated by the demands of time and the attention span of the congregation. As just one example, consider the very detailed description that Bourdaloue gives of the achievements of the Society of Jesus (on the Feast of St. Ignatius) and the way in which John Bolton compresses it:

## BOURDALOUE

*d'une compagnie qui, sans se renfermer dans l'enceinte d'une province ou d'un empire, doit annoncer la gloire de Dieu et son saint nom dans tout l'univers: Euntes in mundum universum; doit prêcher l'Evangile à tous les peuples sans distinction d'âge, depuis les enfants jusques aux plus avancés, sans distinction de qualités et d'états, depuis les plus pauvres et les plus petits jusques aux plus riches et aux plus grands: Praedicate Evangelium omni creaturae; d'une compagnie qui, sans se borner à un moyen plutôt qu'à l'autre, fait profession d'embrasser tous les moyens de glorifier Dieu et de sanctifier les âmes: les écoles publiques et l'instruction de la jeunesse, la connaissance des lettres et divines et humaines, le ministère de la sainte parole, la direction des consciences, les assemblées de piété, les missions et les retraites: d'une compagnie qui, pour se dégager de tout autre intérêt que celui de Dieu et des âmes qu'il a rachetées de son sang, renonce solennellement à tout salaire et à toute dignité; qui, pour être plus étroitement liée au service de l'Eglise de Dieu, s'engage par un voeu exprès à s'employer partout où les ordres du soverain pontife et du vicaire de Jésus-Christ la destineront, fallût-il pour cela s'exposer à toutes les rigueurs de la captivité, à toutes les horreurs de la mort: d'une compagnie qui, par la miséricorde du Seigneur et par la force toute-puissante de son bras, perpétuée de siècle en siècle et toujours animée du même esprit, à la place des ouvriers qu'elle perd, en doit substituer d'autres pour leur succéder, pour hériter de leur zèle, pour cultiver les mêmes moissons, pour soutenir les mêmes fatigues, pour essuyer les mêmes ennemis et avec les mêmes armes, pour remporter les mêmes victoires, ou pour faire de leur réputation, de leur vie, les mêmes sacrifices.*[105]

## Bolton

A Society not bounded to carry the name of Jesus within the limits of one Province or Empire, but must carry that glorious name before all nations, to preach the Gospel to all men without distinction all over the universe. A Society not constrained to any one way, but [one that] embraces all means to glorify God and to save souls, as by public schools, instruction of youth, preaching the word of God, by erecting public congregations of piety or Sodalities. A body of men consecrated to all crosses and afflictions, to the greatest labors and fatigues and even to the terrors of death for the greater glory of God and the salvation of souls. A Society through the mercy of God actuated with the same spirit from age to age, for laborers lost and victoriously fallen can substitute others that inherit their zeal, that willingly embrace their labors, undergo their fatigues, expose themselves to the same dangers, engage the same enemy and equally sacrifice their reputation and lives.[106]

Such condensation of language and imagery is extremely common, especially when the preachers were translating a text from French, though it also occurs even when utilizing an English source.[107]

Finally, it must be kept in mind that the colonial preachers did not limit themselves to a single source when composing (or transcribing) a homily. At least one homily in the collection is drawn from two sources: Manning's *Moral Entertainments* and Darrell's *Moral Reflections*. Bolton, the author, alternates in quoting first a paragraph from one, then the other, and so on through the homily — changing a sentence here and there, and also adding some original material (although a third source may be involved).[108] This was probably a common practice, and may account for some of the additions that were discovered in the homilies that were studied.

However, it is important, despite all the evidence that exists for considering the sermons in the collection to be highly derivative, not to dismiss the idea that at least some of them contain large amounts of original material. It is, of course, much more difficult to prove originality than to establish derivation, but the existence in the Georgetown College Library Collection of such scriptural, patristic and theological compendiums as Houdry's *La Bibliothèque des prédicateurs*, Labata's *Loci communes ad Conciones*, and Claus' *Spicilegium Catechetico Concionatorium*, indicate that at least some of the missionaries were composing part or all of their sermons.

In the opinion of Robert Emmett Curran, the use of published sermons and commonplaces by the colonial missioners leads to "the impression the sermons give of being out of time and place."[109] Yet, while admitting that the style and language employed in them makes it difficult to categorize the sermons as informal and spontaneous discourse, they are comparable to what Anglo-Catholics were hearing in sermons both in England and on the Continent.[110] Furthermore, a partial but representative comparison of the sermons with the sources upon which they were based reveals that the missionaries were more than willing to make additions and deletions to their source text, some of a substantial nature, in order to adapt a sermon to the needs of their audience. Perhaps, considering the demands upon their time and the conditions under which they lived, more could not be expected.

## NOTES

1    Joseph M. Connors, S.V.D., "Catholic Homiletic Theory in Historical Perspective" (Ph.D. diss., Northwestern University, 1962), 77.

2    *Canons and Decrees of the Council of Trent*, trans. Henry J. Schroeder (St. Louis: Herder, 1941), 26, quoted in Connors, 80. Edwin C. Dargan states that the Council's actions were "effective in producing a decided improvement in Catholic preaching." *A History of Preaching*, vol. 2, (New York: Burt Franklin, 1968), 25; Hubert Jedin observes: "The decree on `[Bible] reading and preaching,' published in the fifth session, held on 17 June 1546, was the first, and we may add at once, the only successful attempt to combine Church reform with whatever was sound in Christian humanism." *A History of the Council of Trent*, vol. 2, trans. Ernest Graf (St. Louis: Herder, 1961), 122. For an account of the discussion surrounding the decree, see Jedin, 99-124.

3    Connors, 81.

4   Connors, 82. The Tridentine manual was not ignored by the colonial Jesuits, who quoted the decrees of Trent frequently in their sermons, and kept numerous copies in their libraries. See for example the Bohemia Manor booklist, MPA,16,3, and that of St. Thomas Manor, MPA,15,18.

5   Connors, 97, and Dargan, 25.

6   See Connors, 98-105. For Ignatius of Loyola's *Rules for Preachers*, see the Jesuit *Constitutions*, pt.IV, c.8, Decl. B,C. For Laínez's *Monita*, see Hartmannus Grisar ed., *Jacobi Lainez Disputationes Tridentinae* (Innsbruck, 1886), 2:506-542. For Borgia's *De ratione concionandi*, see Patrick Boyle ed. and trans., *Instructions on Preaching* (New York: Benziger, 1902). For Nadal's *De Ministerio Verbi Dei*, see *Monumenta Historica Societatis Iesu, Epistolae et Monumenta P. Hieronymi Nadal*, Vol. 4, (Madrid, 1905), 653-670. For an excellent life of Nadal see, William V. Bangert, S.J., *Jerome Nadal, S.J., 1507-1580*, ed. Thomas M. McCoog, S.J. (Chicago: Loyola University Press, 1992).

7   Geoffrey Holt, S.J., *The English Jesuits 1650-1829: A Biographical Dictionary* (London: Catholic Record Society, 1984), 126.

8   Holt, 2.

9   It had been anticipated that the Jesuit School Manuscripts Collection, housed at Georgetown University, and consisting of forty-three manuscript texts presumed to correspond to the course of studies at Liège, would have shed some light on the homiletic preparation of Jesuit scholastics. However, an examination of this material revealed nothing relevant to homiletics. For information on the collection, see *Special Collections at Georgetown. A Descriptive Catalog* (Washington, D.C.: Georgetown University Library, 1989), 64.

10  Peter Bayley, *French Pulpit Oratory, 1598-1650* (Cambridge: Cambridge University Press, 1980), 22. For Bayley's description of the Jesuit's curriculum in rhetoric, see 23-29.

11  Bayley, 29.

12  Connors, 135.

13  Conners notes, "This extensive and critical work by a French Jesuit was translated into German and Italian, going through several editions in both languages. Later European writers knew and used it extensively" (149).

14  A further factor which suggests that Gisbert's work played a role in the formation of the Jesuit missionaries of the English province is that a copy of the French edition was located in the rare book collection of the Woodstock Theological Library at Georgetown University, a collection which is drawn from, among other sources, the original mission libraries maintained by the Jesuits and brought with them from the Continent.

15  Blaise Gisbert, *Christian Eloquence in Theory and Practice*, trans. Samuel D'Oyley (London: H. Clements, 1718), 14. The text cited is the only English translation made of Gisbert's work, done incidentaly by an Anglican, but none the less faithful to Gisbert's original French. The particular copy consulted was owned by Richard Henry Lee, and is now housed in the Special Collections of the University of Virginia Library.

16    Gisbert, 44.

17    Gisbert, 311.

18    Gisbert, 58.

19    Gisbert, 101,151.

20    Gisbert, 314. Similar advice was given to Puritan preachers in the colonies by William Perkins in his *Art of Prophecying*. They were urged to: (1) read the text of Scripture distinctly, (2) give the correct interpretation of it, (3) offer a few related points of doctrine, and (4) apply these to daily life in a simple and unadorned way. Cf. *American Sermons: The Pilgrims to Martin Luther King*, ed. Michael Warner (New York: Library Classics, 1999), 889.

21    Gisbert, 325.

22    Gisbert, 149.

23    Georgetown University Special Collections, Rev. John Digges, Jr., S.J., Papers, folder 2. Digges (1712-1746) was a Maryland native, educated at St. Omers and Liège. He was sent back to Maryland in 1742, but died only four years later. See Holt, 80. Practically all that is known of him is the unflattering evaluation made of Digges' scholastic ability by the provincial: "ingenium non promptum." Noted in Thomas Hughes, *History of the Society of Jesus in North America*, *Text*, vol. 2 (London: Longmans, Green, and Co., 1917), 692.

24    John Digges Jr. Papers, 2

25    Ibid.

26    Ibid.

27    ACSC, Dig-1, Dig-2, Dig-3. It is unclear if Dig-2, the incomplete sermon, was deliberately left so—in keeping with the advice offered above—or if this was simply an oversight (i.e., a sermon whose composition was never completed).

28    See, for example, ACSC, Neal-8(a-d), Neal-10(g,h), Pi-8, Pi-9, Car-10, Car-12. While Puritan preachers typically wrote their sermons out, memorized them, and then preached from memory or from numbered outline notes (*American Sermons*, 889), it seems fairly certain that the Anglo-Catholic missioners routinely preached by reading from a written text, at least in the first three-quarters of the century. This can be established not only from the large number of extant manuscripts, but also from comments such as the following by Father Farmer: "I preach in German and English. However, in the latter, only on paper as the English-born do themselves." MPA, 25,5. It would seem that Farmer's German-speaking flock preferred a more fluid homiletic style, as many congregations did by the end of the century. Robert Molyneaux wrote to John Carroll in 1785 from Philadelphia that "I am now near thirteen years at Philadelphia, and I find it harder to preach than formerly. I wish I had the talent of doing it *ex tempore*. To preach with a paper does not suit this place so well; and now from want of time and habit, I should find it difficult to speak without" (quoted in Hughes, 514). Carroll himself wrote to a friend that Holy Week (1802) was so busy "when a moment was obtained, I was forced to employ it in preparing a Passion sermon, as those I had ready, were become stale in this

Congregation and after all, I was under the necessity of going into the pulpit with a half-finished discourse." MPA, 57.5,18 (also in JCP, 2:386-87)

29    Admittedly, the size of the manuscript pages does vary, from the small six-and-a-half by four inch pages favored by John Lewis and Henry Pile, to the expansive nine-and-three-quarter by seven-and-a-half inch sheets used by Leonard Neale. As to length, not all the homilists thought it prudent to limit themselves to eight pages; Benet Neale has a sermon on "Faith and Works" in which he proposes to "solve then this grand question in brief," that runs to *forty* pages in two sections, ACSC, Ne-10.

30    In a few cases these dates span the length of a missioners career, e.g., Joseph Mosley's sermon for the feast of the Ascension, preached 10 times between 1763 and 1784. ACSC, Mos-7.

31    Although a Corpus Christi sermon by James Frambach explicitly designates the "*Exordium*" and the "Conclusion." ACSC, Fr-1.

32    Apart from this problem, and considering their age and the conditions under which they were written, the sermons are remarkably readable. Except for occasional tears and water spotting, the text is unobscured, and the handwriting is fairly legible.

33    Connors, 43.

34    There are many instances of this, e.g., ACSC, Nea-1, and Mat-4.

35    This follows fairly closely the vision of the homily as presented by Gisbert.

36    See Connors' treatment of this in *Catholic Homiletic Theory*, 122-29, and also in his "The Vincentian Homiletic Tradition, II," *American Ecclesiastical Review* 138 (Nov., 1958), 338-50, esp. 343-49.

37    Carol L. Van Voorst comments: "Many of them [sermons] were preached again and again, sometimes in different locations but often in the same church." "The Anglican Clergy in Maryland, 1692-1776" (Ph.D. diss., Princeton University, 1978), 277; Richard Beale Davis notes that many Anglican preachers had the habit "of giving the dates and places where each sermon was preached." *Intellectual Life in the Colonial South. 1585-1763*, vol. 2 (Knoxville: University of Tennessee Press, 1978), 741.

38    The largest collection of colonial Anglican sermons in manuscript form may be found in the Archives of the Episcopal Diocese of Maryland consisting of over one hundred and thirty sermons, of which at least one hundred are by the Reverend Thomas Cradock. For a "typical" sermon, see Cradock's Easter sermon of 1768 in which he discusses in his first part "various irresistible proofs" of the resurrection, and in the second, the effect it ought to have in the life of a Christian. Archives of the Episcopal Diocese of Maryland (AEDM), Baltimore, Cradock papers. For a discussion of Cradock's life and preaching, see David C. Skaggs, ed. *The Poetic Writings of Thomas Cradock, 1718-1770* (Newark: University of Delaware Press, 1983), esp. 32-42. Also his "Thomas Cradock Sermons," *Maryland Historical Magazine* 67 (1972): 179-80.

39    Van Voorst, 278.

40    Gisbert, a3$^r$. The very fact that ministers of the Church of England were

turning to the same book as Roman Catholics for assistance in homiletics is significant in light of the similarities in the style and manner of their preaching. r

41    Gisbert, a4^r.

42    Van Voorst, 277, n. 3.

43    Robert Emmett Curran, S.J., *American Jesuit Spirituality. The Maryland Tradition, 1634-1900* (New York: Paulist Press, 1988), 14.

44    ACSC, Boa-7, Bol-13(a), Bol-13(b), Bol-19, Gr-3, Le-10, Ma-3, Mol-6, Mor-1, Mos-10, Ro-23, Se-22, Wa-3. Notations, however, indicate that they were occasionally delivered on the days following Christmas, most likely due to the missioner's inability to visit all of his flock on Christmas day. Cf. ACSC, Bol-13(a), Bol-13(b).

45    The authors of these printed works were selected for one, or both, of the following reasons: (1) It was previously established—by the colonial clergy's written admission—that the author's work had been referenced in composing a sermon; (2) The work appeared on one of the catalogs of books in the libraries maintained at the Jesuit's mission stations.

46    (1632-1704), one of the most celebrated preachers of seventeenth-century France. Many of his printed homilies were those delivered before Louis XIV and his court, and which earned him the title of "*roi des orateurs et orateur des rois.*" For a treatment of his life and preaching, see H. Chérot, "Bourdaloue, Louis," *Dictionnaire de Théologie Catholique*, ed. A. Vacant *et al.*, vol. 2 (Paris: Librairie Letouzey, 1932), cols. 1095-99. Also Émile-Antoine Blampignon, *Étude sur Bourdaloue* (Geneva: Slatkine Reprints, 1972), Henri Bremond *Histoire Littéraire du Sentiment Religieux en France*, vol. 8 (Paris: Librairie Bloud et Gay, 1930), 310-60, and Dargan, 99-105. A popular version of his life is John Reville, *Herald of Christ, Louis Bourdaloue, S.J.* (New York: Schwartz, Kirwin & Fauss, 1922). The four sermons, all titled "*Sur la Nativité de Jesus-Christ,*" may be found in the *Oeuvres de Bourdaloue*, vols. 1, 2, 3 (Paris: Chez Firmin Didot Frères Librairies, 1840), 1: 64-75, 129-39; 2: 253-63; 3: 565-67. An English translation of the second of the sermons in vol. 1 of the Firmin edition can be found in *Sermons and Moral Discourses on the Important Duties of Christianity*, trans. Anthony Carroll, S.J. (Dublin: James Duffy, 1855), 2-21.

47    (1641-1682), confessor to St. Margaret Mary Alacoque, chaplain to the Duchess of York in London (where he was imprisoned during the unrest surrounding Titus Oates plot), and known for his *Retraite spirituelle*, and *Lettres spirituelles*, Colombière was also a gifted preacher, although, as Henri Monier-Vinard comments, "*Il est regrettable que les sermons aient été rangés dans un ordre si arbitraire.*" "Claude La Colombière" *Dictionnaire de Spiritualité*, eds. M. Viller *et al.*, vol. 2 (Paris: Beauchesne, 1953) cols. 939-43. See also Bremond, vol. 6 (Paris: Librairie Armand Colin, 1967), 401-10. His first and second sermons "*Pour le Jour de Noel*" are found in the *Oeuvres Complètes du Vénérable Père Claude de la Colombière*, vol. 1 (Grenoble: Imprimerie du Patronage Catholique, 1900), 101-25, 127-50.

48 (1652-1689), a seventeenth-century preacher who had, in the words of J. Brucker *"une courte, mais brillante carrière comme predicateur. Il avait le don de toucher les coeurs par une sorte d'onction particulière, que secondait bien le douceur de son débit. Mais il est loin d'avoir la richesse de doctrine et l'éloquente logique de son contemporain et confrère Bourdaloue."* "Cheminais de Montagu, Timoléon" in *Dictionnaire de Théologie Catholique*, vol. 2, cols. 1095-99. His sermon *"Sur la Nativité de Jésus-Christ"* is found in *Sermons du Père Cheminais*, vol. 2 (Paris: Chez George & Louis Josse, 1694), 32-59.

49 (1651-1721) rector and professor at the Jesuit schools of St. Omers and Liège, and author of a defense of St. Ignatius (London, 1688), the *Gentleman Instructed in the Conduct of a Virtuous and Happy Life* (London: 1732), and *Moral Reflections on the Epistles and Gospels of every Sunday throughout the Year* (London: 1711). It is from the latter that Darrell's two sermons for Christmas Night are taken (one for the epistle, and one for the Gospel). For more information on his life, see Joseph Gillow, *Biographical Dictionary of the English Catholics*, 5 vols. (London: Burns & Oates, 1885-1903), 2:17-19.

50 (?-1704), a secular priest who labored for over twenty years on the English mission, was one of the foremost spiritual writers of his day, in addition to which he had the great fortune to instruct the young Richard Challoner in the faith, and was instrumental in directing him to studies at Douay in July 1704. Joseph Chinnici notes that Gother's works were "known for their emphasis on Scripture, the social mission of Christianity, and the apostolate of the laity." *Living Stones: The History and Structure of Catholic Spiritual Life in the United States* (New York: Macmillan, 1989), 9. Gillow calls him "the principal Catholic controversialist during the reign of James II," and notes "his laborious efforts were met with great success." See Gillow, 2:540ff; and Sr. Marion Norman, I.V.B.M., "John Gother and the English Way of Spirituality," *Recusant History* 11 (October 1972): 306-19. Gother's sermon may be found in the *Spiritual Works of John Gother*, vol. 4 (Newcastle: F. Coates, 1792), 68-81.

51 (1627-1704), a preacher known for his elaborate funeral orations, but who also produced a series of sermons for Sundays and feasts throughout the liturgical year. For Bossuet's life and spirituality, see P. Dudon, "Bossuet," *Dictionnaire de Spiritualité*, vol. 1 (Paris: Firmin-Didot, 1937), cols. 1874-83. His two sermons *"Sur le mystère de la nativité de Notre-Seigneur"* are found in *Chefs-d'Oeuvers de Bossuet*, vol. 2 (Paris: Chez Lefèvre, Éditeur, 1844), 216-43, 251-62.

52 (1663-1742), priest of the French Oratory and Bishop of Clermont. See A. Molien, "Massillon, Jean-Baptiste," *Dictionnaire de Théologie Catholique*, vol. 10, part 1, cols. 258-65. The French text for Massillon's Christmas sermon is found in *Oeuvres de Massillon*, vol. 1 (Paris: Chez Firmin Didot Frères, Librairies, 1853), 83-93. An English translation is in *Sermons by Jean-Baptiste Massillon*, ed. and trans. William Dickson (Brooklyn: T. Kirk, 1803), 306-30.

53 The Catechism of the Council of Trent, as mentioned above, contained an outline of a catechism arranged for delivery throughout the Sundays of the liturgical year. That given for Christmas recommends an explanation of the

third article of the Creed, *"Natus ex Maria Virgine." The Catechism of the Council of Trent*, trans. J. Donovan (Baltimore: James Myers, 1833), 45-51, 521.

54    ACSC, Mos-10, Boa-7, Se-22, Gr-3.

55    *Oeuvres*, 2:253-263.

56    ACSC, Mol-6.

57    *Sermons*, 32-59.

58    ACSC, Ma-3. Lewis uses almost the exact same phrasing in Le-10.

59    Manning's *Moral Entertainments* was first published in London in 1742, and consists of sixty-two sermons preached at Ingatestone Hall, where the author was chaplain to Lord Petre (1702-1730/31). The work went through numerous editions, and Gillow comments in regard to this and Manning's other works that he was "remarkable for his easy and flowing style, but still more regarded for the solidity of his arguments and the Christian spirit in which they were couched." Gillow, 4:453-57.

60    Manning, *Moral Entertainments* (Dublin: Richard Grace, 1839), 13.

61    ACSC, Le-4. Greaton (1679-1753) had been superior of the mission in Phildelphia—where he established St. Joseph's church—before returning to Bohemia Manor where he died on 19 August. Notations show that this sermon, while preached at Greaton's funeral, had been written orginally for that of Mrs. Frisby (7 April, 1752), and would be used again in 1754, 1761, 1764, 1765, 1767 and 1773.

62    ACSC, Le-4.

63    ACSC, Le-22. Lewis copies most of Manning's "Twenty Seventh Entertainment" verbatim, except for the introductory paragraphs. Manning, *Moral Entertainments*, 207-14.

64    ACSC, Le-13. Compare with Manning, *Moral Entertainments*, 410-15.

65    ACSC, As-2, As-3, Li-1, Li-2, Li-3, Li-4 (only four sermons by Livers have been preserved, and all are based to some degree on Manning), Bol-23.

66    For the contents of such libraries, the few extant catalogs may be consulted, keeping in mind that the dates of their compilation are generally nineteenth-century. MPA, 16,3 (Bohemia Manor Booklist, compiled 1831); 15,14 (Newtown library account, undated); 15,18 (Booklist for St. Thomas Manor, 1840).

67    Published first in London in 1744. Hornyhold, who was from 1756 to 1778 the Vicar-Apostolic of the Midland District, received much praise upon the publication of this work. Gillow reports Milner's comment that "This was so generally approved of that he received something like official thanks from Oxford for the publication." *Biographical Dictionary*, 3:402. For Gillow's treatment of Hornyhold's life, see 399-402.

68    ACSC, Je-15, Je-25. The first sermon treats the first commandment, while the second sermon explicates the third commandment. Compare with Hornyhold, *The Commandments Explained in Thirty-Two Discourses* (Baltimore: Fielding Lucas, n.d.), 24-36, and 129-43.

69    ACSC, Bol-8, and Hornyhold, *Commandments Explained*, 36-50.

70 Chinnici argues that Challoner "heavily influenced Gother [and] became the most important English catholic devotional writer in revolutionary America. Challoner's works embodied a dignified piety, strong moralism, the promotion, in contrast to any aristocratic pretense, of mental prayer for everyone, and some knowledge of affective prayer. Most important, Challoner's work evinced a conviction of the possibility of a direct personal experience of God. This was important in a community that might not see a priest or any other official representative of the church for months at a time." *Living Stones*, 10. Cardinal Wiseman observed that Challoner "supplied, in fact, almost the entire range of necessary and useful religious literature for his Catholic fellow-countrymen; and that at a time when such a supply must have been truly as a boon from heaven" (quoted in Edwin H. Burton, *The Life and Times of Bishop Challoner, 1691-1781*, 2 vols. [London: Longmans, Green and Co., 1909], 2:280). Challoner's pervasiveness in the colonies can be gauged from an examination of the library records mentioned above (n. 66), and also from memorandum of books ordered from England, MPA, 3,15; 4,2; and those lent out to the laity, MPA, 3,15.

71 "Bishop Challoner: The Devotionary Writer" in *Challoner and his Church. A Catholic Bishop in Georgian England*, ed. Eamon Duffy (London: Darton, Longman & Todd, 1981), 81. This volume contains excellent articles on various aspects of Challoner's life and work, and should be considered essential in any study made of his career.

72 Luckett, 80-81.

73 ACSC, Di-1.

74 Richard Chalenor (sic), *Think well on't. or Reflections on the Great Truths of the Christian Religion* (Philadelphia: Carey, Stewart & Co., 1791), 62.

75 ACSC, Hu-6.

76 Chalenor, 39.

77 ACSC, Ha-4.

78 Chalenor, 44.

79 This is interesting, as the only work of homiletics in the Georgetown College Library Collection (which was assembled in part from volumes owned by the early colonial Jesuit missionaries) that can definitely be linked to one of the homilists is William Darrell's *Moral Reflections*, with Liver's signature on the title page. Surely he must have based some of his sermons on this work; but if he did, they have not survived.

80 ACSC, Li-1. Manning, 207-14.

81 ACSC, Li-4 and Manning, 415-25. His change is to omit Manning's counsel to spend "one half hour at least in spiritual reading," Manning, 423.

82 Manning, 269.

83 ACSC, Li-2.

84 While mixed marriages were not uncommon among the Maryland Catholic community, especially in the early years of the colony, in the eighteenth century the religious leadership became increasingly concerned. For the early situation,

see Michael J. Graham's "Lord Baltimore's Pious Enterprise: Toleration and Community in Colonial Maryland" (Ph.D. diss., University of Michigan, 1983), 91; for later concerns see Beatriz Betancourt Hardy, "Papists in a Protestant Age: The Catholic Gentry and Community in Colonial Maryland, 1689-1776" (Ph.D. diss., University of Maryland, 1993), 89, 185, 346-48; and Tricia Pyne, who reports that in 1753, a "Jesuit not only refused to marry a couple, but physically threw that couple out of a chapel because the bride refused to convert or allow the children to be raised as Catholics." In "The Maryland Catholic Community, 1690-1775" (Ph.D. diss., Catholic University of America, 1995), 286. Cf. as well Robert F. McNamara, "John Carroll and Interfaith Marriages: The Case of the Belle Vue Carrolls," in *Studies in Catholic History in Honor of John Tracy Ellis*, eds. Nelson H. Minnich, Robert B. Eno, S.S., and Robert F. Trisco (Wilmington, DE: Michael Glazier, 1985), 27-59; and the letters of John Carroll where he expresses his own scruples about inter-faith marriages: JCP, 1:275; 2:514; 3:92, noted in Charles E. O'Neill, S.J., "John Carroll, the 'Catholic Enlightenment' and Rome," in ACPP, 24.

85    Manning, 334-35.

86    ACSC, Li-3.

87    ACSC, Be-3.

88    *Oeuvres Complètes*, 1:179-201. Beadnall is not the only homilist to mention "planters" specifically. James Ashby, in his sermon for the First Sunday of Advent, based on a sermon for the same day by William Darrell, follows Darrell in his argument that St. Paul does not require Christians to leave their professions, but then adds in his list of examples that "the planter [may] follow his business...." ACSC, As-5.

89    Translation from *Sermons and Moral Discourses*, 430.

90    ACSC, Ha-2 (emphasis mine).

91    Bourdaloue, *Ouvres* 2:347.

92    ACSC, Mos-7.

93    ACSC, Je-23. This sermon for Sexagesima is taken from Darrell's *Moral Reflections*, which it follows closely for the first paragraph, then somewhat more creatively, dropping the last two pages entirely. Jenkins, a Marylander (1742-1800), returned to his fellow colonists in 1776. Geoffrey Holt, *St. Omers and Bruges Colleges, 1593-1773. A Biographical Dictionary* (London: Catholic Record Society, 1979), 147. He was affectionately referred to by Carroll as, "that man without guile, little Augustine Jenkins. I am told he is almost adored by his acquaintaines; and I dare say very devotedly." JCP, 1:56.

94    See William Darrell, *Moral Reflections on Select Passages of the New Testament*, 2 vols. (London: W. Bickerton, 1736), 1:156. This Protestant edition of Darrell has been consulted occasionally due to the lack of a complete copy of the 1711 edition of the *Moral Reflections* in the United States.

95    Two sermons mention the length of time it took to preach a sermon: Rev. Peter Attwood, who was in Maryland in the first third of the century, notes at the beginning of a sermon of six pages "Let us then descend for the space of a short

half hour...." ACSC, At-3(a). Later, towards the end of the century (1790), Fr. John Bolton notes at the end of his introduction to a funeral homily "I must beg your patience for half an hour...." ACSC, Bol-14. The Attwood sermon was shorter than most, so perhaps the time frame of thirty to fourty-five minutes would be more appropriate. By contrast, Congregational sermons averaged about an hour (which was a substantial reduction from the late seventeenth century average of two hours!) Patricia U. Bonomi, *Under the Cope of Heaven* (New York: Oxford University Press, 1986), 67-68.

96  See, for example, ACSC, Mos-7, Mos-10, Ha-2, Be-2, Be-3.

97  Darrell, 1:3 (emphasis mine).

98  ACSC, As-5. Ashby (1714-1767), vere Middlehurst was born in Lancashire, and educated at the English College in Valldolid. He labored in Maryland from 1742 until his death. In 1757-58 he was the superior of the mission during George Hunter's absence. Hughes, 2:691; Holt, 178.

99  Cf. ACSC, Ha-2, where Robert Harding eliminates some illustrative comparisons offered by the church fathers which Bourdaloue includes in his sermon, e.g., when the latter points out St. John Chrysostom's remarks on the necessity of preparation for death: "*disait ce Père, on n'attend pas à équiper un vaisseau quand il est en pleine mer, battu des flots et de la tempête, et dans un danger prochain du naufrage. On ne pense pas à munir une place quand l'ennemi arrive et qu'il l'investit. On ne commence pas à meubler le palais du prince, quand le prince est à la porte et sur le point d'y entrer.*"

100  Darrell, 1:5.

101  ACSC, As-5. The Jesuits, as managers of substantial plantations upon which they depended for their livelihood, had themselves reason to be concerned about becoming emeshed in the things of the world.

102  This is unlikely considering the willingness of the homilists to preach on this subject, e.g. ACSC, Be-6.

103  As John Lewis did in ACSC, Le-4, which is discussed above.

104  Bourdaloue, *Oeuvres*, 2: 31.

105  Bourdaloue, *Oeuvres*, 3: 464.

106  ACSC, Bol-2.

107  Cf. Ashby's condensation of material in Darrell. ACSC, As-5, and Darrell, 1:8.

108  The sermon is ACSC, Bol-23, for Sexagesima Sunday, and may be compared to Manning's "Fifty-fifth Entertainment," and Darrell's "Reflection for Sexagesima." Cf. Manning, *Moral Entertainments*, 415-25, and Darrell, *Moral Reflections on the Epistles and Gospels for Every Sunday throughout the Year*, 4 vols. (London, 1711), 1:302-16.

109  Curran, 14.

110  This may be established not only from the fact that many of the sermons were drawn from published works of English sermons, e.g., Manning, but also that some of the sermons in the collection show evidence of having been preached prior to the author's arrival in the colonies. For example, Benet Neale's sermon

for the feast of St. Thomas Becket was originally preached to the students and faculty at St. Omers, since it addresses "devout Scholars," speaks of Thomas as sailing to Flanders, to "you, to whom he comes," and finally the fact that St. Thomas was the patron of the student's chapel at St. Omers, and whose feast was solemnly celebrated there. Cf. ACSC, Ne-8, and Hubert Chadwick, *St. Omers to Stonyhurst* (London: Burns & Oates, 1962), 48.

CHAPTER THREE

# "*Fully Instructed and Vehemently Influenced*"

## THE STRUGGLE AGAINST THE WORLD

There can be no doubt that the colonial Anglo-Catholics, living as they did on the isolated frontier of the "New World," looked to their clergy for guidance on matters of faith and morals; advice and direction that the homilists were more than willing to offer. It should not be surprising to find that both the methodology and the aims of these preachers are similar to those of their fellow clergy in England, whose flocks also endured a "frontier" existence, socially if not geographically.

One need only look to the writings of Bishop Challoner to be reminded that for him, as one might imagine for the priests on the Maryland and Pennsylvania mission, uniqueness was not the over-riding concern. Consider the following observation by Richard Luckett. "Utility is...the explanation of the vast amount of adaptation to be found in Challoner's works. He saw no point in creating something new if something that already existed could be made, when adjusted to prevailing conditions, to do the task for which it was intended."[1] If indeed such a rationale informed the preaching of the Jesuit missionaries, and their goals, despite the differences in the medium employed, were similar to Challoner's, then the following description of his ministry can be applied, *mutatis mutandis*, to them: "It can be said of Challoner that to an extraordinary extent writing itself was the mode of his ministry, and that if it had not been he could never have accomplished what he achieved in his episcopate: the preservation of the morale and sense of identity of a community widely dispersed geographically, and at a time when that community, besides the burden of proscription, suffered from the apostasy of a number of the more influential Catholic families, the possible taint of association with armed revolt, and above all, from an intellectual climate not so much hostile to, as contemptuously dismissive of, their beliefs.[2]" All of these factors were concerns for the colonial Jesuits as they sought to minister to a widely dispersed flock suffering from civil disabilities, apostasy, the fear of charges of complicity with revolution,[3] and a hostile intellectual atmosphere; they responded to them by preaching both the necessity and means of living out Catholicism in the midst of an unfriendly, or at most indifferent world. As numerous examples will make abundantly evident in the course of this chapter, great stress was laid upon the need to oppose the world and its influence, and in this endeavor the homilists' emphasis was—using the tripartite division of Cicero and Saint Augustine[4]—less on *delectare* than on *movere* and *docere*. They sought primarily to persuade and teach, not please, and in this endeavor they unashamedly used, as we have seen in the previous chapter, the source materials they had at hand. Theirs was a practical homiletics,[5] tailored to the needs of their community, "pieces of furniture in a home which are intended for use rather than ornamentation."[6] This will become clear in a brief examination of the manner in which the preachers described their own ministry.

## *The Priests Describe their Preaching*

Richard Molyneaux,[7] in his sermon for Sexagesima Sunday on the text "The sower went out to sow his seed," tells his flock that God "sowed his seed to Adam" in the form of a sermon, "in which he gave him the sovereignty of the world, the prohibition of the tree of knowledge, and his approbation of matrimony."[8] Likewise, the seed of God was sown in the Mosaic Law, in the prophets, and finally in his Son. If accepted, this seed "becomes a strong antidote against our bad habits and temptations. It teaches us all sanctity and inclines us to embrace it." Christ, Molyneaux declares, says that his true sheep

Delight in my word delivered to them by my missioners. By it they are taught the vanity and folly of vice; by it they are taught the merit and charms of virtue, and are persuaded to fly from the madness of that to the virtue of this and thus fully instructed and vehemently influenced they make sure their election to an eternal crown.

The role of the missionary is cast here in very moralistic terms. He is called to teach his flock through his preaching of God's word about virtue and vice and the holiness which comes from emerging victorious over "bad habits and temptations." The very phrase "fully instructed and vehemently influenced" points to the primacy that catechesis and moral suasion had in colonial homiletics.

At the end of the century Robert Plunkett echoed the same theme in his sermon for the Feast of the Circumcision. Chiding those who excuse their late appearance at Sunday services by arriving in time to hear the sermon,[9] Plunkett declares:

Sermons only show you what you're bound to do in order to purify your soul and fit you for making a worthy appearance at the august sacrifice that is offered for your spiritual and temporal welfare; so that it is not simply listening to the explanation of the Law, but by practically observing it, that you can avoid the crime of profaning the Sabbath....[10]

Here again sermons are presented in an almost functional way, as aids to living the moral life in the manner necessary to attend Mass and receive the Eucharist.

Plunkett also stresses that sermons must not just be heard but acted upon; more often than not the colonial clergy could be found lamenting that, contrary to their hopes and expectations, their oratorical labors produced little fruit. James Beadnall in a sermon dating from 1758 decries the slothful ways of his hearers, and protests:

They'll go from a sermon filled with the Spirit of God and spoke with all the energy and zeal a preacher is capable of, against lying and detraction, lust and idleness; and that moment, that instant they come out, they begin to lie . . . and enter upon schemes to spend the whole day, though ever so holy and sacred, in vices diametrically opposite . . . .[11]

Though this fickleness of the colonial Catholics was not an indigenous trait, the clergy never ceased to point out their inconstancy. Charles Sewall expresses surprise at the "blind passion of revenge, which daily increases, notwithstanding all the zeal and eloquence of the preachers of the Gospel to correct this vice."[12] Augustine Jenkins comments that, even when a sermon is presented in a pleasing manner, its power of persuasion is not thereby increased: "If a preacher forms his discourse in such a manner that his turn of words or thoughts strikes our fancy, we admire him for the present for his talent, but little reflect on the truths he teaches...."[13] John Boone strikes a note of desperation when he upbraids his hearers: "I preach, I exhort, I beg, I spend my spirits in confessions, at the altar, all to better the world, and still you grow more and more wicked."[14]

Such melancholy thoughts are reflected even by the newly consecrated Bishop John Carroll, in the sermon he delivered on taking possession of his episcopal see of Baltimore on 12 December 1790. Commenting on the "spirit of infidelity" present in the newly erected diocese (which embraced all of the recently independent United States), he notes that "Licentiousness of discourse and the arts of seduction are practiced without shame and, it would seem, without remorse." He preached against these sins before, but

What reformation followed then my earnest entreaties and exhortations? Was prayer more used? Were parents more assiduous in the instruction of their children? Were their examples more edifying? Was swearing and blaspheming diminished? Was drunkenness suppressed? Was idleness extirpated, was injustice abolished?[15]

This experience of frustration was made worse by Carroll's awareness that the growing integration of his Catholic flock into the wider community was only increasing the number of obstacles they faced in living a religiously observant life. Yet this conviction that Catholics could not help but be involved in a fierce struggle with the spirit of the world was present throughout the century, and is reflected in the following comment of James Beadnall: "The sensual man, the spirit of the world, must therefore be utterly rooted out of our souls and destroyed, if we would be replenished with the Spirit of God."[16]

This theme of the necessary struggle against the world was common in the spirituality of the English Catholic community as well,[17] and it forms the backdrop to countless sermons in the collection; both the negative influence of the world considered in general, and the specific sins that are seen to characterize it.

## *The World and its Influence*

We should note at the outset that the world, in the sense of created matter, is not presented as evil in and of itself by the colonial missionaries, though it is often depicted as a place of trial and sadness. For example, Benet Neale asks his congregation why they are attached to a world: "where everyone suffers, everyone grieves, everyone is afflicted; where our whole life is one continued chain of disgraces and afflictions that perpetually succeed one another without giving us the least moment of respite."[18] Living in the world certainly involves more than just suffering hardships and infirmities, but also exposure to what the preachers commonly call the "spirit of the world, that spirit of falsehood and seduction...."[19] which is diametrically opposed to the Christian life. James Carroll notes that, as Christ was condemned by the world, his followers cannot expect any better treatment.

Yes, dear Christians, this world into whose favor you have so industriously insinuated yourselves...has carried its blindness and its injustice to such a pitch, as to condemn even a God-man. Persuade not yourselves, I beseech you, that it will be more favorable to you than it has been to him.[20]

John Lewis is amazed that "Christians should still be so much in love with the world, so fond of its customs, so much guided by its maxims," since there is in the world a "profound forgetfulness of God, of eternity, of all spiritual things, a . . . neglect of everything that relates to our salvation."[21] Thus he insists that the faithful have an "indispensable necessity . . . to hate, to fight against, to overcome the world . . . ." Bernard Diderich exhorts his charges in a similar vein to "Despise . . . contemn, [and] slight in time a deceitful world, that does but despise, contemn, and delude you; raise your heart and thought above the fading, sordid, pleasures and goods of the earth . . . ."[22] This "spirit of the world," however, encompassed a multitude of sinful snares, ones the missionaries were not at all reticent about naming, and which provide some insight into the spiritual struggles that confronted the colonial Catholic community.

## A Multitude of Sins

A constant lament of the preachers concerned the laxity of attendance at Mass and the small amount of time that was spent in prayer and other devotions. Benet Neale bemoans the fact that people are always ready to make excuses for their lapses:

Their temporal affairs, family business, the trouble of a noisy house full of children take it out of their power . . . . And I make answer that that very excuse you allege, will be your own condemnation; because there is no temporal affair ever so pressing, which almighty God does not prefer to the care of your souls. No business ever so urgent will retain you from an assembly, a public meeting, or an horse race, and yet the least vain and frivolous affair is sufficient to make you neglect going to church, frequenting the sacraments, or saying your prayers.[23]

Even legitimate pursuits ought not to intrude on the time that should be set aside for spiritual concerns, yet the homilists alleged that these temporal affairs were merely used as feeble excuses. James Beadnall, in criticizing such rationalizations, notes the reasons people offer him for missing Mass:

"My affairs are perplexed, my family must be looked after, and I must provide for my children...." Others of you say: "I've a plantation that demands all my care, I've business to transact and a charge that requires my presence. My horses are reduced and I can't come in time to perform my devotions."[24]

One would have thought the reasons cited above would have had some degree of validity, given the difficulty that the colonial Catholics encountered in practicing their religion, e.g. the lack of a horse would certainly have presented a dilemma when the nearest location for attending Mass was miles away. That they are listed here in such a dismissive manner, though, would seem to indicate that they were often used to excuse a culpable neglect.[25] Joseph Mosley, in his "Third Discourse upon Mass," certainly has no hesitation in declaring mortally sinful the behavior of those who neglect to come to Mass or arrive late, prevented by nothing other than their own sloth.

A master of a family hindered by some unnecessary affairs never thinks of hearing Mass till it begins to grow too late, he calls for his horse in all haste, or else Mass will be lost; he dress[es] and away he goes, his head full of what he had been about.[26]

Some do not even make the attempt to attend at all, moving Charles Sewall to exclaim that "some of you think it nothing to absent yourselves upon such days of obligation, as if you could be saved without complying with the commandments of the Church."[27]

This cavalier attitude towards fulfilling religious obligations was even more serious when it came to satisfying the Easter duty, as the homilists often lamented. "How many are there," Louis Roels exclaims, "who slight Jesus, by receiving him only once a year...?"[28] Even worse than this was the failure of many to receive the eucharist at all. The widespread incidence of such laxity led Bishop Carroll to despair:

When, on one side, I view the number who call themselves children of the Church; and on the other, the list, the very short list of those, who during this Easter time have offered themselves to partake of Christ's sacred body and blood, I am confounded, and disheartened and terrified.[29]

James Beadnall was surprised to find that even the "thunderclaps of excommunication" failed to persuade some to fulfill this precept of the Church,[30] while Sewall lamented that Christians add thorns to the crown of Christ by their "eating meat on forbidden days and by neglecting the Easter communion...." He continued: "It is with no little sorrow, Christians, I find myself obliged to repeat the same thing so often to you. [But] many of you are so very guilty in these two principal points of religion."[31]

As this last comment indicates, there was a common perception of indifference not only with regard to prayer, church attendance, and frequentation of the sacraments, but also in the practice of obligatory fasting and abstinence. Robert Molyneaux lamented, "At present, I fear, there are but few who observe the fast of Lent; almost everyone claims exemption"[32] — despite the relative leniency of the fast when compared to the rigors of life in the early Church. Sewall accuses his listeners of ignoring the ordinances of Lent, not from laziness, but due to shame.

It frequently happens that upon a fasting day meat is placed before you on the table; the Church commands you to do a good action in abstaining from meat...[but] you are ashamed to obey, though you are not ashamed to eat the forbidden fruit and with it to eat judgment (and damnation) to your souls.[33]

The homilists often, as in the case above, attribute such tepid religious practice to what they term "human respects," which they see as an alarming willingness on the part of some to abandon or modify their faith to avoid the censure of the world. James Ashby comments that Christ, in proposing the maxim "Give to Caesar the things that are Caesar's," provided "us an admirable admonition that no human respects, no obligation whatever of complying with our temporal masters ought to hinder us from performing our duty to God...."[34] Yet, the missioners note, how common it is that Catholics behave otherwise. Robert Plunkett asks: "How often in company has the dread of being taken for a regular pious Catholic made you forget that you were a Christian. How often have you acted the sycophant in praising what you should censure?"[35] Henry Pile accuses such people of entering willingly into slavery, since such a one guided by human respects must "be always ready to obey the humor and inclinations of those he seeks to please, and whom he dare not offend, though God's honor and his own conscience be the sacrifice."[36] Even the act of saying grace before meals, which Charles Sewall considers a "duty" is "half-uttered, and scarcely ever attended to. Yes, there are found Christians who are ashamed of the practice, and fear lest they should be counted too religious."[37]

"Human respects" would have been a very real challenge to the Anglo-colonial Catholics, since the temptation to assimilate with the dominant Protestant culture—and so improve one's social standing—was ever present. Any distinctive Catholic practices, such as fasting or saying grace, would only have made such assimilation more difficult. Neither should one too quickly discount the notion that a temperamental "rugged individualism," which marked colonial Anglo-Americans of all religious persuasions, was coming into play here to some degree.

The faults listed above, like neglecting prayers and missing Mass, might be termed sins of omission, and though they were considered serious by the eighteenth-century Catholic pulpit, they were less commented upon than were sins of commission, whether of an individual or social nature. The cause of most of these sins could be traced to the fact that the Christian

Is so blind and obstinate in his pursuit of pleasure and happiness, as not only to mistake real and true happiness and in its place make use of base, low and limited objects to satisfy his desires; but also should make choice of such things, which in themselves are real evils and miseries.[38]

Among such objects of false happiness, Ignatius Matthews lists: "the gratification of carnal appetite, desire of revenge, gluttony and drunkenness, gaming, and the wasting of both time and health at assemblies and balls...."

It will surely come as no surprise to any student of the Christian tradition that sins of the flesh would merit a place on such a list, but what might be astonishing is that out of more than four hundred sermons only one can be said to deal exclusively with the topic of fornication. This is a homily by James Beadnall for the Third Sunday of Lent, 1763, with the text taken from Paul's Letter to the Ephesians: "Fornication and Uncleanness...let...not so much be named among you." It is a rather dramatic, one might say histrionic, address which declares quite early on:

If heathens or infidels were to enter here among us, to see our actions and hear our discourse, they must think that Venus is no less adored among us, than she is amongst them; nay that we are the most devoted to her. They've only got their set times and place and seldom go thither to perform their diabolical rites and shameful ceremonies; you scarce ever observe either time or place, but abandon yourselves, if not to the blackest crimes, at least to words, they would be ashamed to utter, and to indecencies, these very indians themselves, I know, could not be forced in public to be guilty of.[39]

Though the rhetoric conjures up images of licentiousness attributed to the ancient Romans, the reality is probably indicated by the phrase "at least to words;" namely, that much of this indecency was probably limited to lewd talk and indelicate behavior (the existence of which Beadnall makes a matter of particular—and stinging— reproach by his comparison to the practices of the native peoples). He gives three examples of such behavior: an adulterous relationship between a man and his friend's wife, a woman who "gives up the inestimable treasure she's in possession of...," and a young man who "went into bad company...and imagines all [is] true they have the impudence to boast of." That much of this is occurring in the realm of speech is again suggested by Beadnall's outburst: "O! Parents! O! Masters! What are you doing? What are you thinking of, who permit *this hellish talk?*"[40] Even so, the fact that he thought the subject worthy of a sermon, and further that Beadnall is quick to offer particular examples of forbidden "entertainments," and finally that his sermon continued to be used by his confreres after his death,[41] would seem to indicate that sins of the flesh were as much in evidence then as in other times and places.[42]

Apart from this rather explicit homily there are no other sermons in the collection that treat the subject of fornication exclusively, although many discuss lustful thoughts and the ways to combat them.[43] When sins of the flesh are mentioned, usually as "lust" or "concupiscence," they are presented as the archetype of unreasoning behavior, and a sign that one has fallen under the sway of the world.[44]

One might think that sins of the flesh represented the pinnacle of vice for the colonial clergy, but such an assumption would be erroneous, as a number of transgressions are ranked far higher. In fact one missioner, despite the severity displayed in his sermons, manifests a very humane attitude towards human weakness in this area:

The stronger the temptation and the more violent the concupiscence is; the lesser is the sin.... For instance impurity is a very great sin; but the charm of the pleasure, the frailty of the flesh, the strength of the temptation, [and] the beauty of the creature lessen the enormity of the sin.[45]

If he is somewhat more tolerant of weakness in this area, however, Bernard Diderich reserves his wrath for those who swear, and thus "sin for the sake of sinning" and exhibit such "a perverseness of heart, to be thus wicked without the least motive of pleasure or profit."[46] In an earlier sermon (though they were both delivered to the same congregations only months apart in 1780) on the same text from Exodus 20:7—"Thou shalt not take the name of the Lord thy God in vain"—Diderich connects this sin to the power of anger, and exclaims

Good God, how easily we let loose this passion! For how slight provocations! A child, a servant, has committed a small oversight, and presently the parents or master puts all the house in an uproar and ferment. Nothing is heard but noise and clamor, but oaths and imprecations....[47]

It is truly "the sin of the devils, who are pleased in nothing, but in abusing the holy name of God...."[48]

Nor is Diderich alone in his grave estimation of swearing. Germain Bitouzey—one of the few non-Jesuit priests whose homilies are extant—preached that if the habit cannot be overcome "then all hopes of salvation must be over with them; then they shall certainly be lost...."[49] Robert Plunkett even predicted that swearing would call down the wrath of God on one's material possessions: "You open your mouth to curse your cattle and all that surrounds you; those crimes will not go unpunished. A curse will fall upon your flocks, will consume your substance, blast your lands and dissolve all that belongs to you...."[50]

Notwithstanding the attention paid to profanity, the priests were not unaware that certain other sins often went hand-in-hand with it, as Roels notes when he proposes that the congregation ask themselves how any one of them can pray to God while admitting that he is "still persisting in my detestable habit of drinking, cursing and swearing?"[51]

Drunkenness is certainly another frequently mentioned vice. Ignatius Matthews included it in his list of empty pleasures quoted above, John Bolton suggested that even a brief indulgence in drink was enough to lead to eternal punishment,[52] and Charles Sewall insists as a necessary accompaniment to a conversion of life that one "give up drink and the scandal of drunkenness."[53] As the mention here of scandal suggests, however, the evil of drink was often placed within the context of social relationships, suggesting that the clergy saw this as much more of a communal, than solitary, transgression. James Walton, in a sermon for All Souls Day, advises his hearers to pray for the souls of others whom they have led into sin by bad example: "Twas you that engaged them in the company that carried them to that tavern, where they so often committed excesses in eating and drinking."[54] Augustine Jenkins considers that enticing others to overindulgence is worse than committing the sin itself. He censures those who "press others to sin; as for example in drunkenness....," and notes that since encouragement can be expressed in different ways, it is wise not to jest with another about his habitual drunkenness, as "sinning mortally is too serious a matter to joke at...."[55] Because "fraternal motivation" often led to increased incidents of drunkenness, the clergy expressed a distrust of those social occasions and places where frivolity was taken to an excess, including not only taverns, but also, as Matthews had noted, "assemblies and balls," and, Walton adds, the "barbecue."[56] Sylvester Boarman recommended that the faithful should avoid public gatherings in the village where sinful activity took place; however "If they should be obliged to call in on days the wicked rabble are accustomed to assemble, which are truly the devil's market days, they must stay there no longer, than their urgent business requires...."[57]

As the above comments indicate, the missioners were indeed aware of the social dimensions of sin. James Ashby reminded his congregation that from the one to whom much is given, much will be expected, and asked

Have we been good improvers of the talents given us? Have we been just to ourselves by the right use of them? Have we been just to our neighbor in employing the gifts of God to his spiritual profit and advantage? We are all accountable for others as in some sort as well as ourselves....[58]

Often, though, it would seem that the colonial Catholics were more bent on their neighbors' downfall than his advantage, when one realizes the number of times the homilists mention the presence and effects of such sins as anger and envy. In the early part of the century Peter Attwood told his assembled audience that like the people of Nazareth, Christians

By sin cast Christ out of the city of their hearts. Avarice has your hearts, ambition has your hearts, inordinate love has your hearts; anger, passion, revenge and envy have your hearts...and he who ought to be the sole possessor of it is ejected and excluded.[59]

He goes on to express his amazement that they dare to express this anger and envy by using their "tongue in preaching detraction and uncivil words...."

Detraction—if the sermons are at all reflective of colonial life— was a problem of serious magnitude, as it appears not only in lists of sins to be avoided,[60] but also forms the subject of three separate sermons by James Walton, Louis Roels, and Leonard Neale. Roels notes, "Although our tongues be but a small member of our body, it

[sic] is very often the most hurtful and destructive to Christian souls . . .,"[61] through the sins of calumny and detraction, which Neale defines as "an unjust taking away of another person's good name."[62] Walton comments on its severity when he declares:

Few sins, dear Christians, [are] more detestable in the sight of God and man than this. Its enormity is more conspicuous than that of other sins, since it not only injures almighty God in person, but likewise robs our neighbor of what is most dear and precious to him.[63]

This destruction of another's character has far-reaching effects for, as Neale observes, you "may ruin his trade, you may hinder people from dealing with him, and render him incapable of getting his bread."[64] The severity of this sin was not to be underestimated: both Walton and Roels affirm that without restitution, there is no hope of forgiveness. Roels makes this point in a rather vivid way, stating there is no

Shadow of hope even, of ever obtaining the pardon of this sin, though you was [sic] to discipline yourselves to blood every day...for neither pope, bishop nor priest can absolve from that sin, unless you make restitution, as far as it lies in your power....[65]

Walton recommends that the restitution take the form of draining "the bitter cup, dregs and all, of a faithful...and humble confession of all your impostures, and that not only to one or two, but generally to all those that were witnesses of them."[66] Nor does one have to take an active role to fall under the censure of this sin, as Roels notes that "more Christians will be damned...by almighty God on the day of judgment for giving ear or approving what they hear, than for committing detraction itself."[67]

Another sin that afflicted the community as a whole was revenge, mentioned in at least eight sermons,[68] and made the subject of three discourses by James Ashby, Ignatius Matthews, and Charles Sewall. All of them agree that Christ provided the supreme example of charity and forgiveness, but lament that Christians spurn this paradigm in their daily life. Matthews exclaims, in regard to Christ's forgiveness of his enemies,

Ah, Christians, what an astonishing noble example of charity is this! Yet you, because your neighbor has said some slight thing against you behind your back...you fly out into rancor, hatred and revenge. You try to do him a mischief, you vow you will be revenged....[69]

Ashby admits that this "greatest commandment" is a difficult one to observe, as "Nature teaches us to revenge an injury, not forget it; experience, interest and human prudence are not strong enough to ward off the violent strokes of an irritated passion."[70] Even the most committed and pious Christians can fall prey to this sin, observes Sewall; merely "Show them the least air of contempt, give them the slightest contradiction, [and] they then discover their proud imperious heads, they become mountains of smoke and flames."[71] Yet, as with the sin of detraction, if the vengeful party cannot bring himself to forgive, then he will fail to receive pardon from the Lord. Ashby asks if "the injuries he [our adversary] has done us, equal those we have committed against our maker. How dare we nourish in our hearts hatred and enmity towards the image of him on whose friendship and love depends our all? But he who willfully persist[s] in refusing pardon for an offense will find that he cuts himself off from all hopes of obtaining pardon for his own sins, and consequently has nothing to hope but secure damnation."[72] He adds as a personal note that many people will deny that such anger and revenge play a part in their lives, but observes "I have so frequently been eyewitness to it, yet nobody will think themselves guilty."

Finally, the clergy are mindful of the repercussions that all these sins can have on family life. As an example of this it would be appropriate to repeat a citation from Joseph Mosley's Ascension Day sermon which presents in frank detail the way in which immoral behavior can poison family relations:

The husband answers the contradictions of his wife by oaths and bitter imprecations, and perhaps with blows. The wife bears the ill temper of her husband by foul language or revenges herself on him by opening his failings to the whole neighborhood. The children are treated with bitter curses, or unhumanely and barbarously corrected with kicks and blows.[73]

Such unfortunate situations would not seem to have been common—at least they were not often referred to in the sermons. Rather, it would seem that the issue was more often one of neglect, than actual ill-treatment. James Ashby asks his flock if:

You entered upon the concern of the world and that so entirely as if a livelihood was the only business you came for into this world....What you has [sic] by lawful inheritance you squandered away by dishonest courses whilst your wife and family was in want at home. You neglected the honest education of your children, or advanced them by dishonest and unjust ways.[74]

While the material well-being of the family was obviously important, it was the education of children—especially in the faith—that occupies a position of greater concern in the sermons. Often they depict the parents as culpable in failing to provide this instruction, or even worse, as training their children in vice. Bernard Diderich uses a brutal image when he exclaims:

Thus even parents often times prove murderers of their own children, not as to their bodies, but to their souls, by the bad examples they set before their eyes. ...You are usually so fond of your children that you humor them almost in everything they can wish or propose; they must command and you must obey.... For do we not see often times children 14, 15, 16 or 17 years old and...ignorant of the necessary things for salvation, particularly the sacraments.... Others will allow, at least suffer them, to go abroad during the night, or to be in the company of persons of [a] different sex, which will certainly prove the fatal ruin of their innocence and the occasion of the damnation of their souls.[75]

John Boone comments mockingly that "Time must be found for that little master to dance, [and] to give an impertinent answer. But for his catechism, it is a matter of little or no concern...."[76]

## Conclusion

This brief examination of the various aspects of the "world" against which the colonial clergy urged their flock to fight points to some interesting features of both the sermons themselves, and colonial Catholic life in general. First, we can say that the overwhelming emphasis of the homilies was directed towards individual moral behavior; what Jay Dolan said of the preaching of the parish missions of the nineteenth century applies as well here: "morality, not dogma; right doing, not correct believing was the thrust of the . . . message."[77] The preachers did explicate and defend Catholic teaching, but they were somewhat more concerned with how the individual Catholic dealt with the moral struggles of daily life.

What is intriguing about the various sins and failings of the community highlighted by the sermons is the emphasis placed on the interpersonal and social nature of sin. While one might expect to find criticisms of laxity in religious observance, and what are considered the more ubiquitous vices of lust and intemperance, the attention that is paid to the destructive effects of anger and detraction on the community as a whole, and the way in which societal pressure—in the form of "human respects"—can lead to sin, is indeed fascinating. It suggests that the homilists were responding to the concrete conditions in which they and their congregations lived. These sins would have been especially damaging to the Catholic community: anger and detraction would have eaten away at the all-important cohesion upon which it depended for survival. On the other hand, an excessive desire for assimilation into the dominant Protestant culture, if achieved through the abandonment of the essentials of the Catholic faith, risked the gradual disintegration of the community by other means. The desire of the priests to maintain the cohesion of the community under their care would also explain why they were so concerned about domestic violence within the family— which was the "domestic church" in Anglo-colonial America—and the failure of parents to hand on the faith. A church whose members were never numerous, and who labored under burdensome political restrictions for much of the century (and certain societal ones for much longer), truly could ill afford to excuse or ignore strife of any kind within their own community.

Though the missionaries were aware of their limitations in reforming the lives of their flocks (which included their acknowledgment of the often seeming ineffectual nature of sermons), they were nonetheless confident that the remedies offered to the faithful by Christ and his Church were effective in combating the dangerous temptations of the world, if they were but employed. They were remedies which the homilists truly believed would maintain and preserve the integrity of the Catholic community to which they ministered. It is to these means, as presented in their sermons, which we will now turn.

## NOTES

1   "Bishop Challoner: The Devotionary Writer," in *Challoner and His Church. A Catholic Bishop in Georgian England.* ed. Eamon J. Duffy (London: Darton, Longman & Todd, 1981), 80.

2   Luckett, 78.

3   For a treatment of the suspicions of Catholic complicity in a French/Indian invasion of the colonies, see Timothy W. Bosworth, "Anti-Catholicism as a Political Tool in Mid-Eighteenth-Century Maryland," *Catholic Historical Review* 61 (October, 1975): 539-63; Joseph J. Casino, "Anti-Popery in Colonial Pennsylvania," *Pennsylvania Magazine of History and Biography* 105 (July, 1981): 279-309, esp. 294ff.

4   Found in *De Doctrina Christiana*, Bk. 4, ch. 12: see *Christian Instruction*, trans. John J. Gavigan, O.S.A. (Washington, D.C.: Catholic University of America Press, 1947).

5   It is interesting to note in this context that it has been said of Bourdaloue and his generation of spiritual writers that they "were manifestly men more preoccupied with their matter than with its form . . . ." nor do they "speak to us in abstract form about the matters of the interior life. Instead, what they pass on to us . . . is above all the observations accumulated in their daily work amidst the most fervent Christians." Joseph de Guibert, *The Jesuits. Their Spiritual Doctrine and Practice.* ed. George E. Ganss, S.J., trans. William J. Young, S.J. (Chicago: Institute of Jesuit Sources, 1964), 569.

6   Joseph de Guibert, quoted by Tricia T. Pyne in "The Maryland Catholic

Community, 1690-1775" (Ph.D. diss., Catholic University of America, 1995), 14.

7    Born in 1696, he served in Maryland from 1730 to 1749, nine of these years as superior of the mission (1735-42, 1747-49). He returned to England in 1749, and died in Bonham in 1766. Geoffrey Holt, S.J., *The English Jesuits 1650-1829. A Biographical Dictionary* (London: Catholic Record Society, 1984), 167.

8    ACSC, Mo-1.

9    As noted in an earlier chapter, it was possible for a colonial Catholic to arrive after Mass and still be in time to hear the homily, as the latter was usually delivered following the celebration of the Mass.

10   ACSC, Xb-6. A Londoner, Plunkett was born in 1752 and was a Jesuit scholastic studying philosophy at Liège at the time of the suppression in 1773. Ordained in 1779, he arrived in America sometime between 1791 and 1795, and was readmitted to the Society of Jesus before his death in 1815. Holt, 198. For his tenure as the first president of Georgetown College, see John M. Daley, S.J., *Georgetown University: Origin and Early Years* (Washington, D.C.: Georgetown University Press, 1957), 61-78.

11   ACSC, Be-5.

12   ACSC, Se-20.

13   ACSC, Je-3. This sermon was first preached on Trinity Sunday in 1786, at a time when the desire for well-crafted homilies, even among Catholics, was increasing. Cf. Joseph A. Agonito, "The Significance of Good Preaching: The Episcopacy of John Carroll," *American Ecclesiastical Review* 167 (December, 1973): 697-704, esp. 698-702.

14   ACSC, Boo-6. Boone (1735-1795), a Marylander, returned to the colonies in 1765, but went back to England in 1770, where he remained under something of a cloud until 1784, when he was once more back in America. Thomas Hughes, S.J., *A History of the Society of Jesus in North America, Colonial and Federal: Text*, 2 (London: Longmans, Green and Company, 1917), 696; Geoffrey Holt, S.J., *St. Omers and Bruges Colleges, 1593-1773. A Biographical Dictionary* (London: Catholic Record Society, 1979), 43.

15   ACSC, Car-6. Also reprinted in JCP, 1:476-78.

16   ACSC, Be-5.

17   John Bossy asserts that Challoner himself "certainly maintained, and transmitted in the community, a strong view of the antagonism between Christianity and "the world."' *The English Catholic Community, 1570-1850* (London: Darton, Longman & Todd, 1975), 377.

18   ACSC, Ne-6. Benet Neale (1709-1787), another member of the Neale family of Maryland, was schooled on the Continent and returned to Maryland in 1742. He was the founder of the plantation at Deer Creek, referred to as "Priest Neale's Mass House," where he labored for many years. Hughes, 692; Holt, *St. Omers*, 188; and John W. McGrain, "Priest Neale, His Mass House, and His Successors," *Maryland Historical Magazine* 62 (September 1967): 254-284. Although the sermons, on the whole, evince a spiritual anthropology that, in

Curran's words, is "moderately positive about human nature," occasionally one encounters statements that betray a more negative mindset. For example, John Lewis refers to the body as "a little filthy corrupted matter...a sack of dung...meat for worms...." " (although he is here quoting Saint Bernard, who is not known for a negative anthropology), ACSC, Le-6; for Curran, see *American Jesuit Spirituality* (New York: Paulist Press, 1988), 14. For a treatment of Bernard's anthropological views, see John R. Sommerfeldt, *The Spiritual Teachings of Bernard of Clairvaux* (Kalamazoo: Cistercian Publications, 1991), 3-41.

19    ACSC, Ro-11. Louis Roels, alias Rousse (1732-1794), was born in Watten, Belgium, and arrived in Maryland in 1761, where he labored until his death at St. Thomas Manor. Hughes, 693; Holt, *St. Omers*, 226. Little is known of his character, though Carroll told Charles Plowden in 1779 that "as for Lewis Roels, if you can get his cup of Grog, i.e., rum and water, he will never overturn states, or resettle our Independency." JCP, 1:52.

20    ACSC, Car-3. James Carroll, an Irishman who was not directly related to the archbishop of Baltimore, was born in 1717 and arrived in Maryland in 1749, laboring there until his death in 1756. Holt, *English Jesuits*, 53.

21    ACSC, Le-7.

22    ACSC, Di-28. John Baptist (Bernard) Diderich (1726-1793) was born in Luxembourg, and arrived in the colonies in 1770. He labored in both Pennsylvania and Maryland, dying at Notley Hall. Hughes, 698. Carroll described him in 1784/85 as a "good, but wrongheaded Waloon J[esui]t," and "truly a zealous, pains-taking clergyman; but not sufficiently prudent, and conversant in the world....," JCP, 1:151, 165. Carroll was later forced to withdraw Diderich's faculties due to his contentiousness. See JCP, 1:320-21, 322-25.

23    ACSC, Ne-3.

24    ACSC, Be-9. These specific examples may be thought to be especially exemplary of colonial Maryland and Pennsylvania as they do not appear in the sermon by Bourdaloue on which Beadnall based this homily. Cf. *"Sermon pour le Dimanche dans l'Octave du Saint Sacrement."* in *Oeuvres de Bourdaloue*, vol. 2 (Paris: Chez Firmin Didot Frères Libraries, 1840), 22-31.

25    The objection could perhaps be made that the colonial clergy were simply ignorant of, and/or indifferent to the hardships suffered by their flocks, but such a supposition is not borne out by the evidence that the Jesuits did seek to have onerous burdens on the people altered. For example, in 1724/25 the Jesuit Provincial Thomas Lawson wrote to George Thorold, the Superior in Maryland, that the Vicar-Apostolic of London had granted faculties to the Jesuits to dispense from precepts requiring fasting and a cessation of labor on holydays. MPA, 3,8. Hughes, 2:588.

26    ACSC, Mos-4.

27    ACSC, Se-9.

28    ACSC, Ro-8.

29  ACSC, Car-35. Also in JCP, 3:397-399. In his 1785 report to Cardinal Antonelli upon becoming Superior of the American Catholic missions, Carroll commented on the difference in piety between the established Catholic community and more recent immigrants, noting "while there are few of our native Catholics who do not approach the sacraments of Penance and the Holy Eucharist, at least once a year, you can scarcely find any of the newcomers who discharge this duty of religion...." In John Tracy Ellis, ed. *Documents of American Catholic History* (Milwaukee: Bruce Publishing Company, 1962), 149.

30  ACSC, Be-4. The obligation of the laity annually to confess their serious sins and receive the Eucharist—fulfilling the duty during the Easter season, hence the name "Easter Duty"—had been binding on Catholics since the time of the Fourth Lateran Council in 1215. Cf. H. Denzinger and A. Schönmetzer, *Enchiridion Symbolorum, Definitionum et Declarationum de rebus fidei et morum* (Freiburg im Breisgau: Herder Verlag, 1965), no. 812.

31  ACSC, Se-19.

32  ACSC, Mol-2. Robert Molyneaux (1738-1808), an Englishman from Lancashire, arrived in the colonies in 1770, and was for many years in charge of the mission in Philadelphia. He became the first superior, in 1805, of the restored Society of Jesus in America, and was widely held to be a man of erudition and charm, well-suited to the cosmopolitan life. Hughes, 698; Holt, *St. Omers*, 182. Carroll described him to Plowden in 1779 as "the same good-natured creature you ever knew him, as fat as a porpoise, which occasions his neck to appear much shorter than it ever did, and therefore fills him with a dreadful apprehension of going off in an apoplexy." JCP, 1:52. He also noted in 1782 Molyneaux's "natural talents for elegant life and manners...." JCP, 1:67. In 1787 he described him as "*fat comme un cochon*. He laughs as much as ever. He is wonderfully proud...." JCP, 1:246. For more on Molyneaux and his life, see Philip S. Hurley, S.J., "Father Robert Molyneaux, 1738-1808," *Woodstock Letters* 67 (October 1938): 271-292.

33  ACSC, Se-9.

34  ACSC, As-11.

35  ACSC, Xb-1.

36  ACSC, Pi-3. Pile was a Marylander, born in 1743, who attended St. Omers from 1754 to 1761, studied theology at Liège, and was ordained in 1768. Serving on the English mission till 1784, he returned to his native land in that year, where he remained until his death in 1813. Holt, *English Jesuits*, 194.

37  ACSC, Se-4.

38  ACSC, Mat-7. Ignatius Matthews, who was born in Maryland in 1730, had the somewhat rare experience (for a colonial boy) of spending only two years at St. Omers (1754-56) before transferring to the English College at Valladolid (1756-63). Upon completing his studies, he was ordained in 1763, after which he entered the Society of Jesus, returning to Belgium to begin his novitiate at Watten, up the hill from St. Omers. Following his novitiate he returned to serve his native Maryland (1766), and died there in 1790. Holt, *English Jesuits*, 161.

39   ACSC, Be-6. Note the unflattering reference to "indians."

40   Emphasis mine.

41   Peter Morris adds a line to the beginning: "I'd have thought, if I had not been acquainted with you, there would have been no need to have mentioned this filthy and abominable vice...." Morris (1743-1783), arrived in the colonies in 1768, and served at various missions in Maryland till his death from apoplexy. Hughes, 697; Holt, *St. Omer*, 185.

42   We know that sexual license was a problem in colonial Maryland from the letters of Anglican ministers to various correspondents in London. For example, Rev. Skippon writes from Annapolis on 19 January 1714/15 to the Bishop of London: "But what gives me the greatest uneasiness is, that dissoluteness of manners...which has universally spread itself over the Province, of which the frequency of polygamy, fornication, and such like sins is a flagrant instance." William S. Perry, ed., *Historical Collections Relating to the American Colonial Church*, vol. 4 (New York: AMS Press, 1969), 73. Raphael Semmes also cites numerous instances of adultery and fornication in the legal records of early Maryland. See *Crime and Punishment in Early Maryland* (Baltimore: Johns Hopkins University Press, 1938), 174-206. One could also point to the toleration of an adulterous relationship among the staff at Charles Carroll's estate, and his annoyance at his priest's condemnation of it. Beatriz Betancourt Hardy, "Papists in a Protestant Age: The Catholic Gentry and Community in Colonial Maryland, 1689-1776" (Ph.D. diss., University of Maryland, 1993), 325.

43   Cf. for example, Neal-7, where Leonard Neale warns his listeners that "you should always remember that at the judgment seat of God, you must render an account even of your thoughts, and therefore should keep yourselves pure and spotless in *mind*, as well as in body."

44   ACSC, Ro-11.

45   ACSC, Di-8.

46   Ibid. It could be said that Diderich is obsessed with this particular vice; of his thirty-three sermons, eight deal either in whole or in part with this topic: Di-1, Di-2, Di-6, Di-8, Di-11, Di-15, Di-21, Di-22.

47   ACSC, Di-6.

48   ACSC, Di-2.

49   ACSC, Bi-3. Lest anyone in his audience be in the dark as to which expressions constitute the sin of swearing, Bitouzey enlightens them by reciting the oaths most common to the day. He does, however, protest to God that "I do repeat them here in thy divine presence only to show to thy people the sacriligious, impious, and diabolical meaning of these words...."

50   ACSC, Xb-4. He brings this image closer to home by suggesting that one who curses his wife and children will lose them when he most has need of them, and cites a story from St. Augustine about a mother who curses her children at the font, leading God to take their life.

51   ACSC, Ro-12.

52   ACSC, Bol-7. John Bolton (1742-1809), arrived in the colony with Robert

Molyneaux in 1770, and served for all his life in Maryland, first at Newtown and St. Thomas Manor, and later, upon the death of Joseph Mosley, at St. Joseph's, Talbot County. Hughes, 698. Carroll described him as "a good fellow, an active Miss[ione]r, and fully as much a good fisherman and Hunter." JCP, 1:52.

53   ACSC, Se-18. This example was later crossed out in his text. Raphael Semmes notes: "There seems to have been quite a lot of drinking done in early Maryland. Two Dutchman visiting the province said that Maryland planters upon the arrival of any vessel in port would spend so much in buying wine and brandy that they would often neglect to buy enough clothing for their children." 145-161, here 147.

54   ACSC, Wa-2. James Walton (1736-1803), born in Lancashire, arrived in Maryland in 1766, and served at Newtown and St. Inigoes, where he laid the foundation of the present church in 1785. Hughes, 696, Holt, *St. Omers*, 276. Carroll admitted that, although he was not a good farmer, he was "indefatigable in his spiritual occupations." JCP, 1:56. Walton lists drunkenness with `mortal and deadly sins' in Wa-5, and Sylvester Boarman is amazed how many "drunkards" are to be found equally among heathens and professed Christians. ACSC, Boa-11.

55   ACSC, Je-9.

56   ACSC, Wa-2. Eighteenth-century barbecues must have been of a more riotous character than many of their twentieth-century cousins, as not only Walton but also John Boone criticize them by name, the latter noting that they are "lewd places" which "the Church absolutely forbids." ACSC, Boo-7. Leonard Neale might be referring to such gatherings when he warns against "assemblies where nothing immodest is transacted *openly* and yet modesty is upon the very brink of a precipice." At such places, he predicts, "one false step, one unguarded look, maybe more fatal than the loss of life." ACSC, Neal-7.

57   ACSC, Boa-8. Sylvester Boarman (1746-1811) of Maryland, returned to the colonies in 1774, and labored zealously for twenty years at Deer Creek (1780-1800), the mission founded by Benet Neale. See Clarence Joerndt, *St. Ignatius, Hickory, and Its Missions* (Baltimore: Publication Press, 1972), 370-75.

58   ACSC, As-9.

59   ACSC, At-2(d). Peter Attwood (1682-1734) is one of the few priests represented in the collection who labored in the early years of the century. He was a native of Worcestershire, and was sent to America in 1711, becoming superior of the mission in 1720. See Curran, 73.

60   ACSC, Bol-3, Se-10, Bi-1, Wa-5. Semmes comments: "From the number of cases of defamation in early Maryland, it is quite obvious that the colonists were very zealous in guarding their reputations." 207. Among the routine accusations he lists are: cheating, adultery and theft (especially hog-stealing).

61   ACSC, Ro-16.

62   ACSC, Neal-6. Leonard Neale (1747-1817) was another of the Portobacco, Maryland Neale clan. He studied at St. Omers and Bruges, and returned to Maryland in 1783, after spending a period as a missionary in Guiana. He was

appointed as Carroll's coadjutor in 1795, but was not consecrated until 7 December, 1800. Hughes, 700; Holt, *St. Omers*, 189. His tenure as Archbishop of Baltimore in his own right lasted only from 1815 to 1817. Thomas Spalding judges the effects of his short-lived but ineffective rule "calamitous." Cf. *The Premier See. A History of the Archdiocese of Baltimore, 1789-1989* (Baltimore: Johns Hopkins University Press, 1989), 74-77.

63   ACSC, Wa-6. Despite the seriousness he attaches to this sin, Walton does not lose his sense of humor, as may be seen from this passage in the same sermon: "How many do we still meet with that make it their constant business to muster up together whatever is said or done in a whole town, and communicate their venom to every company they are engaged in. One would imagine they were the common genealogists maintained at the public expense, and living gazettes, where all the failings of each particular are exposed to the view of all."

64   ACSC, Neal-6.

65   ACSC, Ro-16. Roels insists on restitution just as strenuously in the case of theft, and even comments that priests are often forced "to make use of the discipline of the church, and to refuse absolution...." to those who will not restore what they have obtained through injustice. ACSC, Ro-1.

66   ACSC, Wa-6.

67   ACSC, Ro-16.

68   ACSC, As-2, At-2(c),(d), Mat-6, Mos-7, Se-10, Boa-10, Pi-1.

69   ACSC, Mat-4.

70   ACSC, As-6.

71   ACSC, Se-20.

72   ACSC, As-6.

73   ACSC, Mos-7.

74   ACSC, As-9. James Beadnall likewise, in his compendium of "innumerable sins" and "abominable actions," mentions "that dissipation of your substance and goods...[and] that irregularity and ruin of your family...." ACSC, Be-2.

75   ACSC, Di-25.

76   ACSC, Boo-7.

77   *Catholic Revivalism: The American Experience, 1830-1900* (Notre Dame: University of Notre Dame Press, 1978), 111.

# CHAPTER FOUR

# "The Example of Your Crucified Savior"

## PREACHING THE SPIRITUAL LIFE

Never one to mince words, John Boarman warned his congregation:

> Till you renounce the maxims of the world, till you resolve to reform your judgment and manners, till you conform them to the doctrine of Christ, you cannot be accounted among his disciples; you remain excluded from his blessings.[1]

Yet, it would have been remiss of the colonial clergy had they only pointed out the difficulties of living in the world, and neglected to offer any advice on the means of acquiring the virtues appropriate to a Christian life. As we have seen, their preaching was practical in nature, an approach which was a characteristic of all the apostolates of the Society of Jesus. Joseph de Guibert, in his invaluable study of Jesuit spirituality, remarks that an important feature of their method "to overcome defects and acquire virtues is that there is a question above all of a direct struggle and a direct effort."[2] This undertaking is animated primarily by the personal example that Jesus Christ left his Church; indeed Guibert observes: "It is truly noteworthy that in the innumerable writings on Christ, His passion, and His Sacred Heart, the dominant idea is that of imitation. For them [the Jesuits] Jesus is above all the leader and model, the one to be loved, followed, and imitated. The examples of His mortal life make up the concrete ideal of the "true life", and this ideal is tirelessly kept before the eyes to guide and encourage the efforts at reformation."[3] This imitation is rooted in concrete progress in the spiritual life, and it always "comes back explicitly to the practical consequences of that love."[4]

The program of spiritual reform preached by the colonial missioners takes much of its impetus from this idea of imitation; not only the imitation of Christ, but also of Mary and the saints and even, we shall see, of heroic fellow Catholics. However, their preaching would have been deficient—as loyal sons of St. Ignatius—had it failed to include, as Guibert noted, practical suggestions on the means to put this imitation into practice. The homilists were hardly reticent in their advocacy of a variety of ways to live out the spiritual life, including recommendations on prayer, spiritual reading, penance, reception of the sacraments (especially Eucharist and Penance), and works of charity. But before examining these various counsels, it might be helpful first to examine the ways in which the priests set forth the idea of imitation.

## The Way of Imitation

The season of Christmas was a time when the clergy were very busy making the rounds of their mission stations, saying Mass and preaching on the theme of the Nativity throughout the Octave that followed the 25th of December.[5] A recurring theme in their discourses was not only the poverty and humility of Christ in becoming human, but also the necessity this placed on Christians of following his example. For example, consider Peter Morris' sermon on John 1:14, "And the Word became flesh," delivered at St. Inigoes in 1769. In his introduction, Morris declares he will talk of the "moving example of our new-born Savior to excite us to renounce the wicked principles of this world which are so contrary to those he came to teach us." After describing the "ruinous stable" and the severity of the "rigorous season" in which Christ was born, Morris states: "Behold dear Christians an example worthy of your imitation." Indeed, such imitation is the way to demonstrate love for Christ, as "To love Jesus Christ, and to follow the example he has given, is one and the same thing; for the love of Jesus Christ necessarily includes a fulfilling of all his commands."[6] Joseph Mosley also stressed this point in his Christmas sermon, when he affirmed that the purpose of Christ's humble state was "to teach us how to follow his example. Attend, dear Christians, if you please, I said to teach us to follow his example."[7] John Bolton, in one of his sermons for Christmas, likewise states that Christ "preaches to us by example only...."[8] Robert Molyneaux provides some explanation for the necessity of a divine exemplar, when he discloses that Christ "began by practicing what he *taught*. A long experience had sufficiently shown the weak influence of the noblest maxims of the purest morality, unenlivened by practice. The only sovereign remedy is the divine example."[9]

Another popular feast day on which the theme of the imitation of Christ was stressed was Ascension Thursday. Henry Pile states: "To follow Christ is to imitate and practice his virtues; it is to be meek and humble of heart with him...."[10] Bernard Diderich (in the conclusion to a sermon, the body of which has been lost) offers a few examples of what these virtues might be, and encourages his people: "Follow then...the example of your crucified Savior. If we are like to Christ by penance, by patience, by crosses and afflictions, we may be sure to be in the way as to a happy eternity."[11] Louis Roels concludes his Ascension sermon by warning his flock in a similar vein:

There is no way to reign with Christ, than by following his footsteps, [and] we ought to follow them as closely as we are able, and blush even to desire an easier way than that which Christ has chosen, which is the way of pains and afflictions.[12]

John Lewis, after describing the joys to which Christ ascended in heaven, and declaring, "in order to obtain this happy end, we must follow and imitate his example," continues:

Now [if] it was by sufferings that our Savior Christ entered into his glory, what other way can we pretend to go? I cannot do penance, says one; I cannot fast, I cannot bear affronts as people put upon me, says another; I cannot endure the least sickness and infirmity, I cannot undergo any mortification, I cannot suffer any kind of contradiction, says a third. Alas, Christ, who are we, that for us poor miserable sinners a new way to heaven must be found out?[13]

Indeed, no alternative is offered by the preachers to this following of Christ, which, despite its unpleasantness, is deemed essential to the Christian life. John Carroll expresses this well when he remarks:

The life of Jesus, and the instructions contained in it, are the most useful book, and the most advantageous for meditation, to which we can resort. There are to be found the most perfect models of Christian virtue, and the best encouragements to practice them.[14]

Though the missioners preach first and foremost the imitation of Christ, they do not ignore other sources from which Christians might receive instruction in virtue, namely the vast company of saints, and especially the Virgin Mary. The example of the saints was perhaps even more important to the colonial Anglo-Catholics than their Continental co-religionists, as their invocation was a witness to that which was distinctively "Catholic" in the midst of a society which was overwhelmingly Protestant. Lacking what might be termed a "sacralized landscape,"[15] excluded (except in Pennsylvania) from worshipping publicly for much of the century, the "family" of the saints was an invaluable means by which Catholic identity could be both defended and substantiated.[16]

The sermons present the Mother of God as a particularly good example to imitate, since, in their view, Mary's great dignity was a result of the virtues she expressed in her life, especially fidelity and humility. James Ashby, drawing his thoughts from Bourdaloue, comments:

The Blessed Virgin was not raised to so eminent a degree of glory merely because she was chosen to be the mother of our Blessed Redeemer; but because she was faithful to God's commands, because she was humble in his sight, and by means of these two virtues in a singular manner his servant.[17]

If the practice of the virtues had such a wondrous effect in the life of Mary, then, the homilists claim, it can have a similar—if less exalted—impact on the life of the average Christian. Charles Sewall affirms that if Mary was glorified "because she was obedient and humble, we may hope to enter the kingdom of heaven by means of the same virtues, as these are the ways God has marked out for the salvation of his elect."[18] Thus Bernard Diderich encourages his flock "to imitate the virtues of the Blessed Virgin Mary, let her be your pattern...resolve upon following her steps as the sure way of being in God's favor."[19] Ashby, in discussing Mary's virtues, recommends in a similar vein:

'Tis in our power to make use of the same by following her example. For we may be faithful as well as she to Almighty God's commands according to the measure of grace he has been pleased to offer us. We may obey his voice speaking interiorly to our hearts as she did....[20]

Finally, William Hunter concludes his sermon for the feast of the Assumption with an analogous thought:

Thus you see, Dear Christians, the means by which the Blessed Virgin Mary mounted to the happiness which she now enjoys. No other way is open to us. The same path, which conducted her to glory, will also lead us thither. We shall be partners in her reward, if we copy her witness. But from her assumption into heaven, we also derive another advantage, which is that of her powerful patronage.[21]

As Hunter's final phrase bears witness, the colonial missionaries were quite emphatic in stressing that Mary should not only be imitated, but also invoked to intercede for others on their behalf.[22] Ashby describes such intercession as follows:

Amongst all the elect she has received a supereminent degree of grace and favor in virtue of which she may intercede for us to God. Consequently we may piously and profitably have recourse to her prayers and protection.[23]

Peter Attwood, in the first half of the century, not only assumes that such prayers are routine, but also boldly states, "We must neither hope to receive anything without her assistance, nor despair of anything with her help."[24] Sylvester Boarman refers to petitions to the Virgin as commonplace, and in the past tense, when he admonishes his flock: "let none of us be so base, so mean-spirited, as to refuse to give public testimony of the favors Mary has obtained for us, which are both numerous and edifying."[25]

Boarman lists as one of the ways that the congregation has implored Mary's help "reciting the beads," and he is not alone in his reference to the rosary. John Lewis, in his sermon for the Feast of Purification, speaks of it: "as a devotion suited to all capacities and states: for a traveler may perform it on the road, a laborer at his work, a tradesman in his shop, a gentleman in his walks...and a sick man confined to his bed."[26] John Bolton also advises having recourse to the rosary, "if used according to the direction of those books which prescribe the method, by leading the mind through all the mysteries of man's redemption."[27] He rejects the charges of repetition and idolatry that were often leveled against it, and indeed offers a defense of all Marian prayer by noting:

When we desire the Blessed Virgin to pray for us, it is not because we have a greater confidence in her than in God—no, God forbid, this is what we utterly abhor as blasphemy itself—but because we have a greater confidence in her prayers than in our own.[28]

As much as Bolton approves and encourages devotion and prayer to the Virgin Mary, he offers the important caveat that, in regard to such pious practices, "none of them, however approved, are enjoined by the Church; and so far from being made a term of communion, that all members of it are at full liberty of using them if they think fit, and likewise of letting them alone."[29]

Looking to the homilists' views on the imitation of the saints, we will see that they are presented in terms quite similar to the imitation of Christ and his mother. Louis Roels tells his audience on the Feast of All Saints that the Church encourages her children to imitate the saints, and "follow in their glorious footsteps...in hopes of arriving one day at their happy company...."[30] Sylvester Boarman, in a sermon for the same feast, calls their example a "perfect model, by which we may all regulate our lives," and declares that it will not only "convince all deluded Christians of their errors," but also "rouse the tepidity and animate the courage of the tepid and slothful to practice true sanctity."[31]

It is not surprising to discover that the saint most often presented by the homilists as worthy of imitation is none other than St. Ignatius Loyola, the founder of the Society of Jesus.[32] George Hunter, after recounting at length the wonders of Ignatius' life, concludes by urging his listeners:

Christians, let us...endeavor to copy in our own persons what we so much admire in his life and conduct. Let us then resolve from this time to be faithful in corresponding with all God's graces and inspirations as our saint did, and we may be sure almighty God will be faithful in seconding us on all occasions as he did our saint.[33]

John Boone offers a similar thought when he exclaims:

Arise then, my brethren...and after the model shown in the person of Ignatius...let us endeavor to grow in virtue, in faith, in extensive charity to each other, and in unbounded love of God, and that to the end of our lives.[34]

Thomas Poulton anchors his exhortation to the imitation of the saint in the solid foundation of the imitation of Christ when he concludes his sermon for Ignatius' feast on the text "I have created him for my glory" (Is 43:7) with the following: "me thinks I hear our saint addressing himself to this assembly with the great apostle of the gentiles...'be ye imitators of me as I am of Christ.'"[35]

However popular the presentation of Ignatius Loyola as a role model in the Christian life was, it certainly did not exclude the proposal of other individuals for this office, both canonized saints (such as the Jesuit Francis Xavier and Mary Magdalene)[36] and even in one case a much beloved fellow missioner. In his "Funeral Sermon on the Death of the Rev. Ferdinand Farmer"—which was published in Philadelphia in 1786—Robert Molyneaux listed the admirable virtues which had made Farmer a much-beloved figure in Philadelphia among people of all faiths, and then concluded by exhorting the assembly: "It remains with us...carefully to follow in the steps he has traced out to us, by his bright and edifying example."[37] Thus even a non-canonized missioner could be held up to the community as an example worthy of imitation.

The foregoing examples will serve to suggest how powerfully this idea of imitation was ingrained in the minds of both the Jesuit missioners of Maryland and Pennsylvania and the spiritual tradition from which they drew their teaching. Yet this imitation of specific virtues visible in the lives of Christ and his saints, such as humility and fidelity, could only occur if the faithful were nourished and supported by the active use of prayer, spiritual reading, penance, the sacraments and the practice of charity—which were themselves vital elements in the lives of the saints. It is to an examination of the treatment in the sermons of these all-important aspects of the spiritual life that we now turn.

## The Life of Prayer

Private prayer was consistently encouraged by the colonial homilists as one of the few spiritual practices that was available to all, regardless of their state in life. At a time when the nearest chapel might be so distant as to render it inaccessible on a regular basis, the priests were adamant in their insistence that everyone had an obligation to develop a structured, regular prayer life. Indeed, when one realizes the infrequency with which organized liturgical prayer (especially the Mass) was available to the colonial Catholic community, it is obvious why the preachers insisted on the cultivation of a life of personal prayer, for only this would allow the faith to survive in such difficult diaspora conditions. Yet the Jesuits were aware that their counsels were all too often ignored, and they were quick to draw attention to the sinfulness of such carelessness. Ignatius Matthews points out that the neglect of morning and evening prayers

1. St. Francis Xavier Church, Newtown, Md. (present-day Compton), ca. 1906. The oldest Roman Catholic church structure in continuous use in Anglo-Colonial America, it was built in 1731 on land farmed by the Jesuits, and was originally "disguised" as a tobacco barn to belie its real function.

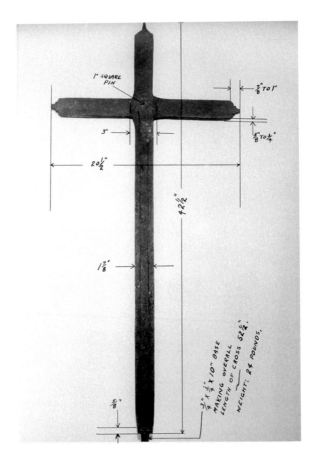

2. This wrought iron cross, now hanging in the Dahlgren Chapel of Georgetown University, is said to have been brought to Maryland by the colonists who arrived on the Ark and Dove in 1634. It first graced the Catholic chapel at St. Mary's City, then, following the closure of the chapel, the cross was taken by Fr. Thomas Mansell in 1704 to the mission he founded on the Eastern shore at Bohemia Manor.

into execution. Let us say with S. Austin,
too late, O my God, have I loved thee! and what
wd. be my lott, if I deferred any longer. It's not
too much, but all. too little to consecrate the
short remains of my life to your service,
that so by yr. mercy I may deserve eternal
life. Amen

Thus the Church addresses her children in the beginning
of this holy season, exhorting them in the words of the
Prophet to seek the Lord, while he may be found; that
is to say, while still allows us in his mercy, this acceptable reprieve of his justice, these forty days
of humiliation, abstinence, fasting and prayer.

Permit me, Dr, to address you, in these words of Prophet
at the entrance of this solemn occasion, on entering
on a course of devotion, perfect contrition
and reconciliation of Heaven with the sinner
in the Holy Jubilee, wch we begin to day. But
above all, Let me call on & Let me know this
from you Robt. Molyneux R. Molyneux

3.  The concluding page of an Ash Wednesday sermon of Fr. Robert
    Molyneux, on the text: "Seek the Lord, while He may be found…"
    (Is. 55:6). Note the two alternate opening paragraphs, and
    Molyneaux's signature. [ACSC, Mol-5]

In the Name of God. Amen.

I Ferdinand Farmer make this my last Will & Testament. I give & bequeath all my wordly Estate unto my beloved Friend Robert Mollineux, Gentleman, of the City of Philadelphia, to have & to hold the same for himself, his heirs, Executors, or Administrators, or Assigns for ever: whom I also appoint my only & sole Executor. In witness whereof I have written this with my own hand, & have set my seal thereunto this sixth day of October A.D. One Thousand Seven hundred & Eighty.

Testes
Moses Bussy
Anthony + Gorven
Mark

Ferdinand Farmer

4. The Last Will and Testament of the tireless German missionary Ferdinand Farmer (*vere* Steinmeyer), dated 6 October 1780.

A

# FUNERAL SERMON,

On the death of the

## Rev. FERDINAND FARMER,

Who departed this Life the 17th Aug. 1786,

In the 66th year of his age.

BY THE

## Rev. ROBERT MOLYNEUX.

---

PSALM cxi. VERSES 7, 8, 9.

*"The juſt ſhall be in everlaſting remembrance :*
*" he ſhall not fear the evil hearing.—His*
*" heart is ready to hope in the Lord : his*
*" heart is ſtrengthened : he ſhall not be*
*" moved until he look over his enemies. He*
*" hath diſtributed, he hath given to the poor:*
*" his juſtice remaineth for ever and ever."*

---

PHILADELPHIA :

(Printed by C. Talbot, in Front-ſtreet. 1786.)

---

5.　　Such was the esteem in which Ferdinand Farmer was held by the citizens of Philadelphia, that Robert Molyneaux's sermon for the funeral of his fellow missioner was printed for public distribution.

what will grieve you at yt hour! how you will wish to have
acted on such an occasion, to have spoke in such company,
to have complied with such a charge, to have acquited yrself
of such exercises of penance, of charity & Religion! being
influenced by such sentiments you will esteem nothing they
nothing & nothing, but what is agreable to yt Law of God.
Lastly, to enter often into yrself; to examen yrself; in order
to be acquainted with yr self: what I call being acquainted
with ourself, is to know our obligation, ye good we ought
to practice & do not; what we ought to take care of in our
state of life, ye obstacles we meet with ye helps to salvation,
with what progress we advance & to what miscarriages we
are liable. to have stated times in ye year, ye month ye week
for this solide & important inquisition. Thus our fear
according to ye Royal Prophet will prove our strongest
defence, because it will serve to excite our vigilancy.
such was ye fear of ye saints, & ye fruit they derived from it.
Every day of their lives, they not only contemplated death
they not only watched to prepare emself for death for it,
but they learnt this science of death, by making life,
as it were an exercise of death.
O God, enable us with thy grace to live so, yt we may
die ye death of ye saints, & conduct us thro' whatever
way thou pleasest, so they but bring us at last to ye happy
end, for weh we were created. weh God &c

at Philad: Dom: 15ª. post Pent: 1751
ibidem Dom: 15ª. Pent: 1753
ibidem Dom: 15ª Pent: 1756
Frederick Town. Dom. 24

6. A sermon of Fr. Robert Harding for the 15th Sunday after
   Pentecost, on the text "And when he came nigh to the gate of the
   city, behold a dead man was carried forth, the only son of his
   mother"; delivered in Philadelphia in 1751, 1753 and 1756. [ACSC,
   Ha-2]

he sinks beneath the dignity of man, & descends down nearer to the level
and capacity of mere animals, which have no knowledge of any thing
that is spiritual. Hence it is that such sensual people have no conception
nor right understanding of the mystery of the cross, of humility, of self
denial, of penitential austerities, of crucifying the flesh & its concupiscence. Their eyes are too weak to bear the light of these sublime doctrines
of a spiritual life. They esteem it all no better than folly, no good & less
and unreasonable restraints. Whereas it is in reality true wisdom,
the wisdom of God, not to be understood perfectly, but by those that
practise it. And if you desire to learn this true wisdom, to relish the
doctrine of Christ crucified, you must begin the important study
by fasting and mortification. These are the first lessons of wisdom, that
will open your eyes, to see the emptiness of this world, to teach you to
despise it, and to make the better choice of walking in the road of the
cross, which is the only road that leads to heaven. + 1772.

Dom 3ᵃ Quadrag. Ser 5ᵃ post Dom 2ᵈᵃᵐ
Erat hoo quidam dives qui induebatur purpura
& bysso & epulabatur quotidie splendidè
Luc. 16. 19

There was a certain rich man who was clothed
in purple & fine linen, & feasted sumptuously every day.

Though the good things of this life, as power, possessions, health &c are very un-
equally distributed, much being given to one & little to another; yet you must
not ascribe this to blind chance. It is a disposition made by an all-wise providence, on purpose to keep up a certain subordination & dependence of one upon
another; which is absolutely necessary for the well being of this world. And whatever rank God has allotted you in this subordination, it is your duty to discharge the obligations annexed to that rank; by the doing of which, you will
save your souls. If he has blessed you with plenty, it is not for yourselves
alone, to waste it in excess & superfluous expences, but that you may act as
his stewards, & have the merit of relieving others who are his children, as
much as you are. Or if he has afflicted you with want & with sickness, it is that
you may sanctify yourselves by patience and by submission to his holy will,
under which you may have this consolation, that, though your lot be the harder

8. The only extant manuscript of a sermon by Ferdinand Farmer on the importance of offering prayers for the dead, delivered at Lancaster, Pa., in 1782, and at Donegal, Pa., in 1783. [ACSC, Far-1]

9.   A sketch of St. Thomas Manor at Port Tobacco, Md. Founded in 1641, it was the residence of the superiors of the American mission for 150 years, and the site of the restoration of the Society of Jesus in 1805. The present church of St. Ignatius was built in 1798, and blessed by Bishop John Carroll, and is honored as one of the oldest Catholic parishes in America in continuous existence.

Ad Majorem Dei Deiparæ Sti Ang: cuff: Gloria.
1728

Apprehendit Pil: Jesu et flagellavit. 9.19.1.

Salomon seeing in spirit ye Coronation of our Sr invites all
faithfull souls seriously to contemplate yt mistery. Egredimini
filiæ Sion & videte Reg Sal: in diademate quo coronavit illu M sua in
die desponf: illius. i.e. Go forth O pious souls & behold X ye true Salo
in ye crown of thorns wch his Mr ye Sinagogue or rather Stephen
has put on his head in ye day of his espousals to ye C. He allud
to ye ancient custome of crowning Bridegroom & bride on ye day of
marriage, with flowers. The day of X ts death was ye day of his mar
riage to ye C. yn he is crownd o with roses but with thorns. In my
former discourses I treated of our L grief in ye garden of ye injuries
in ye house of Caiphas. now I shall profs ye cruel scourging at ye
pillar & crowning wth thorns. Go forth thfre pious souls, contemplate
your L cruelly torn with whips & crownd wth thorns to espouse
you to himff. Behold &c.

2    It was ye custom of ye jews at Easter to release to ye people
a malefactor out of prison whom ye wd. Pilate thfre desirous
X fd be ye man proposd him & Bar: & doubting but yt ye wd choo
X before Bar: who was a thief a murderer & seditious fellow. But
ye priefts & elders went about to raise persuade people to
preferr Bar: saying undoubtedly yt X was more deserving of death
yn Barrab: yt he was more seditious having disturbd ye whole
nation, yt he was an enemy to Cæsar pretending to make him
ff king. yt he was an imposteur, a friend of ye divel Blasphemer
fo yt movd wth ye authority of grace & fe learned persons
& more through spleen ye cryd out release to us Bar: away
wth X & crucify him. O Loving Sr how fron are you forgot
by men. O ye ingratitude & perverfness of mankind. a thief a
murder can gain ye peoples favour, can find patrons & advocate

10. A Good Friday sermon of Fr. Joseph Greaton, founder of the
mission in Philadelphia, first delivered in 1728. [ACSC, Gr-1]

OLD ST. JOSEPH'S IN 1776

11. Conjectural sketch of Father Greaton's residence in Willing's Alley, Philadelphia, by E. A. Jones, S.J., c. 1870. This sketch presents a highly romanticized view of the residence, yet the artist writing in 1887 from Collège Ste.-Marie, Montreal recalled, "I don't recollect much about it now save that I followed very minute written and oral directions—which were very explicit with regard to the vines between the windows, etc."

betrays a lack of charity to God,[38] and John Carroll includes the "habitual, and therefore willful omissions of morning and evening prayers" among his list of venial sins.[39]

The preachers preferred, however, to motivate their congregations to prayer by presenting it as a discipline that required relatively little time. Arnold Livers asks of those whose schedules seem crowded with occupations (quoting Robert Manning): "What reasonable pretense can hinder them from daily saying the short office to our Blessed Lady, and the penitential psalms, with the long Litanies, besides a short half hour devoted to their evening prayers."[40] Robert Manning's "Fifty-Fourth Entertainment" is restated by John Lewis, who recommends that Christians should never "begin or end the day without putting ourselves under the protection of the Blessed Virgin, by saying some short prayer in honor of her...."[41] Joseph Mosley, in his "First Discourse on the Mass" tells his audience that even though they cannot attend Mass every day: "You might every day allot yourselves one half-hour in your chamber to be there present in thought and intention, saying what prayers your devotion commonly suggests in [the] time of that awful Sacrifice...."[42]

John Lewis purports that the neglect of such daily prayers causes an individual to accede more willingly to sinful temptations, noting that such a one will discern "Either some preceding neglect in the duty of prayer, or his not having armed himself with vigorous resolutions in the morning...has always been the forerunner of those consents...."[43] Charles Sewall argues the case for morning and evening prayer slightly more poetically when he tells his congregation:

At least, in the beginning of each day, when rising from that sleep which is the image of death, we enter, as it were, upon a new existence...[how] shocking is our ingratitude, if we neglect to pay a tribute of praise to that eternal Being, who stationed around us his blessed angels...to shield us during our slumbers...if we do not let our hearts run to him with thankfulness, and our breasts send forth amorous sighs to so much goodness. Again, at the return of the night, is it not a shameful insensibility, to retire...without looking back with grateful emotions on the blessings of the day past?[44]

One should not think of this prayer as wholly private and personal; though the sermons often advocate and assume this, it is not the only form of prayer that they encourage. John Bolton, in his discourse on Pentecost, draws a lesson from the witness of the apostles united in fervent prayer: "Dear Christians, you must imitate their example, not only by assisting at public prayers in the church, but by setting an example of it in your families, praying together like the apostles: father, mother and children, all with one voice and heart."[45] Joseph Mosley offers a reminder that the family unit in the eighteenth century often included more than father, mother and children when he encourages his hearers as follows:

Let us rise in the morning to labor for the greater glory of God; for that end let us timely offer all our actions by a daily pious morning oblation. Let fathers and mothers see their children *and servants* perform duly this truly Christian exercise.[46]

Familial prayer is thus extended to include all for whom the parents are responsible, including the servants and slaves, who otherwise would surely lack the requisite time for personal prayer. John Carroll urges this duty upon his audience, although he recommends night, as opposed to morning, prayer, saying: "The practice therefore, which I would suggest...is to collect all your family to prayers every evening, whenever it can be done without great inconvenience. . . ." He astutely seeks to head off excuses of loss of precious time (presumably to servants) arguing that "by adopting a regular and constant method and time of gathering your family to prayers, you will suffer no loss, no diminution of labor."[47] Once again, considering the scarcity of corporate worship led by a priest, such family based prayer, presided over by the parents, would have been the staple of colonial Catholic "frontier" life. Domestic prayer provided a powerful and effective way for the influence of Christ and his Gospel to be present on a daily basis.

Morning and evening devotions were not the only types of prayer advocated by the colonial clergy. They also, true to their institutional heritage, placed a great deal of stress on the particular examen, a spiritual practice which Ignatius himself considered of primary importance in the improvement of one's life.[48] Robert Harding counsels the particular examen as an aid to the constant preparation for death, and recommends that Christians:

Enter often into yourselves, to examen yourselves, in order to be acquainted with yourselves...to know our [sic] obligations, the good we ought to practice and do not...the obstacles we meet with, the helps to salvation, with what progress we advance, and to what miscarriages we are liable.[49]

In a similar spirit Louis Roels plainly advised his congregation to prepare for death by means of "serious examens,"[50] whereas Henry Pile provided a little more detail when he urged his flock, "to examine how far we practice what we know, and by constant endeavors never cease, till, by degrees, we reform in ourselves what we observe to be contrary to the maxims of Christian discipline, of justice and of truth."[51]

For the practice of the examen to be successful, it was important for the Christian to find a respite from the world, and indeed one serious obstacle to prayer which the Catholics of colonial America experienced was the degree to which the cares and demands of daily life intruded into any time which they attempted to set aside for spiritual purposes. We have seen evidence of this in the comments of the preachers on prayer, and we can also intuit it from the importance that they place on a time of retreat from the world.[52] John Lewis insists: "Retirement then is the only means to give us a clear prospect of our danger and leisure to find a way to avoid it."[53] Augustine Jenkins, in a sermon for the Sunday after Easter, calls upon his audience to: "Set apart some little time in the year, wherein renouncing all worldly distractions as much as possible, we might with more than ordinary recollection, employ ourselves wholly in heavenly things...."[54] That this was intended to be a set, specified time might be inferred from Jenkins' concession that it was valuable to set aside "even a day in each month, or a few minutes every day, to make some serious reflections upon eternity...." Benet Neale testifies to the existence of such a practice not only when he urges his listeners to "frequently retire into solitude,"[55] but also when he predicts that some will be lost, despite "all their exercises of piety and devotion, after several days spent in solitude and retirement...."[56] Leonard Neale sees the life of St. John the Baptist as a model of the benefits that can accrue from a retirement into the desert (literally or symbolically), and he advises that all "must retire into the wilderness, by taking some stated times for solitude and prayer, laying aside all worldly thoughts at that time."[57]

The existence of such formal spiritual exercises in the colonies is certainly suggested by surviving retreat notes used by the Maryland clergy.[58] In addition there is also the heading on a sermon of Charles Sewall, first preached on 14 January 1787: "At a Retreat's Beginning," indicating that such undertakings were what would today be termed "preached retreats." In it Sewall counsels that Christians must live

At certain regulated times in a proper separation and a holy retirement from the world. For...it is only in this spiritual retreat from the noise and perplexity of temporal business, where we can find a repose of mind.... [At such times] we examine our past life, we regulate our present conduct, and look into futurity....

He continues that while it is never difficult to "embrace a time of retirement when the health of your body requires it," yet an endless number of excuses are offered when a spiritual retreat is discussed. Nevertheless, our

Interest requires that we should make it a rule to retire from the tumult and perplexity of worldly occupations at certain moments and on certain days.... For it is in these little retirements from the noise of the world, that almighty God speaks to the heart, illuminates the mind, convinces us of our faults, gives us a horror of vice and a love for the things of heaven.[59]

In their zeal for encouraging the faithful to make time for a retreat, the missioners were quite willing to combine the social with the spiritual. In 1705, for example, when William Hunter, heard that Clement Hill, Jr., planned on spending Easter in the neighborhood of the Jesuit farm at Port Tobacco, Maryland, he wrote him a letter declaring, "you shall be very welcome to our house, at any time you please." He then urged him to make a retreat "to consider the affairs of your soul," adding "I don't say this as if others had not as much need of a small retreat as you."[60]

Closely tied to the development of a fruitful prayer life was the practice of spiritual reading, a discipline that the missioners strongly advocated both in word and action. They often listed it as a component of the spiritual life, along with the practices discussed above, as in a funeral sermon of James Ashby: "Is there a time set apart for prayer, spiritual reading, examination of conscience, and other devotions....?"[61] Augustine Jenkins advises: "I would recommend a short lesson in some pious book every day. It is in the reading of pious books we draw wholesome lessons for our salvation, and do not easily lose the remembrance of them."[62] Henry Pile discusses the importance of spiritual reading at greater length than many of his confreres, declaring that it is, "a very laudable if not a necessary practice for all Christians, who have any sort of leisure, to give their souls as daily an allowance of this spiritual food, as they do nourishment to their bodies, by being constant in reading some good book every day...."[63] However, Pile cautions in another sermon that such reading cannot be undertaken or carried out haphazardly, as one would read a secular work, noting that "we must read profitably, not for curiosity and only to please the mind, but out of a desire to learn to live well...." He emphasizes the importance of this reading by observing that the Fathers of the Church believe that, "when we pray, we speak to God, and when we read, he speaks to us," and he continues with practical advice on both what and how to read:

Read not many books, but only a few well chosen, which may be proper to stir you up to virtue...such as the *Imitation of Christ* by Thomas à Kempis, the *Introduction to a Devout Life* by St. Francis de Sales, the *Guide to Sinners* by Father Granada, the *Christian Directory* by Father Parsons, or some other according to the advice of your confessor. Read but little at a time and attentively; make some reflections upon what you read and endeavor to draw some good resolutions from thence, and beg of God the grace to put them in execution. Content not yourself with having read a book once over, but peruse it often.[64]

The last piece of advice about reading a book often made sense not only from a spiritual, but also a practical standpoint, since for most of the eighteenth century works of Catholic spirituality were a precious commodity in the colonies. However, as both Thomas Hughes and Robert Emmett Curran point out, the Jesuit missioners were actively involved in procuring works of spirituality for the use of their congregations, and also maintained lending libraries which gave these works a wider circulation than would otherwise have been possible.[65] Here was an instance where the missionaries were able not only to recommend a spiritual practice and take concrete steps to achieve its implementation, but also have the pleasure of seeing their advice heeded.

The priests of colonial America advocated other spiritual observances besides prayer to their flocks, including the rigors of such penitential practices as fasting and mortification. A brief examination of these recommendations will help to illuminate their understanding of the importance of these disciplines.

## The Rigors of Penance

James Walton, in a sermon for the Sunday in the Octave of Christmas, offers a common rationale for the mortification of the body through penance, noting that there are three enemies of human salvation, namely:

The flesh, the world and the devil; and there is not one of these that is able to hurt us, or to drive Jesus Christ out of our souls, but by the assistance and treachery of our passions. The flesh that is able to hurt us, is an unmortified flesh, a flesh whose passions are all alive and are always soliciting it to rebel against the light of reason and divine grace....

He observes a little later: "An excellent means to conquer passions is to refuse them sometimes the satisfaction of this and that which are lawful and innocent, so they may be the more easily conquered.... So, to debar ones' self, sometimes, the satisfaction of drinking, when one is dry...."[66] Walton is here recommending the practice of fasting as an aid in controlling the body's unruly passions. The discipline of fasting was mandatory for Catholics during the forty days of Lent, as well as Ember and Rogation days, and every Friday; however, the homilists often encouraged Catholics to go beyond what was compulsory and fast on their own as an aid to self-control. In addition, a few preachers also advocated it as a means of procuring the deliverance of souls from purgatory.[67]

Yet it was primarily in reference to Lent that preaching on the necessity and rationale of fasting was directed, most often on Ash Wednesday, the beginning of that most penitential of seasons. Robert Molyneaux, in his homily for Ash Wednesday, explains that the manifold reasons for the Church's imposition of a universal fast for forty days are:

To appease the anger of God; to punish our past offenses; to bring us back into the ways of mercy from which we had gone astray; to draw out anew the image of virtue, disfigured in our hearts by sin; to call back the children of darkness to that admirable light from which they had departed; to raise in sinners a true compunction of heart; to renew and animate the fervor of the just; and to prepare us *all* to receive the great  benefit of his passion and blessing of his resurrection....[68]

Leonard Neale offers as the paradigm for this period of fasting the experience of Christ (the theme of imitation again) commenting: "This fast of our divine Redeemer, is the pattern which the Church follows in the forty days fast of Lent...." His homily provides an insight into the regimen of the fast in the eighteenth century when he declares that it requires that all over the age of twenty-one have only one meal a day, and abstain from flesh, eggs and cheese in the following way: no cheese allowed on Ash Wednesday and Good Friday, no eggs on any Wednesday and Friday, and flesh only on Sunday, Tuesday and Thursday during the first four weeks of Lent. He notes that these requirements were once much more rigorous, and that now even a "refreshment" is permitted at night, though this has resulted in people becoming even laxer, with the result that "now the severity of Lent seems to vanish away by degrees, as our negligence and sins are increased and multiplied." He admits that legitimate exceptions are allowed for a good cause: "If a bad state of health or hard labor make it reasonable, the pastors have power to dispense with the law," but cautions: "you must not imagine that every trifle, or a little headache or such like pain...is cause sufficient to be exempted...."[69] The rush to claim exemption from the discipline of fasting must have been common, for other preachers lamented this trend as well. Francis Beeston, for example: "Too many Catholics, it is to be feared, under one pretext or another, ask to be dispensed or dispense themselves from observing the fast of Lent."[70] Charles Sewall twice accuses his listeners of flouting the rules of abstinence, especially in public.[71] Robert Molyneaux even declares, "At present, I fear, there are but few who observe the fast of Lent: almost everyone claims exemption."[72]

Yet for all their discouragement over the widespread neglect of the practice of fasting, the homilists still insisted on its necessity, sometimes with morbid humor. Witness an Ash Wednesday sermon by Henry Neale, delivered in Philadelphia in 1748:

By pampering the flesh, we only fatten a victim for death, and prepare a greater trophy for the grave. You are afraid of looking pale, and yet by and by this will be your only color. You have a horror of becoming lean; how fat will you be in the grave? Let not only the ashes be upon your forehead by way of ceremony, but...moderate your body with fasting, with praying, with watching, with hair cloth, and the other pious artifices of self-denial and Christian abnegation.[73]

It should be noted that Neale recommends the hair shirt as an approved manner of penance; indeed, this is not the only mention of physical mortification apart from fasting. Peter Attwood uses vivid language when he urges, as a help to reach a state of sanctity, that one should: "Let a sharp pointed chain gore our sides till the blood spurt out, let a rough hair shirt [illeg.] our skin, let disciplines open our veins to bathe us in a sea of blood...."[74] Nor is Attwood the only one to use such gory imagery. In 1779 Ignatius Matthews speaks of the Holy Spirit prompting those in search of virtue to "put on the hair shirt, or chastise their flesh by whips and disciplines to blood...."[75] As we noted above, the sin of detraction was considered so grave that the homilists declared that without restitution, it would not be forgiven, *despite* the use of bloody mortifications.[76]

Penances of this sort might well have been both recommended and practiced in colonial America, although such severe routines were not normally assigned to the ordinary believer. Rather, they were usually reserved for those who were well-advanced on the path of Christian perfection: i.e., members of religious institutes, or laity of extraordinary fervor. Another sermon suggests that in all likelihood such language was exaggerated and meant for rhetorical effect. Charles Sewall, in praising the spiritual combat of the saints, uses the form of *occupatio* to ask: "But perhaps you'll say that, must we punish our bodies as the saints did theirs, must we make use of long and rigorous fasts, must we wear rough hair shirts, and discipline ourselves to blood...?" He answers his question in the negative, reassuring his audience:

No, Christians, such austerities are not to be undertaken without a particular inspiration from almighty God. But this at least we must do, if we have a mind to conquer our grievous temptations. We must [illeg.] all our inordinate desires, we must deprive ourselves of all vain, superfluous and unnecessary pleasures, we must keep a strict guard over our senses, especially our eyes and tongue, and we must be moderate in our drink, temperate in our meals....[77]

Such reasoned advice, one imagines, is characteristic of the counsel that many of the priests would have given publicly or privately to those who wished to make use of such severe penances in their spiritual lives. Indeed, they would most likely have argued that such non-bloody mortification was the more effective, though less dramatic, of the two. Nevertheless, that such extreme penances were referred to openly suggests that they enjoyed a qualified approval in certain circumstances.

The most powerful remedies available to Catholics in the spiritual life are the sacraments, and the colonial clergy continuously stressed their use, as we will see in the following consideration of the sacraments of Penance (confession), Eucharist (communion), Matrimony (marriage).

## The Sacramental Life in Colonial America

Joseph Chinnici, in his detailed work on Catholic spirituality in America, *Living Stones*, observes in regard to the preaching of John Carroll: "The centrality of Penance and the Eucharist emerged clearly throughout Carroll's sermons. They provided, along with the observance of Sunday, the cycle of feasts and the use of Scripture, the essential structure of his Catholic Christian piety."[78] As in a number of other areas, what was true of John Carroll was also true of his confreres on the Maryland and Pennsylvania mission, and it is indeed a characteristic of the sermons that they stress the importance of the sacraments of Penance and the Eucharist. It is not surprising that these two sacraments should appear most often in the homilies, considering the fact that they were, of the seven, the two most often celebrated. Indeed, these two sacraments were tied closely together, as all Catholics were required to confess their grave sins (if conscious of any) and receive the Eucharist at least once a year during the Easter season. Quite often the homilists would discuss the sacrament of Penance as a preparation for their reception of communion, as Robert Moylneaux did on the Fourth Sunday of Lent in 1778. After explaining the directives of the Fourth Lateran Council requiring annual confession and communion, he told his audience: "Now that your confession may be good, it must be in the first place faithful and sincere," including a declaration of "the whole guilt of your consciences to your ghostly father," intending a "true and sincere change of heart, which is the most important thing of all in the sinner's conversion to God...."[79] Ignatius Matthews insists on the necessity of receiving the sacrament of Penance before approaching the Eucharist, arguing: "Faith alone will not do for a preparation to come worthily to this sacrament.... [You must offer] an humble, sincere and faithful confessing of your sins, joined with a most hearty sorrow for them and such a resolution never to do the like again...."[80] A number of priests expressed concern about their people's lack of preparation for the sacrament, surmising that this explained its seeming lack of effect. Augustine Jenkins declares that the reason why sinfulness continues unabated, is because Christians "are not sufficiently acquainted with the dispositions which the sacrament requires; or . . . they do not use the proper endeavors to acquire them." This has come about because most of what Catholics know about Penance "is owing chiefly to the instructions they receive in their infancy; a time, when they were not in a capacity to understand thoroughly the extent of their obligations.[81] John Lewis likewise observes that, though many may go to confession, it is to be feared that a great number "abuse this sacrament to their own ruin and destruction, through the want of a sufficient preparation, and due dispositions for the receiving of it...."[82] Germain Bitouzy noted in a humorous vein, "Everybody knows how to fall into sin, but very few know to do penance for it...."[83]

Because of this widespread ignorance, a number of homilists sought to provide a catechesis on the sacrament, explaining what was required for its proper reception. Bitouzy's approach is typical when he lists the three parts of the sacrament (contrition, confession, and satisfaction), and then expounds on them as follows:

A penitent sinner who sincerely wishes for the forgiveness of sins has three things to do. First he is to be sincerely sorry from the bottom of his heart for all his sins, secondly he is to confess them rightly to a priest, thirdly he is to make atonement to God for them.[84]

Much effort was spent explaining the first of these steps, that is, the nature of the sorrow that a penitent was to express. Both Lewis and Leonard Neale describe it as being interior, supernatural and universal, and both are concerned about their penitents' habit of relying on a simple act of contrition read from their prayer books. Lewis states that Trent describes contrition as:

Interior, that is, from the heart. Many deceive themselves in this point; they imagine their business is done when they have read an act of contrition or two which they have in their prayer books, though in their hearts they still retain the same criminal affections to creatures, and cherish their darling passions as before.[85]

Leonard Neale notes similarly, "For to read over an act of contrition, and to be truly contrite of heart, are two very different things," and adds comically that such rote reading of an act of contrition is "of no more service than if a parrot were to utter the same words."[86]

In regard to the actual confessing of sins, the main concern expressed by the clergy is that the people fail to approach the sacrament with any frequency, either through shame or indifference. John Bolton observes that many penitents try to find a "confessor that's both blind, deaf and dumb,"[87] while Henry Pile laments that some, after committing a sin,

Instead of quickly raising themselves, and having recourse to the sacrament of Penance, yield to all occasions, neglecting to confess themselves, whether for fear, shame, remissness, or negligence of their salvation, until some great feast or indulgence obliges them... This abuse is very common among you, and the cause that many fall back after their good resolutions....[88]

That so many relapse into sin is a great concern of the homilists, and they use a variety of images to encourage their flocks to resist the temptations that inevitably arise. Louis Roels uses the analogy of a snake bite when he remarks that the confessor only "pressed out the venom of your sins, so that the wound remains still wide open, and if no care is taken of it, will soon fester again." The moral he draws from this is that one should not

Trust to present resolutions, without taking proper measures; no end can be obtained without proper means. Never make peace with flesh [and] blood and God almighty will give the peace of a good conscience in this world, and a happy eternity in the next.[89]

Leonard Neale uses a different approach to convey the necessity of resisting those temptations that seek to lead the forgiven penitent back to a life of sin. He notes that bad habits "leave behind them certain remnants, which are, with regard to the soul, much the same as old wounds, fractures and bruises are to the body." Just as the latter act up when weather is bad, so the former: "When they are put to a stress by temptations, and especially by the presence of dangerous objects, then will they begin to throb and give pain, and perhaps the old sore will break out afresh, and bring death to the soul." Neale goes on to note that the reason why many return so quickly to a life of sin is that they "never had a real purpose of amending their lives."[90]

Since the struggle against ones' faults is a relentless one that requires the aid of God, the priests urged their flocks to seek this help by a frequent reception of the Eucharist. Most of the homilists would have agreed with Carroll's assertion that the "sacrifice of Christ's body and blood" was "the greatest act of religion" and they stressed this not only because of its intrinsic excellence but also because of the effects which it wrought in the lives of those who received it.[91] In fact, these two are often linked together, with the latter flowing out of the former, as in the following quote from a sermon by Louis Roels for the Feast of Corpus Christi in which he claims that the special grace of the Eucharist is:

To cause us to live in a more holy and perfect manner. The effects of the other sacraments are more limited; for Baptism blots out original sin, Confirmation strengthens us to profess our holy faith, Holy Orders qualifies us to exercise the sacred functions, Extreme Unction fortifies us against death and the devil, but the Blessed Sacrament diffuses its virtue through the whole man.

The effects of receiving the Eucharist, which is "nothing else than Jesus Christ veiled under the appearance of bread and wine" will be, Roels insists, to: "change you quite into a new man: `tis the bread of angels; it will extinguish and calm in your hearts the fire of concupiscence, it will pacify your thoughts, it will regulate your inordinate desires.... "[92] James Frambach gives a typical presentation of the efficacy of the Eucharist in supporting a life of virtue and resisting vice when he declares:

This Divine Sacrament supports our spiritual life by the abundance of graces which it furnishes for the food and nourishment of our souls. [This is the bread] that gives us force against all temptations, that weakens our passions and concupiscences, that enables us to grow daily in virtue....[93]

Bernard Diderich points to the witness of the early Christian community as an example of this transformative power when he notes that for: "Primitive Christians...daily communion was in practice among the faithful. How great was their innocence of life and manners! But above all how unshaken their constancy in faith...." He goes on to emphasize that the Eucharist "ought to be received frequently, being the health of soul and body, the remedy against all spiritual diseases by which our vices our cured [and] our passions bridled...."[94]

Of course all Catholics were under the obligation of receiving the Eucharist once a year at Easter time—the "Easter Duty" mentioned above—and the preachers were zealous in their admonitions that it be fulfilled.[95] These ranged from a simple catechesis on the reasons for the establishment of the requirement, like that given by James Farrar in 1734,[96] to more impassioned discourses like those of Charles Sewall, who claimed that those who received communion only once a year, and that with scanty preparation, "do an outrage to the Sacrament, and expose themselves to unavoidable scandal."[97] The textual evidence is unclear on the question of just what percentage of the Catholic community fulfilled their Easter Duty, ranging from Henry Pile's remark on Easter day that "Most of you have approached this morning the adorable sacrament of the altar...."[98] to John Carroll's more pessimistic indictment of those who "have continued year after year to seclude themselves" from the Eucharist. "How many," he laments,

Ah how many, contented with a public and notorious violation of this yearly salutary commandment of the church, openly ridicule its observance, and without reason or inquiry impute to ignorant simplicity the most exalted acts of virtue and religion? Such persons as these we may truly call the pests of a religious society, the corrupters of Christian morality.[99]

The preachers, were however, even more strenuous in castigating the sentiment among their flocks that infrequent, if yearly, communion stood them in good stead. Diderich states it as an obvious fact that "those who communicate very seldom or never are the worst portion of the church of God," whereas "those who communicate ofter, are the most eminent for piety and religion, the most regular in their lives and most virtuous...."[100] Farrar observes that "we seem to be afraid lest an attentive regard to his presence [the presence of Christ in the Eucharist] should be some curb upon our inclination, or restrain the freedom of our entertainments."[101]

In his zeal to recommend frequent communion Diderich even asks if it is possible to receive too often, while Roels exclaims "how many are there who slight Jesus, by receiving him only once a year, whom they ought to receive *daily*, or at least be worthy to receive him...."[102] Beadnall (echoing Bourdaloue) urges his hearers with similar enthusiasm to remain in the state of grace exclaiming, "Fear not therefore, Dear Christians, to approach and even to approach daily, or as often as possible, with this disposition to the sacred Mystery."[103]

Jesuit spirituality strongly recommended frequent communion, and in advocating it the colonial missioners were only being true to their formation. But we might wonder if they actually encouraged daily communion. Such a practice would have been unusual in the eighteenth century, and moreover the scattered nature of the Maryland and Pennsylvania Catholic community and the sporadic opportunities its members had of attending Mass would seem to argue against its existence.[104] On the other hand, there is the following observation of Joseph de Guibert: "For the Jesuits on the eve of the suppression of the Society Communion received even daily was fairly close to achievement, at least in those environments where they could speak freely without risking too violent collisions with an opinion influenced by Jansenist rigorism."[105] Though such may have been the case in the cities and universities of Europe, it still remains unlikely that the Jesuits had advanced this far in the colonies. In light of that fact the following recommendation of Augustine Jenkins seems to represent the "typical" approach of the Jesuits in colonial Anglo-America: "It were to be wished that all Christians would dispose themselves weekly for this holy table. However, since this is rather to be wished, than hoped for, at least no business ought to hinder anyone from communicating at least once a month."[106]

The homilists were well aware that many in their flock failed to receive the Sacrament even monthly, so they did not fail to explain the benefits that would accrue to them from at least a devout attendance at Mass. Arnold Livers, quoting Manning, urges a presence at Mass as a remedy for tepidity, and counsels his flock to assist "upon all days of obligation at the Divine Sacrifice of Holy Mass with a religious attention, respect and devotion" as a way "to withdraw your affections from the things of this world...."[107] Jenkins, drawing on Hornyhold, provides an excellent summary of the spiritual benefits of Mass attendance when he advises his audience:

Wherefore, Dear Christians, never fail when in your power to hear Mass devoutly, that thereby you may through Jesus Christ worthily adore God, return him thanks for his benefits, make atonement for your sins and obtain of him all that grace and assistance you need....[108]

A devout and pious disposition was an important component of hearing Mass, and one which the homilists so often found lacking. Mosley is particularly caustic (and also revealing of contemporary church-going behavior) when he condemns women who "gaze about admiring each new dress, considering every fashion that newly appears, noticing to a nicety every flower or ribbon in a headdress."[109] Nor does he spare:

Undevout tepid men; do you think you hear Mass, while you place yourselves in some unbecoming posture, either seated at your ease, or standing...or at best only one knee on the ground, while...you devoutly lean till you drop asleep? While you are at talk under a tree, or lolling in the shade...or carrying off two or three of your idle companions to divert yourselves at a spring and quench your thirst...?[110]

Contrary to such undevout behavior, Mosley recommends an "exterior reverence [which] ought to appear in keeping yourselves on your knees, your eyes cast on the altar or fixed on some pious, proper book."

Though the reading of printed prayer books and manuals at Mass was common in English Catholic piety of the eighteenth century,[111] there were those who tried to cultivate a more participatory attitude on the part of the laity.[112] Mosley himself, in his "Third Discourse on the Mass," notwithstanding his above comments, declares:

I can't sufficiently conceive the reason of an infinite number of Christians, who, when they have a mind to apply their thoughts . . . can't hear Mass devoutly unless they read some prayer book, or say their prayers. One single part of the Mass ought to occupy an interior Christian with sufficient matter to meditate upon for whole years.... Yet if any one finds that he can't have sufficient command over himself as to recollect his wandering thoughts, it's better to pass the time in reading prayer books that treat of the holy Mass, than be entirely wandering on worldly pleasures....[113]

Such an approach encouraging participation in the Mass, as opposed to mere bodily presence, was urged not only by Mosley but also by those homilists who sought to explain the Mass by preaching on the meaning of its different parts. For example, Peter Attwood, in a sermon entitled "How to Hear Mass with Devotion," defines the word "Mass" in Latin and Hebrew, comments on the symbolic significance of the priest's vestments, relates the appropriate posture to maintain during the service, and then proceeds to explain what occurs at every part of the liturgy and what the people's role should be.[114]

In addition to stressing the importance of the frequent reception of the Eucharist and attendance at the sacrifice of the Mass, some homilists also encourage their flocks to make visits to the Blessed Sacrament, and to pray in the Lord's eucharistic presence. This should not be surprising, as even after the prohibition of public worship in 1715 Catholics were still permitted to attend Masses celebrated in the chapels or rooms of private houses (whether those owned by the wealthy laity, e.g., the quite substantial chapel of the Carrolls at

Doughoregan Manor, or the "plantation" residences of the clergy, e.g., the "Mass House" of Benet Neale at Deer Creek[115]), and it would be logical to assume that the Eucharist was reserved in at least some of these.[116] For example, during a discourse on Saint Mary Magdalene, "the penitent sinner," Benet Neale asks his audience:

> Why does this God-Man reside personally upon our altars, but that I may have frequent access unto him and...may like Magdalene spend some time at least bathing his sacred feet with my penitential tears, [and] in conversing with him....[117]

Yet the colonial clergy were aware that many of their flock found the journey to a chapel to attend Mass difficult enough, let alone a separate expedition to spend time in eucharistic adoration. Charles Sewall, in describing the means that may be used to acquire a love of God, notes:

> Many holy souls...make three visits a day to the most Blessed Sacrament with the intention of obtaining this love. But as it is not in your power to visit the chapels so often you may at least make the same petition in your private chambers, or when you are at work or walking about....[118]

George Hunter offers similar advice: "Often adore, praise and glorify with all fervor possible the Sacred Heart by frequent visits to the Blessed Sacrament; devout meditations, pious aspirations in the presence thereof, or in your chambers or private oratories."[119] Thus, the focus of one's prayer was to be eucharistic, even if it could not be undertaken in the physical presence of the Blessed Sacrament.[120]

Besides the prayer that could be offered during the private adoration of the Eucharist, there is no doubt that many Catholics had experience of Eucharistic exposition and Benediction. Certainly by the end of the century Benediction was a fixture at afternoon vespers in the town churches, as recommended by the Synod of 1791.[121] Yet even in the middle of the century there is evidence that Eucharistic adoration was popular on the Pennsylvania mission.[122] One sermon from 1799 even makes mention of a Corpus Christi procession, albeit in an indirect way. John Bolton addresses his hearers as follows:

"It might be asked what foundation is there for that ceremony usually practiced on this day in Catholic countries, in carrying her Savior's body in procession and pomp."[123] Although Bolton is careful to distinguish that he is referring to "Catholic" countries and a "usual" practice, he does presuppose some familiarity with the custom on the part of his audience (certainly enough to presume that they wouldn't find the question incomprehensible). While in Maryland the practice certainly could never have taken place in public—as it did in Europe—there is a mention of a procession occurring in 1808 during the dedication of the chapel of Saint Mary's Seminary in Baltimore within the enclosed property of the seminary.[124] If there were any processions prior to 1800, they would have taken place in seclusion—a condition not impossible at many of the remote Maryland missions. That such a possibility should even be considered is demanded by the existence of public processions in Pennsylvania, which were conducted by the Jesuit clergy (though it must be noted these priests were mostly *German* immigrants serving a largely *German* population). A public procession at Goshenhoppen in 1757 was mistaken by Protestant eyewitnesses for a military drill, and resulted in a law preventing Catholics from bearing arms.[125] If public processions were taking place in Pennsylvania it is not impossible to imagine that the Maryland Catholics might have indulged in a furtive march around a rural chapel.

Before concluding this overview of the sacramental life of the Catholics of Anglo-colonial America, it would be illuminating to review what the homilists had to say about one other sacrament that was an important milestone in their lives of many in their congregations: matrimony.

All of the preachers who treated the subject in a homily[126] were in agreement concerning its admirable nature; witness Bernard Diderich, who declared that marriage was:

Instituted and sanctified by God himself...and since raised to the dignity of a sacrament by his Son Jesus Christ.... 'Tis great by that particular grace which is annexed to it, and by which the married people are enabled to bear, in a

Christian manner, all the tribulations incident to that state...to bring up their children...as good Christians, so as one day to be happy in heaven.[127]

However much the homilists may have esteemed marriage, though, they were quick to point out, as Diderich himself did, that "a life of purity is more excellent, more perfect, and more acceptable to God, than the married state." But, he continues, any individual who has not received this grace of chastity, "may lawfully have recourse to marriage, to preserve himself from the danger of ruining his soul...."[128]

Apart from such sentiments, the priests did not spend an exorbitant amount of time discussing the theological nature of Christian wedlock. Their concerns were much more practical; and perhaps the principal anxiety evinced by them in their sermons is the careless and misguided way in which many of their flock approached the sacrament of marriage. Roels exclaims:

We have abused this divine institution and changed it into a state of slavery and bondage, though it was instituted for our happiness. I must own as it is now a days managed matrimony is a soil fertile in nothing but thorns and discontents. [It is entered] without prudence, and without consulting almighty God.... Interest alone for the most part settles all matches, and reason seldom has a vote in it...."[129]

One motive of self-interest identified by Roels is monetary gain. He laments that "men court not women for women's sake, but their money," noting that "one hundred pounds more atones for one hundred ill qualities and as many good ones make no compensation for a penny less."[130] He is particularly critical of those families who arrange marriages for financial advantage, declaring: "When the obligation runs for life, parents have no right to threaten their children into matches for which they have any aversion, merely to support a sinking family...."[131]

Another poor motive for matrimony much criticized in the sermons is the physical attractiveness of one's spouse. Roels observes in this regard: "a fine complexion is not always a sign of a fair disposition, nor charming features of a beautiful soul. Though a woman seem an angel without, she may be a devil within...."[132] Closely related to this caveat are the warnings the homilists issue against entering marriage to gratify fleshly lusts. Diderich is typical in this regard when he observes that many miseries in married life can be traced to the "bad intention of those who enter into the state of marriage and propose to themselves no other end in that state than carnal pleasure...."[133]

Diderich also deplores in another sermon the incidence of mixed marriages in the community, and urges that the first consideration for a young person seeking a spouse be that he or she "fix upon a person of your own religion...." He offers three reasons for this: the first is the salvation of the Catholic partner; for though "in certain circumstances the Church finds it necessary to overlook such dangerous connections," often the faith of the Catholic spouse is weakened, and soon they begin to believe that "they may serve their soul in any religion, provided they be good moral Christians," and cease to frequent the sacraments. Another concern is the welfare of the children the couple may be blessed with: "What is to be expected from children who hear one thing from the one parent, and the contrary from the other...," but that they become "cold and indifferent about all religion...." Finally, a difference in creed often becomes a source of conflict in a marriage, leading to "dissension and disturbances."[134] Diderich's sermon suggests not only a growing incidence of mixed marriages in a climate of ever increasing religious pluralism, but also the clergy's increasing concern about the trend.

To offset or avoid these dangers, and to secure a blessed marriage, the homilists offer a number of recommendations. First, young people should prepare for marriage by leading chaste and prayerful lives,[135] and should make every effort to approach the sacrament of Penance before their marriage.[136] Once married, the couple should endeavor to cultivate conjugal fidelity and purity,[137] as well as to seek each other's perfection, render mutual assistance and avoid reproaches based on flaws in character, for as Roels observes: "you are in this world, where...thorns spring up with roses; men and women without faults are found only in heaven among the blessed."[138]

These few comments on marriage reveal yet another way that the missioners had of stressing the "communal" aspect of the spiritual life. A further dimension will be illuminated as we turn now to their counsel that charity extend beyond the bounds of the domestic hearth and church to embrace those in need in the wider community.

## The Practice of Charity

Sister Marion Norman comments that the spirituality of John Gother and "the English Way" in general reveals a "surprisingly strong sense of social justice..."[139] and one finds this echoed in the sermons of Anglo-colonial America. A number of sermons stress the importance of aiding those in need as essential to the Christian life. For example, Louis Roels recommends, along with examens, confession, communion, and spiritual reading, that his flock "give alms to the poor, as far as you are able...."[140] James Beadnall likewise, in his sermon on fornication, counsels "alms and good deeds" as a preventative for falling into such sins.[141] In his sermon for the Third Sunday of Advent, John Lewis addresses the charitable obligations of the wealthy, and tells them they ought not to think that

Pre-eminence will wait upon you any further than the dust. The worms have no respect of persons, and will as greedily prey on thy putrid corpse as on that of thy vilest slave. As thou art rich and placed in a higher station than others, so thou art more strictly obliged to virtue. [You must] find work enough to manage your estate, to support your family, to defend the oppressed, to protect orphans and widows, to relieve the poor.[142]

John Carroll, using the theme of the imitation of Christ, describes the compassion of the Lord, and then asks his assembled listeners not only to admire it, but also "Take care at the same time that it be not a barren admiration, but such as may encourage every one of us, suitably to our stations in life and our opportunities, to bestow consolation on the wretched...."[143]

Though many homilists make passing references to the importance of the care of the needy and other acts of charity, James Walton, in a sermon for the Sixth Sunday after Pentecost on the text "Jesus took bread, and when he had given thanks, distributed it" [John 6:11], preached a whole discourse on "the obligation of giving alms...." In it he claims, like Carroll, that Jesus' example should be an impetus to aid those in need; that the rich "should concur with him in his charity towards them [the poor] and should be the ministers of his liberality." The excuses that the disciples made to Jesus at the feeding of the multitude are the prototype of those offered by the rich today, Walton claims. To those who say the time and place are inconvenient, the preacher answers: "If the rich are somewhat more pinched than ordinary, what must be the case of these miserable wretches, who scarce ever enjoy the benefit of a plentiful season." If some claim their own needs, Walton protests:

We seem to rely more upon men than God, and doubt of his promises. Shall we never try whether God will not prove more faithful, and whether our liberalities to the poor will not render him more favorable to our designs. I know not whether my eyes deceive me: I see on all sides ample fortunes ruined, families disgraced...and that by gaming, ambition, idleness, debauchery and prodigality. But I see nobody that is reduced to these deplorable circumstances by alms.

When some object that others can give better than they, Walton demurs: "There's no other fund destined by the Divine Wisdom for the maintenance of the poor, than what is in the hands of the rich" and scathingly continues:

All rich persons consequently must look upon themselves as the stewards of the poor appointed by God to supply their wants.... How can anybody suffer to behold the most nice and delicate persons take a sensible satisfaction and delight in feeding useless animals with their own hands, and yet should find an aversion merely to see the poor.

Finally, some will complain that the poor are numberless, and that their demands infinite, but the homilist counters: "Christ only demanded what they had, what they were able to afford. For 'tis not God's design that you should ruin your fortunes to raise theirs, but only by your superfluities to supply their necessities.... "[144]

One must bear in mind that in preaching the need for their flock to care for its most vulnerable members, the priests were hardly innovators, as the Maryland Catholics had been known for their commitment to the welfare of the whole community from the earliest days of the colony. Through business, religious associations and the dispositions of their wills, the early colonists sought to ensure that the needy and marginalized among their number were cared for.[145] This tradition continued throughout the eighteenth century—if the bequests recorded in wills are any guide[146]—and was carried on not only by the laity, but also by the missioners themselves,[147] who embodied their spoken message in their deeds.

Besides urging that charity be shown to those who were in need of material assistance, the homilists also were quite consistent in their exhortations that another neglected and mistreated group of Catholics be properly cared for and ministered to: the African slaves owned by many of the Catholic faithful.

## The Jesuit Homilists and the Slave Question

By the end of the eighteenth century, African slaves comprised an ever-growing number of the population of the Church in Anglo-Colonial America, making up roughly 20% of Maryland Catholics.[148] The circumstances of the Maryland plantation economy made reliance on slave labor more and more of an economic necessity, as even the Jesuits themselves found. Yet while many Protestant slave-owners displayed a certain disregard when it came to the spiritual and moral welfare of their slaves, Gerald Fogarty notes that "The Jesuits ... strove to have their own slaves instructed and baptized and ordered Catholic slave-owners to do likewise."[149]

It must be acknowledged, though, that the colonial homilists (with one exception) did not challenge the institution of slavery.

Typical in this regard was Bernard Diderich, who exhorts "even" the slaves in the congregation to pursue a spiritual life by admitting that "though you have been appointed by . . . providence to be slaves to men, yet [you] have not been slaves to sin . . . ."[150] The priests often attempted to make slavery appear to be an attractive state in life, John Lewis telling those who are slaves to: "Rejoice! You are in a happy state both in order to this life and next. You are free from innumerable cares of the world, and supposing you live in a regular Christian family art in an easy road to eternal felicity in the world to come."[151]

The homilists did stress that all Christians were bound, in Benet Neale's words, by "reciprocal duties," which included those linking "servants to their masters, [and] masters to their servants...."[152] For slaves, this included primarily obedience, Richard Molyneaux urging all in service "to obey your earthly masters with fear and trembling in the simplicity of your hearts as Christ himself...."[153] Lewis is a bit more explicit, cautioning slaves not to be mere "eye servants," who seem "to be diligent when the master's eye is over you," and summarizing three duties that slaves must follow to gain salvation:

Be nicely faithful in what is committed to your charge; to be punctually obedient to the commands of those over you; and to be extremely careful in loving and keeping peace and quietness among one another. These, my dear children, are no hard commands....[154]

It is surely no coincidence that, just as Lewis addresses the slaves as "children" in the quote above, the responsibilities that the preachers detail for masters parallel the duties that parents have towards their children. Lewis tells masters to:

Look upon your servants and slaves as your fellow creatures, as your brothers in Jesus Christ...and abhor your unchristian practice of treating them with injurious language. You are obliged to compassionate their miseries and above all to watch over their souls, to see that they frequent the sacraments, that they are punctual at their prayers...in fine that they are instructed and comply with all the duties of a Christian....[155]

Mosley speaks of the spiritual duties of masters in a similar manner, and urges in regard to the morning offering: "Let fathers and mothers see their children and servants perform duly this truly Christian exercise."[156] Ignatius Matthews criticizes those slave owners who neglect their own spiritual lives, and add to this sin by "infringing" the sanctity of Sunday "by working or permitting your servants to work."[157]

There is, however, one sermon that goes completely against the grain by denouncing slavery and the slave trade in frank and forthright language. The priest responsible was an Irish Dominican, Francis Fleming, who arrived in America from Portugal late in 1789, and who John Carroll described as "a well-informed, decent and sweet-tempered man,"[158] though he did have a reputation as a "progressive" on certain issues. During a sermon preached on the Feast of Saint Patrick in Saint Mary's Church in Philadelphia on 17 March 1790 (shortly after his arrival), Fleming, commenting on the fact that the saint was kidnapped into slavery at the age of sixteen, declared:

The infamous traffic in human blood is not a modern invention. [Patrick underwent]...the same hardships, the same severities, which many of our fellow creatures yet suffer in slavery, but with this difference, that Patrick experienced this cruel usage from unenlightened heathens, and our African brethren from those, who live in the sunshine of revelation, and join in the cry of universal benevolence.[159]

Later Fleming would exclaim, in regard to Patrick's escape, "The most violent apologists of the slave trade cannot dispute the right of God, to rescue his creature from unmerited oppression." What Fleming's confreres in Maryland would have thought of such critical language is debatable, but the very fact that he was able to preach the sermon at all (and its later publication suggests that it was well received) indicates that a breach was already evident between the attitudes of Catholics north of the Mason-Dixon line, and those who lived in Maryland and the South.

## Conclusion

It is important to recall in concluding how practical and pragmatic we have found eighteenth-century homiletics to be. How Christ and the saints were presented so often as models of conduct whose virtues were to be imitated, not only as powerful intercessors whose aid was to be implored. This was true even of the Blessed Virgin Mary who, while she was praised for the efficacy of her intercession, was also lauded as one who showed forth the way to eternal life, "if we copy her witness."[160]

To aid their flocks in living this way of imitation, the clergy recommended a life of devotion suited to their particular circumstances. Their exhortations focused on the centrality of the "domestic church" in the lives of the Catholics of the Maryland and Pennsylvania "frontier," where priests were scarce, and organized public corporate worship was a rarity. Since formal religious worship was thus infrequent and often accessible only with difficulty, the priests stressed the importance of a regular and structured practice of prayer, either communally within the family or neighborhood or privately in the seclusion of one's room, in both cases based on the use of some book or manual. Included in this cycle of morning and evening prayer was the recurring observance of the examen, to help the person to better know the state of his soul, and to recognize any progress he had made in the spiritual life.

Besides this regimen of vocal and silent prayer, the preachers also emphasized the importance of penitential practices in the life of the committed Christian. Whether this involved fasting and the spiritual discipline of the passions alone or included physical mortifications such as a hairshirt is unclear. What is apparent is that the homilists were in agreement that a person lacking in discipline had little chance of advancing in the spiritual life, especially those who lived in the midst of a culture which often lured Catholics away from the practice of their faith.

Another important component in the life of personal devotion was spiritual reading, and here the colonial homilists not only encouraged the use of spiritual classics (by Kempis, de Sales, Granada, and numerous English Catholic authors), but also actively sought to procure suitable works for their people and circulate them by means of lending libraries.

The faithful were encouraged to make full use of the opportunities they had to worship together as a community, most especially in the celebration of the Eucharist. The clergy strongly advocated the frequent (at least monthly) reception of Holy Communion, and accompanied this with a plea to be well disposed by a regular reception of the sacrament of Penance. Even when not communicating, the people were urged to consciously participate in the Mass, and numerous sermons were delivered to aid them in their understanding of that most holy Sacrifice. Eucharistic devotion was fostered, more openly in Pennsylvania, where eucharistic processions were popular, and discreetly in Maryland, which boasted its Society for the Perpetual Adoration of the Blessed Sacrament.

Marriage was praised by the preachers as a grace-filled estate in which to live out one's life, provided one was not called to the higher state of consecrated chastity, though they expressed numerous concerns about the questionable motives with which Catholics entered into matrimony, including the dangers inherent in mixed marriages. That this would be a concern in the socially confined atmosphere of the colonial Catholic community is hardly surprising, especially considering the ever-present possibility that it would result in the Catholic partner relinquishing his or her faith.

Catholics of colonial Maryland and Pennsylvania were urged to remember the poor and those in need, and be generous in assisting them in their wants. Indeed, the giving of alms was presented as an obligation to those who had the means to be generous, and there is evidence to maintain that the Catholic community was more than ready to assist those it found in need.

Finally, while the homilists were assiduous in their attempts to encourage those Catholics who owned slaves to see to their spiritual welfare and humane treatment, with the exception of Fleming they made no attempt to critique the system of slavery itself. Indeed, in a few cases they became almost rhapsodic about the advantages it could offer to the Christian soul. The Jesuits themselves would own slaves until the late 1830s, and though there is evidence that they were at times uncomfortable with this situation, they made little effort to change it.

The Catholic community, however much it may have been isolated by its distinctive character and civil disabilities, was not so introspective that it was unaware of the world around it. The homilists had much to say about the Protestant faith that dominated the religious scene, and about the state of society in general. Yet besides offering a critique, they also provided a defense of Catholic life and practice, and it is to these issues that we now turn.

## NOTES

1    ACSC, Bo-3. John Boarman, often incorrectly identified as the older brother of Sylvester, was born in 1743, studied at St. Omers and Liège, and was ordained in 1769. He returned to Maryland in 1773, and labored there until his death in 1797 at Newtown. Geoffrey Holt, S.J., *The English Jesuits, 1650-1829: A Biographical Dictionary* (London: Catholic Record Society, 1984), 36.

2    *The Jesuits. Their Spiritual Doctrine and Practice.* ed. George E. Ganss, S.J., trans. William J. Young, S.J. (Chicago: Institute of Jesuit Sources, 1964), 569.

3    Ibid. That this should be a central theme in Jesuit spirituality should not come as a surprise, when one remembers that Ignatius read the *Imitation of Christ* early in the process of his conversion at Manresa, and it remained his "prefered, if not his exclusive, spiritual nourishment" for the rest of his life. Guibert, 155.

4    Guibert, 570.

5    This can be established from the notations on the sermons listing the places and dates they were preached; for example, one of John Bolton's sermons on the Nativity records that it was preached on the Feast of St. John (27 December) in 1786, two days after the feast of Christmas. ACSC, Bol-13(b).

6    ACSC, Mor-1. This is the only sermon of Morris' to have survived in the collection. He was born in 1743, studied at St. Omers and Liège, was ordained in 1767, and arrived in Maryland in 1768, dying at Newtown fifteen years later. Holt, 171.

7    ACSC, Mos-10. This sermon (as well as those of S. Boarman, Sewall, and Greaton) is based on Louis Bourdaloue's "*Sermon sur la Nativité de Jésus Christ,*"

in *Oeuvres de Bourdaloue*, vol. 2, (Paris: Chez Firmin Didot Frères Libraires, 1840), 253-63.

8    ACSC, Bol-19. The reason for the frequency with which this image occurs in Christmas sermons may be linked to the popularity of St. Bernard's image of Christ preaching in his infancy, not by word, but by the example of his poor and humble condition. Cf. *Sancti Bernardi Opera*, vol. 4, *Sermones*, eds. J. Leclercq, O.S.B., H. Rochais (Rome: Editiones Cistercienses, 1966), *"Sermo Tertius in Nativitate Domini,"* 260, 1-3. This image is quoted without attribution in the *Catechism of the Council of Trent*, trans. J. Donovan (New York: Catholic Publication Society, 1880), 42. For a translation of Bernard's sermons, see *St. Bernard's Sermons for the Seasons and Principal Feasts of the Year*, vol. 1 (Westminster, MD: Carroll Press, 1950).

9    ACSC, Mol-6. This sermon is taken almost verabtim from that of Timoléon Cheminais, and may be found in *Sermons du Père Cheminais*, vol. 2 (Paris: Chez George and Louis Josse, 1694), 32-59.

10    ACSC, Pi-7.

11    ACSC, Di-27.

12    ACSC, Ro-20.

13    ACSC, Le-17.

14    ACSC, Car-27. Also in JCP, 3:448-50. There are many other descriptions of the life of Christ as a "pattern" for Christians to follow, cf. esp. ACSC, Je-13, Neal-3(a).

15    For a thought-provoking examination of the relationship between geography and the sacred, see Belden C. Lane, *Landscapes of the Sacred: Geography and Narrative in American Spirituality* (New York: Paulist Press, 1988).

16    John Bossy argues persuasively that the cult of the saints in medieval Europe played an important role in the strengthening of social bonds among Christians. One imagines this aspect of the veneration of the saints, if still as effective in the eighteenth century as in the fifteenth, would have been valued by the scattered Catholic flock of colonial America. See *Christianity in the West, 1400-1700* (Oxford: Oxford University Press, 1987), 11-13.

17    ACSC, As-4. The text of Bourdaloue's sermon may be found in vol. 3 of the *Oeuvres de Bourdaloue*, 225-236.

18    ACSC, Se-3.

19    ACSC, Di-30.

20    ACSC, As-4.

21    ACSC, Hu-4. William Hunter (1659-1723), like Peter Attwood, is one of the few missioners represented in the collection who labored in the early decades of the century. Already in 1696 he was the superior of the Jesuit mission at Portobacco, a post he would hold until 1707. He was described as *"Talento ad gubernandum plane excellenti et singulari."* Thomas Hughes, S.J., *A History of the Society of Jesus in North America, Colonial and Federal: Text*, 2 (London: Longmans, Green and Company, 1917), 683.

22    This should come as no surprise to those familiar with English spirituality, as

traditional English devotion included a strong emphasis on Mary and the saints. See, for example, Sister Marion Norman, I.B.V.M., "John Gother and the English Way of Spirituality," *Recusant History* 11 (October 1972): 310. Though some have questioned the influence of these devotions in the eighteenth century, J. A. Hilton observes: "In view of the claim that eighteenth-century English Catholic piety was lacking in devotion to the saints, especially to Mary . . . it had better be stated at once that Butler practiced and advocated such devotions." In "'The Science of the Saints:' The Spirituality of Butler's *Lives of the Saints*." *Recusant History* 15 (May 1980): 190. Alban Butler (1710-73), a priest of the English mission, was a well-known spiritual author, and served as President of the English College at St. Omer.

23   ACSC, As-4.

24   ACSC, At-1(b).

25   ACSC, Boa-6. Father Boarman gave this sermon at the dedication of an unidentifed church named St. Mary's; most likely it was St. Mary's at Boarmans Rest, Charles County, Maryland, the family estate. Note also here the reference to "testifying" publicly to this distinctive aspect of one's Catholicity.

26   ACSC, Le-13. Lewis is here quoting Robert Manning's Fifty-Fourth Entertainment; see *Moral Entertainments on the Most Practical Truths of the Christian Religion* (Dublin: Richard Grace, 1839), 412. Manning (and Lewis) also recommend the recitation of the Angelus and Marian litanies as well as the observance of Marian feasts. Hilton notes that Butler always recommended the recitation of the Angelus and Rosary to others, and comments: "Butler's esteem for the Rosary is of a piece with his insistence, like Challoner's, that mental prayer is not merely possible but also neceessary for all Christians." Hilton, 140.

27   ACSC, Bol-9.

28   Bolton here displays a typical sensitivity to Protestant objections to Marian piety, and instructs his hearers in how to respond.

29   For a more extended treatment of the role of Mary in the missioner's preaching, see Michael Sean Winters, "Marian Spirituality in Early America," in ACPP, 87-105.

30   ACSC, Ro-3.

31   ACSC, Boa-5.

32   The following sermons have the glories of Ignatius as their theme: ACSC, Pu-1, Be-7, Hu-2, Mos-6, Boo-4, Bol-2.

33   ACSC, Hu-2. Besides giving an excellent example of the way in which the homilists called on their flocks to be imitators of the virtues of the saints, this quotation also hints at the closeness the missioners felt to their founder, e.g. "our saint." That lay Catholics also had a devotion to Ignatius may be infered from the name's ubiquity among Catholic men of southern Maryland in the eighteenth century. Cf. Charles H. Metzger, S.J., *Catholics and the American Revolution* (Chicago: Loyola University Press, 1962), 189-90. George Hunter (1713-1779), born in Northumberland, arrived in Maryland in 1747, and

immediately took up his post as the superior of the mission. Hughes, 2:692-93. He was, according to Carroll, "truly a holy man, full of the spirit of God, and the zeal of souls." JCP, 1:56.

34 ACSC, Boo-4.

35 ACSC, Pu-1. Born in Northamptonshire in 1697 and educated at St. Omers and Liège, Poulton was ordained for the Society ca. 1724. After teaching at St. Omers and the English College in Rome, he was sent to the Maryland mission (holding the office of Superior from 1742-ca.46), where he died in January, 1749. Hughes, 2:690; Holt, 203.

36 ACSC, Boa-1, Ne-7.

37 ACSC, Mol-nn. Many copies of this printed sermon are extant. For more information on Farmer's admirable life and ministry, see "Pioneer Missionary. Ferdinand Farmer, S.J.: 1720-1786," *Woodstock Letters* 75 (June, October, December, 1946): 103-15, 207-31, 311-21.

38 ACSC, Mat-6.

39 ACSC, Car-14.

40 ACSC, Li-4. The same text may be found in Manning's "Fifty-Fifth Entertainment" with one small change, namely, that Livers omits Manning's recommendation to spend "one half hour at least in spiritual reading.....," perhaps because he feared presenting too onerous a regimen. Cf. Manning, 423.

41 ACSC, Le-13. Cf. Manning, 410-11.

42 ACSC, Mos-3.

43 ACSC, Le-12.

44 ACSC, Se-4. He continues by declaring critically that evening prayer is usually "deferred till men are so wearied with other pursuits, as to be almost incapable of reflection; and then they are under the necessity of neglecting that prayer, which did they continue it, would from their langour and drowsiness, appear rather like a mockery of devotion, than a tribute of adoration and gratitude."

45 ACSC, Bol-24.

46 ACSC, Mos-6 (emphasis mine). Richard Challoner, in his prayer book that lent its name to a whole era of Catholics, *Garden of the Soul*, provided a rather complete series of prayers and devotions in his "Morning Exercise:" *The Garden of the Soul: or a Manual of Spiritual Exercises and Instructions* (Philadelphia: Joseph Cruikshank, [1774]), 21ff.

47 ACSC, Car-55. In JCP, 3:436-43. For a set of "Evening Devotions for Families," see Challoner, 167-83.

48 Guibert writes that for Ignatius "The examen was not a mere glance over the manner, more or less perfect, in which his actions had been performed, but also a humble search for faults that had escaped him" (67). Ignatius practiced this exercise every hour, and he prescribed it for members of his Society. Guibert notes that for the Jesuits, "The particular examen, which they have vigorously recommended, is . . . [a] type of . . . direct and methodical labor for the reformation of life" (570).

49 ACSC, Ha-2. Born in Nottinghamshire, Harding (1701-1772) arrived in

Maryland in 1732, where he served at various posts until in 1750 he became superior of the mission in Philadelphia, a responsibility he held until his death. Hughes, 2:689-90; Geoffrey Holt, S.J., *St. Omers and Bruges Colleges, 1593-1773: A Biographical Dictionary* (London: Catholic Record Society, 1979), 123. Carroll reported to Rome in 1790 that Greaton was succeeded in Philadelphia by Harding, "whose memory is still in benediction in that city; and under whose auspices, and the untiring energies of whose zeal, the beautiful church of St. Mary's was erected." JCP, 1: 406. He was described by a Protestant minister, Jacob Duche, as a "well-bred gentleman, much esteemed by all denominations of Christians in this city for his prudence, his moderation, his known attachment to British liberty, and his unaffected pious labors among the people to whom he officiated." In *Historical Sketches of the Catholic Churches and Institutions of Philadelphia* (Philadelphia: Daniel Mahony, 1895), 39.

50    ACSC, Ro-13.

51    ACSC, Pi-13.

52    For the importance of the retreat in Jesuit spirituality see Guibert, esp. 301-306.

53    ACSC, Le-3.

54    ACSC, Je-8.

55    ACSC, Ne-3.

56    ACSC, Ne-2.

57    ACSC, Neal-10(e).

58    A text entitled "A Spiritual Retreat for the use of Religious Persons" may be consulted in the John Digges, Jr., Papers in the Maryland Province Archives, as well as other writings useful for those on retreat, e.g., the "Spiritual Dialogues."

59    ACSC, Se-5. Such "preached" retreats might have been similar to what in the nineteenth century would be called "parish missions." The "retreats" of Jean-Baptist David at the turn of the nineteenth century, in the words of Jay Dolan, "exhibited many of the features of a parish mission. They sought to revive religion in "congregations cold and neglectful of their Christian duties;' conversion and instruction were the goals of his preaching.... Like many preachers, David based his retreats on the *Spiritual Exercises* of Ignatius Loyola." *Catholic Revivalism: The American Experience, 1830-1900* (Notre Dame: University of Notre Dame Press, 1978), 16-17.

60    Quoted in Beatriz Betancourt Hardy, "Papists in a Protestant Age: The Catholic Gentry and Community in Colonial Maryland, 1689-1776" (Ph.D. diss., University of Maryland, 1993), 100-101.

61    ACSC, As-3. For other sermons that list spiritual reading as an essential element of the devout life, Cf. ACSC, Hu-5, Le-6, Le-16, Li-1, Li-3, Di-21, Je-8, Je-11, Boa-6, Se-1.

62    ACSC, Je-8. Such advice was given by Anglican ministers as well. Sally Schwartz notes that Reverend Richard Backhouse insisted that "Books were more influential than an 'orator's most moving discourses on ye Same Subject' delivered from the pulpit, and might convince individuals 'Ignorant off, or prejudiced agst ye principles & Ceremonies of our church' of their truth."

*"A Mixed Multitude". The Struggle for Toleration in Colonial Pennsylvania* (New York: New York University Press, 1987), 106.

63 ACSC, Pi-13.

64 ACSC, Pi-25. Challoner also notes this saying of the Fathers, and insists on the importance of pious reading, urging: "Let not a Day pass without employing at least one Quarter of an Hour in reading some spiritual book; and a more considerable Time on Sundays and Holidays...." Challoner, 190.

65 See Hughes' extensive comments in *History of the Society of Jesus in North America, Text,* 2:517, fn. 7, and R. Emmett Curran, S.J., *American Jesuit Spirituality: The Maryland Tradition, 1634-1900* (New York: Paulist Press, 1988), 15. A list of books lent at Newtown Manor ca. 1767, as well as books ordered for the laity (including Manning's *Sermons* and Challoner's *Think Well On't*) may be found in the Newtown "Memoranda Book," MPA, 3,15. The Memoranda mentioned by Hughes, which desires James Carroll to buy a number of books for the widow Jones (August, 1716), and which includes the Rheims *Testament* and the *Introduction to a Devout Life* is in MPA, 57,1. James Walton's diary records that he received a shipment of books including twelve copies of *Garden of the Soul,* lent out a book on St. Aloysius and a catechism, and was given money to purchase books and beads. Cf. MPA, 4,2. Mosley's Account Book also records a steady stream of books being lent out in 1764 and 1765 including, as Hughes notes, the *Christian Directory* of Parsons and the *Catholic Christian Instructed.* Cf. MPA, 49,2. Tricia Pyne points out that "In addition to the lending library, the Jesuits also circulated numerous spiritual writings to educate the laity in the teaching of the Church." "The Maryland Catholic Community, 1690-1775" (Ph.D. diss, The Catholic University of America, 1995), 43. It is interesting, though not surprising, to note that although there is a record of Bibles being ordered for the colonial laity, homiletic exhortations to read the Scriptures directly are non-existent.

66 ACSC, Wa-5.

67 See Walton's All Souls' Day (2 November) sermon, in which he tells his audience, "Frequently fast, or undergo some other mortification for their releasement...." ACSC, Wa-2. Nor should it be forgotten that days of fast were often proclaimed both by civil and religious authorities to plead for the mercy of God. One printed sermon in the collection, by the irrepressible Simon Felix Gallagher, dates from 9 May, 1798, and implores a "safe and honorable deliverance from impending dangers and calamities." Cf. the "Sermon Preached on the Ninth Day of May, 1798, Observed as a Day of Fasting and Prayer, to Implore the Divine Aid and Protection in Favor of the United States." (Charleston: W. P. Harrison, 1798) in ACSC, Ga-nn. For information on Gallagher, see: Peter Guilday, *The Life and Times of John England, First Bishop of Charleston* (1786-1842), 2 vols. (New York: America Press, 1927), 1:164-261.

68 ACSC, Mol-8.

69 ACSC, Neal-4(a). Documents in the Maryland Province Archives show that

the missioners were granted the ability to dispense Catholics from the fast; e.g., on 28 November, 1723 Vicar-Apostolic Bonaventure Gifford granted the Superior of the mission the power to dispense "in relation to the observance of the fast of Lent, and of Holydays, etc." MPA, 3,8. Even in such cases Neale warns: "If you cannot abstain or fast, there are other good works which you may do to make amends for it, and you are bound to do them...." ACSC, Neal-15.

70   ACSC, Bee-1. Beeston was a Jesuit who was not ordained until after the suppression of the Society, at an unknown date, and did not arrive in the United States until 1786. Holt, *English Jesuits*, 29-30.

71   ACSC, Se-9, Se-19. This public flouting of the fast by some of their own number under the eyes of their Protestant neighbors would have only made the life of faithful Catholics more difficult.

72   ACSC, Mol-2.

73   ACSC, Nea-1. This sermon is even more grim when one learns that only three months after it was delivered, Fr. Neale died at the age of forty-five. A Marylander of the prodigious Neale family, he was ordained a priest in 1738, after study at St. Omers and Liège, returning to the colonies by 1740. Holt, *English Jesuits*, 176.

74   ACSC, At-1(b).

75   ACSC, Mat-5.

76   Walton speaks of those who attempt to "macerate their bodies with reiterated mortifications and austerities...." ACSC, Wa-6; and Roels claims forgiveness is denied, even if one were to "discipline yourself to blood, [or] wear a hairshirt and fast for a whole year...." ACSC, Ro-1.

77   ACSC, Se-1.

78   Joseph Chinnici, O.F.M., *Living Stones. The History and Structure of Catholic Spiritual Life in the United States* (New York: Macmillan, 1989), 28.

79   ACSC, Mol-1.

80   ACSC, Mat-3.

81   ACSC, Je-5.

82   ACSC, Le-5.

83   ACSC, Bi-4.

84   Ibid.

85   ACSC, Le-5. For an illustration of the acts of contrition and examinations of conscience recommended to penitents in prayer books of the period, see Challoner, 217-55 and *The Roman Catholic Prayer Book, or Devout Christian's Vade Mecum* (Baltimore: William Warner, 1814), 79-104. The latter lists as a sin against the third commandment, "Not cared to hear Catholic sermons" (86)!

86   ACSC, Neal-C.

87   ACSC, Bol-3.

88   ACSC, Pi-25.

89   ACSC, Ro-21.

90   ACSC, Neal-16.

91   ACSC, Car-4 and JCP, 2:56-57.

92 ACSC, Ro-4.

93 ACSC, Fr-1. For a fuller description of the spiritual effects of the Eucharist as presented in the sermons, including its function as a pledge of eternal life, see my "The Eucharist as Presented in the Corpus Christi Sermons of Colonial Anglo-America," in ACPP, 27-53, esp. 43-46. James Frambach (1729-1795), a German, arrived in the colonies in 1758. Hughes, 695. He served ably at Conewago, Hagerstown and Frederick; though in the late 1780's he became involved in a dispute with Carroll over financial matters, as well as his refusal to cease ministering to the Frederick congregation. Carroll wrote that "His unhappy temper, and, I fear, an attachment to money, without one reasonable view of enjoying or employing it, always have, and always will make him an impracticable man." JCP, 1:295.

94 ACSC, Di-11.

95 This requirement was restated by the Decree of the Synod of Baltimore in 1791, although it urged against making rash judgments to deny Christian burial to one who had failed to make the Easter duty. Cf. the "Report of the Synod," Session 4, 24 in JCP, 1:534.

96 ACSC, Fa-1. He states that "since we are all equally sharers of the sacrifice and merits of his death, we are all of us also equally in power to benefit ourselves and apply those his merits to our advantage especially now at this approaching time of Easter when the Church obliges us to frequent both the sacrament of Penance and Eucharist...." Farrar (1707-1767) served in Maryland from 1734 to 1747, at which time he returned to England. Hughes, 690.

97 ACSC, Se-15. Sewall gives an invaluable insight into the social implications of religious observance in the Catholic community when he remarks that he would be tempted not to admit such ill-prepared people to communion, but if he didn't they would join the ranks of those for whom "There is no Easter...no sacrament, no religious worship; others will mark them with ignominy and will say with reason, such persons have not made their Easter and are in the state of disobedience." (The word `damnation' was crossed out here and replaced)

98 ACSC, Pi-11.

99 ACSC, Car-46, also in JCP, 3:403-404.

100 ACSC, Di-11.

101 ACSC, Fa-3.

102 ACSC, Ro-8.

103 ACSC, Be-9. The sermon is based on one by Bourdaloue for the Sunday within the Octave of Corpus Christi, Cf. *"Sermon pour le Dimanche dans l'Octave du Saint Sacrement,"* in *Oeuvres*, 2:22-31.

104 It is interesting to note that Saint Elizabeth Ann Seton, known for her devotion to the Eucharist, only received the sacrament three times a week, the most permitted by the spiritual director of her community, William DuBourg (who admittedly was not a Jesuit). See Ellin Kelly and Annabelle Melville, *Elizabeth Seton: Selected Writings* (New York: Paulist Press, 1987), 69.

105 Guibert, 385.

106 ACSC, Je-7. Ignatius Matthews echoes this when he remarks that the special children of the Church "never miss once a month at least" and "in a word who can be call[ed] pious or ferverous who stay away longer...." ACSC, Mat-8. Since few in the colonies had the ability to attend Mass more than once a week for most of the century (except perhaps in Philadelphia), it is possible that "weekly" communion was the equivalent of "daily" in this milieu. The advice of Jenkins and Matthews agrees with the mainstream of thought for the Society of Jesus for most of its history up to 1773, as Guibert reproduces Suarez's advice: "It seems proper only rarely to counsel anyone to receive Communion more than weekly as a habitual practice," and comments that these guidelines were "going to remain [those] of the Jesuits in general," though it was said that "monthly Communion is a minimum for devout persons" (380).

107 ACSC, Li-3.

108 ACSC, Je-15. For Hornyhold's sermon, see Joseph Hornyhold, *The Commandments Explained in Thirty-Two Discourses* (Baltimore: Fielding Lucas, n.d.), 24-36; Jenkins bases his comments here on material found on 36.

109 ACSC, Mos-3.

110 He also criticizes those who try to hear Mass while standing under the windows of the chapel, never entering even when there is room.

111 John Bossy notes: "For an eighteenth-century English Catholic Mass was 'prayers' *par excellence*, and though the use of this term was partly the consequence of a legal taboo, it represented with some accuracy what an average Catholic would expect when he came to Mass. ...'devotional' and 'liturgical' traditions were in conflict in the Catholic's attitude to Mass, and the former more deeply ingrained...." *The English Catholic Community, 1570-1850* (London: Darton, Longman & Todd, 1975), 369.

112 Sister Marion Norman comments that John Gother, at least, "gently deplored the habit of saying the rosary or 'getting in' one's breviary or other devotion during the Holy Sacrifice." "John Gother and the English Way of Spirituality," *Recusant History* 11 (October, 1972): 311.

113 ACSC, Mos-4.

114 ACSC, At-3(b). At the consecration, for example, he urges individuals to remember with humility and admiration Christ's love for humanity, and "adore your Savior truly and really present. When the priest says the Pater Noster recite the same with him with such an affection as the presence of your Savior there readily to hear these petitions cannot but move you to."

115 See John W. McGrain, Jr., "Priest Neale, His Mass House, and His Successors," *Maryland Historical Magazine* 62 (Sept., 1967): 254-84.

116 The clergy would at the very least have reserved the Eucharist for distribution as Viaticum. A wooden tabernacle once used in the chapel of John Carroll's mother's plantation at Rock Creek—where he carried out his priestly ministry upon his return from Europe in 1774—is preserved in the archives of the Visitation Sisters at Georgetown. Hardy mentions that in 1723 the Carroll family recorded having a monstrance and tabernacle among the contents of

their Annapolis residence, 201. Also, Joseph Mosley refers to blessing oneself when passing "before the Blessed Sacrament," and Ignatius Matthews attests that the house or chapel of God is "sanctified by the corporal presence of God himself." ACSC, Mos-8, Mat-8.

117  ACSC, Ne-7.

118  ACSC, Se-14.

119  ACSC, Hu-1.

120  A document from St. Thomas Manor at Chapel Point, Charles County, Maryland, dated August, 1768, lists the names of people who had pledged to participate in a "Perpetual Adoration of the Blessed Sacrament." The terms were as follows: "The subscribers oblige themselves to employ every month through the year, the half-hours to which their names are annexed, on their knees, in honor of the Blessed Sacrament, by meditating or saying of vocal prayers, either relating to the Blessed Sacrament or to the Sacred Heart." The roster provided for a half-hour, twice a month, i.e., on the first and fifteenth, the second and sixteenth, etc., and included members of Maryland's oldest Catholic families: the Neales, Brents, Boarmans, etc. This author does not believe that the possibility should be ruled out that some of these families would have had access to the Blessed Sacrament to carry out this adoration in its presence. MPA 57,2. See also John LaFarge, S.J., "Our Pioneer Adorers of the Blessed Sacrament," *Emmanuel* 35 (July, 1929): 176-79.

121  See Chinnici, 27; and the "Report of the Synod," Fourth Session, 17-18, in JCP, 1:531-32.

122  Ferdinand Farmer wrote to his brother that "You have made possible, my dear brother, through your generosity, the devotion to this most Holy Sacrament. A crowd of people came to my church to see the new monstrance which I received through your generosity, and they adored with tender devotion our dear Savior on his throne. O would that I also had been presented with a censer and cape! Our simple folk here are deeply stirred to an increased devotion through holy vessels and vestments." From page 60 of a typescript of unknown authorship, quoting *Der Neue Welt-Bote* in MPA,25,5.

123  ACSC, Bol-21.

124  Annabelle M. Melvile, *Louis William DuBourg: Bishop of Louisiana and the Floridas, Bishop of Montauban, and the Archbishop of Besançon, 1766-1833*, 2 vols. (Chicago: Loyola University Press, 1986), 1:145. A public display certainly would not have been welcomed by Carroll; in a letter of 1811 to Enoch Fenwick he remarked that "the essential object of the Institution of the festival will be obtained better by confining the procession within the limits of Catholicity, I mean, the possessions of the Church." JCP, 3:153. See also, Thomas Spalding, C.F.X., *The Premier See: A History of the Archdiocese of Baltimore, 1789-1989* (Baltimore: Johns Hopkins University Press, 1989), 61-62.

125  Gerald Fogarty, S.J., "The Origins of the Mission, 1634-1773," in *The Maryland Jesuits, 1634-1833*, eds. Robert Emmett Curran, S.J., *et al.* (Baltimore: The Corporation of Roman Catholic Clergymen, 1976), 24;

Edward H. Quinter and Charles L. Allwein, *Most Blessed Sacrament Church, Bally, Pennsylvania* (Bally, Pa.: by the authors, 1976), 4. The negative results of such a procession would justify Carroll's later concern, but the people were quite taken with such worship. Kirlin writes: "Devotion to the Blessed Sacrament by means of prayers, songs and processions was definitely part of the services of the colonial German Catholics," and adds: "It may be presumed, however, that if the people at Goshenhoppen and Lancaster observed the day with a sacramental procession, Conewago, likewise, very early honored the Lord of Hosts." Joseph L. Kirlin, *Catholicity in Philadelphia from the Earliest Missionaries down to the Present Time* (Philadelphia: John Joseph McVey, 1909), 60-61.

126  Six sermons in the collection deal exclusively with matrimony: Ro-15, Di-23, Di-32, Neal-A, Pi-12 and Car-43. The missioners apparently had little difficulty in solemnizing marriages, at least in Pennsylvania, where, "Marriage licenses were given to clergymen of all faiths, including Roman Catholic priests. One official stated that when he issued them to Catholics, `I insert one of their names instead of the words [any Protestant minister] which I always blot out with my pen.' He did `not see any good reason why they may not marry their own People by a License (sic)...since they are allowed the public Exercise of their Religion in this Province.'" Schwartz, 262.

127  ACSC, Di-32.

128  ACSC, Di-33. Leonard Neale advises young people to seek to know through prayer "what is the state to which they are called," for "there is one state appointed for them...." Neal-A.

129  ACSC, Ro-15.

130  Neale had also discouraged those who sought what he called "pecuniary" advantages in marriage.

131  Roels comments on the folly of seeking riches by observing, in one of the many witty maxims in this homily (which is not characteristic of Roels at all!), "satisfaction on foot is preferable to discontents in a coach and six...."

132  ACSC, Ro-15.

133  ACSC, Di-32. He even warns the couple to beware the consequences of too riotous a wedding reception, deploring the sins "that are committed in the celebration of the nuptials, as well by the married, as by those who are invited." He later laments that many invite to their wedding, not Mary (as at Cana—the Gospel text of the day), but the devil, who "belches out so many words of double meaning, to pervert innocent souls. It is he that speaks with such a freedom and licentiousness, as to make all that are not lost to all shame blush. It is he that kindles more and more the fire of impure love particularly in the young people that are invited."

134  ACSC, Di-33. Intermarriage between Protestant and Catholic gentry was quite common, at least in the early years of the eighteenth century. Hardy notes that "one of the really striking facts about the Catholic community from the late 1600's well into the eighteenth century is not so much how few converted

to Anglicanism, but how many Protestants converted to Catholicism or allowed their children to be raised as Catholics" (86, also 84-86). By mid-century the number of Catholic gentry marrying Protestants would decline, and clergy disapproval of such unions would grow more marked. Witness an incident referred to above, in which one Jesuit in 1753 was said to have physically ejected a couple from a chapel, when the bride refused to convert, or agree to allow her children to be raised as Catholics. Pyne, 286. See also Hardy, 346-48.

135  ACSC, Neal-A.

136  This is recommended by Diderich and Neale; cf. Di-32, and Neal-A.

137  ACSC, Neal-A.

138  ACSC, Ro-15. Neale remarks that if some people have "a patience...of so delicate a texture, that every trifle will break it, like a spider's web, they should never have entered into this state in which there must unavoidably be some occasions for patience."

139  Norman, 310.

140  ACSC, Ro-13.

141  ACSC, Be-6. James Ashby argues similarly that "the most powerful and efficacious means he [God] has furnished his Church with of procuring the salvation of her children...[are] the sacraments, giving alms to the poor, assisting distressed neighbors, shewing to the world by their behavior the character they bear, the faith and religion they profess...." ACSC, As-8.

142  ACSC, Le-6. Leonard Neale makes a similar comment in regard to death, when he observes: "All things abandon a Christian at his death; nothing accompanies him...besides his good works, and the poor whom he has sometimes succcoured." ACSC, Neal-3(b).

143  ACSC, Car-55. Carroll deftly points out here that there can be actions of charity corresponding to any station in life, without questioning the validity of such class distinctions. In fact, most of the preachers throughout the century defended class distinctions based on wealth; John Lewis for example, telling those who are poor that they ought to "adore the wise and merciful hand of Providence, who has placed you in the humble state and thereby taken from you innumerable occasions of offending God." ACSC, Le-6. James Carroll likewise tells an audience of poor laborers that "Little do you reflect that it was his [God's] special will that your circumstances should be low, that you be obliged to gain your living by hard labor and fatigue." It is difficult, he continues, for "those who have raised themselves above the state they were placed in by Providence" to attain spiritual perfection. ACSC, Ca-4.

144  ACSC, Wa-1.

145  See James Michael Graham, S.J., "Lord Baltimore's Pious Enterprise: Toleration and Community in Colonial Maryland" (Ph.D. diss., University of Michigan, 1983), 85-102. Also his "Meetinghouse and Chapel. Religion and Community in Seventeenth-Century Maryland," in *Colonial Chesapeake Society*, eds. Lois Green Carr *et al.* (Chapel Hill: University of North Carolina

Press, 1988): 242-74, here 251-53, 270-71.

146 For example, the 1763 will of Joseph Semmes declares: "I give and bequeath unto the poor of this parish where I now dwell thirty pounds current money to be disposed or distributed to them by the Rev. Mr. George Hunter [S.J.] or his successors at his or their discretion." MPA, 25,8. One might object that such generosity is characteristic of those on their deathbed, and yet one of the wealthiest Catholics of his day, Richard Bennett, III, provided for the needy not only in his will, but throughout the course of his life. His obituary of 18 October 1749 noted: "As he was the greatest Trader in this Province, so great Numbers fell in his Debt, and a more merciful Creditor could not be, having never deprived the Widows or Orphans of his Debtors of a Support; and when what the Debtors left was not sufficient for that purpose, frequently supply'd the deficiency." The paper noted that "by his Death, the poor and needy have lost their greatest Friend and Benefactor." Quoted by Michael D. Coyne, "Richard Bennett, III" in Edward B. Carley, *The Origins and History of St. Peter's Church, Queenstown, Maryland, 1637-1976* (Baltimore, 1976), 148-53, here 148.

147 Witness the record of benefaction left by Joseph Mosley in his "Accounts: 1765-67," using the common monetary notation of "pounds:shillings:pence." He notes, for example, giving 0:7:6 to John Cullen on 16 July, 1765 "for charity on burning his house." On 14 March 1766 he records: "In charity, to a poor woman to school her child, for one quarter. 0:8:0." Another entry is less specific: "Given in charity to a poor woman. 0:2:6." MPA, 49,2. In addition to giving alms, Pyne notes that the missioners frequently offered employment to those of their neighbors in need of work, hiring individuals "to perform tasks around the plantation, from digging ditches and building fences to sewing suits and clothing for the Jesuits and their slaves" (296).

148 Cyprian Davis, *The History of Black Catholics in the United States* (New York: Crossroad, 1990), 35.

149 "The Origins of the Mission, 1634-1773," 18. Fogarty also remarks that "Jesuit treatment of slaves was notorious for its gentleness. 'Priest's slave' came to mean one who was granted a large measure of freedom of movement, did not work too hard, and was well cared for" (19).

150 ACSC, Di-22. It is clear from the sermons that slaves were often in attendance.

151 ACSC, Le-6. Henry Pile likewise observed that, as opposed to voluntary slavery (i.e., to sin), "to be made a slave unjustly is far from disgraceful, and what's more I maintain, that slavery so far from being disadvantageous to man's character...is the badge of his honor, and the source of his happiness," provided he suffers for the sake of Christ. Pi-3. However, two priests do refer to the hardships involved in slavery (Nea-1, and especially Be-3).

152 ACSC, Ne-10.

153 ACSC, Mo-1.

154 ACSC, Le-6.

155 Ibid. Bitouzy recommends similarly that masters "make use of your power

according to the rules of humanity and justice." Bi-6; and John Carroll questions whether "inconsiderateness and hard-heartedness of masters towards their servants...is ever a venial sin...[as the] extremity to which it is often carried is most certainly mortal?" Car-14. Such comments cause one to wonder about the incidence of mistreatment of slaves by Catholic masters.

156 ACSC, Mos-6. Other sermons linking the spiritual care of slaves with that of children are: Je-9, Ro-26, As-9, Be-2, Be-4.

157 ACSC, Mat-6.

158 JCP, 1:431. Carroll placed so much faith in him that he was soon made his vicar for the Northern District of his diocese. Sadly, Fleming, who by 1794 would be described by Carroll as one of "our most respectable and valuable ecclesiastical members," died along with Father Graessl as a result of their labors during the Yellow Fever epidemic of 1793 in Philadelphia. JCP, 2: 120.

159 ACSC, Fl-nn. This sermon was also printed in *The American Museum, Or, Universal Magazine*, 3 (April, 1790): 177-80.

160 ACSC, Hu-4.

# Chapter Five

# "The Dangers and Storms of This Tempestuous Sea"

## Catholic Faith and Colonial Society

So far we have concentrated on an examination of what the preachers had to say concerning the "internal life" of the community; that is, its spiritual and moral existence. While not neglecting the role that society—the "world"—had in the living out of their religious duties, we have until now refrained from examining the ways in which the homilists reflected on the position of the Catholic community vis-à-vis the world at large. That community was confronted with challenges presented not only by the churches of the Reformation and the growing tide of rationalism and libertinism, but quite often by political hostility. It is to the first of these issues that we will now turn.

### Catholics and Protestants

That the Catholic community would possess a keen awareness of the religious environment surrounding it is not to be wondered at. Most churches in the colonies during the eighteenth century were keenly conscious of the diversity which enveloped them, and which, interestingly enough, rarely resulted in anything approaching indifferentism. As one scholar notes, "Though religious diversity no doubt perplexed many middle-colony inhabitants, very few responded so uncharacteristically for their time as simply to reject religion. [Many] responded to diversity with a positively sharpened religious self-awareness and an enhanced attachment to the doctrinal uniqueness of their own denomination."[1]

Yet if there was one area in which some semblance of unanimity could be discerned among the divergent Protestant denominations, it was in their opposition to the Roman Catholic Church. "Differ as they might and did in almost every other point, the various sects were sure to agree in their hatred of Rome. In theory every sect except the Baptists and the Quakers followed Locke in believing Catholics dangerous to the civil government. [And even] In Rhode Island and Pennsylvania as in all other British colonies, Catholics were disenfranchised and ineligible for any office of trust and honor."[2] Nor was this discrimination separating the colonial Catholics from their neighbors limited to the realm of religion and politics, for it even pervaded contemporary literature and education.[3]

In the unlikely event that these ever-present reminders of the gulf separating Catholicism from Protestantism lost their impact on the Catholic community, it "possessed a highly trained corps of Counter-Reformation clergy to help them remember the difference between the two."[4] The members of the Society of Jesus did this in a number of ways: negatively by the rhetorical stance they adopted with regard to the Reformation and their critique of Protestant teaching, and positively by their exposition of controverted Catholic doctrine.

Many of the missioners could not be said to have evinced a charitable attitude when referring to those Christians separated from the Roman Catholic Church. Indeed, quite a few did not shrink from calling them "heretics." For example, John Boarman, in recalling the spread of the Church throughout the world, boasts that it has "proved superior...to the malice of heretics, who have employed every art of seduction to corrupt it...."[5] While these references can often be construed to refer to the historical past, as in Augustine Jenkins' unambiguous mention of the "Novatian heretics" of the third century, and John Bolton's remarks concerning "Origen and some heretics,"[6] frequently homilists experienced no difficulty in referring to contemporaries in identical terms. For example, Jenkins refers to "heretics...who deny...all tradition, [yet] are nevertheless obliged to have recourse to it and contradict by practice what they profess in words," and Bolton criticizes "Heretics of this and the last two centuries...."[7]

Although frequently the epithet is used as a blanket term, as when John Boone lists "heretics" as a type of enemy which attacks the Church,[8] often this term occurs within the discussion of a specific theological issue. The word was all the more likely to be used if the matter under discussion was one possessing an inherent shock value to Catholics, such as the denial or desecration of the Eucharist. Bernard Diderich exclaims, while describing the insults offered to Christ in the Blessed Sacrament: "How many heretics vomit blasphemies against him?" Sylvester Boarman, after evoking the image of one who can "trample underfoot the consecrated host and throw it into the fire [as well as murder priests]," thunders: "Behold the heart of the heretic!"[9] Yet the term also occurs within the context of far less heated issues, such as the value and necessity of fasting, which John Digges notes is "contested by heretics."[10]

It would be a mistake to assume, however, that the colonial clergy could refer to their separated brethren by no other term than "heretic," though the alternatives were not necessarily any more flattering. Henry Neale seems to have preferred the term "sectaries" for those separated from the Roman Church, as does Benet Neale, and John Bolton makes use of it as well.[11] The latter homilist, in the same sermon in which he denounces "Heretics of this and the last two centuries," also refers to "our adversaries" agreeing with the church on a controverted topic, demonstrating the fluidity of reference to non-Catholics that was characteristic of his co-workers.[12] Interestingly enough, the word "adversary" is here used to replace "heretic," which has been carefully scrawled out. A similar device is also found in the extant homilies of Charles Sewall, where the word "heretic" is excised in two separate sermons; once by itself, and once as part of a larger paragraph.[13]

Though examples of the use of "heretic" by the homilists can be found throughout the eighteenth century, from John Digges (who was on the mission from 1742 to 1746) to Leonard Neale, there is reason to believe that its use may have been falling out of favor by late in the century. For if the emendations referred to above are indeed those of Bolton and Sewall—whose labors extended into the nineteenth century—and not the work of a later redactor, then one might venture to surmise that the sensibilities of at least some of the clergy were undergoing a gradual transformation.

A further compelling reason for suspecting that a change in tone took place late in the century is the fact that not only does John Carroll never make use of the term "heretic" in any of his sermons that are included in the collection, but furthermore such terminology would have been completely out of keeping with his vision of Catholicity. Carroll is capable of bluntly stating the dangers that accompany religious  pluralism, noting in his inaugural sermon that he has been charged with preserving the faith of his flock "untainted amidst the contagion of error, surrounding them on all sides." Yet even in this context he continues by immediately stressing the importance of his congregation's preserving "in their hearts a warm charity and forbearance towards every other denomination of Christians...."[14] Likewise, though he may through veiled references to other Christian denominations warn of "adversaries" who might "artfully insinuate themselves into our confidence, and under the fair pretense of teaching a purer doctrine, or delivering us from rigorous observances, to which we are bound by religion, attempt to weaken our faith...,[15] he never stoops to name-calling, which was, nonetheless, all too much in evidence among his confreres."

Some of the homilists, not content with referring merely to anonymous "heretics" or "adversaries," mentioned the founders of the reformed traditions themselves, in varying ways. Martin Luther is singled out five times, only once in a manner that indicates some understanding of the gradual development of the Reformation.[16]

James Beadnall notes: "Luther only began to find fault with an abuse that might perhaps have been in the manner of applying or denouncing the indulgences. And this might have been right, but it belonged not to him to find fault or correct it."[17] Ultimately, Beadnall will continue, this quibbling led Luther to reject the teaching of the ecumenical councils on a whole range of subjects.

Other homilists preferred to find the beginnings of the Protestant movement, not in a legitimate—if unwise—dispute over one area of church doctrine, but rather in a monumental act of hubris. George Hunter, for example, takes an extreme position when he describes the genesis of the Protestantism as follows: "Luther was erecting his standard and declaring war against the true Church, aiming at nothing less than its total overthrow and a total abolishing of all religious worship and veneration instituted and established by the Redeemer of mankind."[18] Often the missioners were similarly blunt when it came to assigning a motive for the undertaking of the Reformation. Hunter himself was willing to offer a possible incentive for this "total overthrow" when he depicts as "impious" deluders of humanity those "voluptuous heretics greedy to gratify their sensual appetites...."[19] The excuse of libido is also offered by Henry Pile in his characterization of King Henry VIII, the spiritual father of the Church of England, as a "monster of lust [and] debauchery," adding for good measure that Luther and Calvin can be judged no better.[20]

The mention of Henry VIII brings to mind the particular circumstances of the English Reformation and the founding of the Church of England. Since this was the reformed church that had affected the English Catholics most directly, it is no surprise to find it mentioned frequently by the homilists. Often these references occur in tandem with reflections on the hardships of Catholic life with its attendant disabilities, as in Pile's sermon, wherein he laments that to be a professed Catholic is to be "contented to be rebuked and reviled by friends and relations."[21] Richard Molyneaux, in one of the older sermons in the collection (which may have been delivered during previous work in England) begins by blaming the sins of the pre-Reformation Church for the advent of the Reformation:

And certainly...the sins of England as of Israel were very great and provoking by a vast excess both in number and malice, and the crimes of the priesthood and the laity were the scandal and disgrace of the Church, when the Catholics, God's people, were made a prey to the adversaries of truth.[22]

Thus began what Molyneaux satirizes as a "blessed reformation," which he judges to be as "deplorable as it is ridiculous." In a more personal vein he continues:

This is that cloud which interposes its darkness between God and us which has hung over us two ages obstinately and immovably, and small are the prospects which human prudence can hitherto pretend of its removal and of the appearance of the Sun of Justice to shine again among us. And therefore the Word of God is still very precious in England, the flock is but little to hear it and the shepherds are but few to speak it. O miserable condition of this unhappy kingdom! England is Mary's dowry and yet the devil still triumphs in its possession....

Years later, in 1758, Joseph Mosley, recently ordained and new to the Maryland mission, preached a sermon on 1 Thessalonians 1:6, on the importance of standing firm during trials. This was quite a timely theme considering the rising tide of cultural and political anti-Catholicism both in Maryland and Pennsylvania as a result of the French and Indian War.[23] Mosley declares that it is his

Indispensable obligation to encourage you to bear firmly and steadily all calumnies and persecutions that are raised in our heretical country by our inveterate enemies.... For I see you no less oppressed, than the flock of Saint Paul, and your enemies not less numerous....[24]

He continues:

There is no one, I believe, that sees how our unfortunate country lays wallowing in the mire of heresy and sin, how it is plunged into error and darkness, filled with the enemies of the Catholic church . . . that does not at the same time perceive that of consequence those who profess this Catholic religion must be oppressed, persecuted, calumniated, injured....

Yet Mosley urges his flock to see these tribulations as a blessing from Jesus Christ, who predicted that his followers would be persecuted. Though their suffering does not at present include the loss of life,[25] he observes:

I believe there is [none], that has experienced it, will deny injuries, affronts, loss of estates, afflictions, tribulations, incapacity of public offices, to approach the nearest death as anything can in this life.... You see then, Dear Christians, it is by tribulations that our love is put to the test....[26]

Reflecting on the pressure that many of his listeners were under to renounce their religion, Mosley tells them they must make a choice, but if that choice is to "deny Christ and his holy religion" then they "will be lost." He concludes by encouraging them to:

Fight on the battle that you are engaged in, for God will reject you if you look back as unfit for the kingdom of heaven. But if you persevere, his grace will be given you through all the dangers and storms of this tempestuous sea, and crown you at last with eternal bliss....

It should not be thought that the priests were content with merely issuing blanket condemnations of the Reformation churches and their founders. On the contrary, they were quite willing to enumerate the features of Protestant doctrine they found most troubling, usually in the process of delineating Catholic doctrine. If the sermons provide any indication, the aspect of Reformation teaching they found most troubling was, not surprisingly perhaps, its claim to "reform" the teaching of the Roman Church. The very concept that any individual had the ability, on his own authority, to introduce changes to the doctrine or worship of the church, quite apart from the validity of these alterations in and of themselves, is roundly condemned by the homilists. John Bolton enunciates this position rather succinctly when he declares: "It has always been a settled principle with us, that novelty in faith is an infallible mark of heresy."[27] Germain Bitouzy explicates this at greater length, and in more impassioned language, when he exclaims: "What was true at the beginning of the Church is still true, and what was false at the beginning of the

Church is still false and ever shall be so. All reformation, all innovations, all protestations in matter[s] of faith are wrong...."[28] Formulating his own rule of thumb to aid his flock in recognizing false doctrine, he advises them to ask themselves if a questioned teaching is old, for "if it is a new one you may be sure that it is false."

The preachers thus present the antiquity of its teachings as one of the glories of the Roman Church, while also maintaining that it has preserved the purity of its beliefs unsullied throughout the ages. James Walton states that "its doctrines have been transmitted from age to age free of error, subject to no variation...,"[29] while John Boone affirms in a similar vein that the Church has been "one in the constant and immovable profession of the one and same faith, taught by Jesus Christ and his apostles...."[30]

The homilists further declare unhesitatingly that the Roman Catholic Church is infallible in its doctrinal teaching, as a logical consequence to the fact that Christ founded the church and promised to remain with it. Thus Diderich asks God rhetorically:

Could your tender mercy suffer you to oblige man under pain of damnation to embrace your faith, and not afford him some infallible rule, whereby to know it? Merciful God! Is it possible...that you could leave him without an infallible guide, whereby to distinguish your divine salutary truths from the abominable inventions of the devil?[31]

He quickly answers his own question by instructing his listeners:

If we believe the divinity of Christ, we must believe his promises cannot fail. If we believe his promises cannot fail, we must believe that the Church is protected by Christ, and so directed by the Holy Ghost, that she cannot be deceived in matters of faith, and consequently that in all points of doctrine she is infallible.

Germain Bitouzy firmly attests to the infallibility of the Church when, after citing his text from John 16 on the promise of Jesus to send his disciples the Spirit of truth, he continues: "This assistance Jesus Christ promised to his apostles to be with them to the end of the world proves the infallibility of the Church. It proves that the

Church has ever been, and shall ever be, infallible."[32] The central importance of this infallibility becomes apparent when Bitouzy maintains that:

The infallibility of the Church once proved and agreed upon, cuts off all at once all other difficulties upon matters of faith. For if the Church is truly infallible, then everything it teaches must be true. [In that case] we must submit our judgment and our reason to its doctrine. So you see that the infallibility of the Church is an answer to all the difficulties and to all the contestation in matters of religion.[33]

Louis Roels uses a story drawn from the history of the early Church to reinforce his declaration that Christ has "commanded us to hear and obey the Church, as God himself, under pain of eternal damnation...."[34] He tells of a young boy who, upon being cruelly interrogated by a Roman prefect, cried out "Christ is the true God." When asked how he knew this, the child replied "my mother told me, and God told my mother." Roels exclaims: "This is the true and solid answer every Catholic ought to give, when any point of belief is called into question: My holy mother the Catholic Church has told me, and almighty God has told it to my mother the Church."

Such an approach flies in the face of one of the central tenets of Protestantism, at least as depicted in the sermons, that is, its affirmation of private judgment. Roels, in the above sermon, maintains that all those:

Who believe their own private interpretation of the Scripture or any other private person's or particular Congregation's interpretation have no divine saving faith, because no private person or particular Congregation can claim any promise from Christ of an absolute assistance of God's Holy Spirit, to preserve them from errors....[35]

Roels' critique of private judgment even goes so far as to call into question the actions of one who

Compares without prejudice the doctrine of all the churches, with the text of the infallible word of God, and follows that which he impartially judges most conformable to the sacred text. This person, I say, does not believe with a divine saving faith, though he embraces the Catholic religion...because he does not ground his faith upon the divine authority, but upon his own private judgment...."[36]

Though Roels appears to be distrustful of the very existence of independent human reasoning in one's decision to enter the Catholic church, other homilists have no reluctance in offering various motives to convince either believers or skeptics of the legitimacy of the Church's claims to be the one founded by Christ.[37] A number of them, for example, point to the witness of the early Fathers of the church as a confirmation of Catholic belief and practice. Bernard Diderich, for example, appealed to the "universal concurrent testimonies of all the holy Fathers," and declared that a particular statement echoed "the language of the holy Fathers."[38]

John Boarman takes a different tack when he marshals a series of arguments to demonstrate the authenticity of the "Catholic Christian religion," beginning with the existence of miracles in the spread of Christianity, as a demonstration that "this religion must necessarily have God for its author."[39] He then lists a number of factors indicating how difficult it was for Christianity to spread throughout the world, such as the necessity of overcoming superstition, the challenge that the teaching of Christ presented to the corrupt morals of the world, and the humble origins of its first disciples. All these elements, he declares, suggest how formidable the obstacles were to the spread of Christianity: "What rashness, folly and madness one might have thought, and what prospect of success in such a chimerical undertaking?" Yet despite this, "nothing has been able to prevail against it. Therefore it must have God as its author, and it cannot be false."[40]

Henry Pile discounts the possibility that the Church could ever have failed to grow and prosper, maintaining:

It would be no less impious than ridiculous, to suppose that Jesus Christ had no sooner planted his Church by his sweat and labor, and watered it with his precious blood, but he would withdraw his assistance and let it fall into error and abomination....[41]

John Boone notes that the apostles were merely poor fishermen, despondent after Christ's death, and asks, "Could anything in appearance be more unlikely to succeed in such a design, than men in these circumstances?"[42] Yet he declares the Church has had the assistance of Christ, which has produced overwhelming results:

She has maintained herself against the attacks of her more formidable enemies, viz., politicians, heretics, and new heresies that daily rise up against her, but still remains, and ever shall remain the One, Holy, Catholic, and Apostolic Church of Jesus Christ.

One can imagine a listener protesting this line of argument, though, noting that a multiplicity of different churches all claim to be the true church of Christ. In such circumstances, how can the believer identify the church truly founded by Jesus Christ? Such objections were certainly raised in Pennsylvania. Sally Schwartz notes that "The variety of competing faiths engendered confusion among religiously inclined Pennsylvanians. The father of one young man who came to [Henry Muhlenberg] for baptism, when asked. . .why his son had not been baptized as an infant, replied 'because there were so many sects in this country he had not known which was the best.' When he made inquiries of the teachers of each party, every one of them would say, 'Here is Christ; we have the best medicine and the nearest road to heaven.'"[43] Henry Pile offers a traditional response to such objections, stating the four marks by which the true Church may be recognized:

First therefore for our church to be the Church of Christ it must have existed, and we must be able to prove its existence, since the time of the apostles to the present day. [Second] its faith must have been uniform, without...contradiction.... [Third] we must also show that the faith she teaches is holy.... [Fourth] the faith we embrace must have been spread through the whole world....[44]

Germain Bitouzy, however, takes a rather innovative approach to the question of the identity of the Church of Christ. He is aware that the average person, "sees in this world bishops of two different churches, the bishops of the Catholic church, and the bishops of the

Protestant church, and he does not know to whom of these he is to apply...."[45] This dilemma, though, admits of a solution, as Bitouzy is convinced that serious examination will demonstrate that:

> In matters of faith the doctrine of the Catholic church is the best, that it affords a greater security, and therefore that it deserves the preference over the Protestant church. Why is it so? Because the Catholic church believes everything that is believed in the Protestant church. If therefore the Protestant church is right in its faith and doctrine, then the Catholic church is also right...and the Protestant church cannot say the same. For if the faith and doctrine of the Catholic church is right, then the faith of the Protestant church is wrong, because they don't believe everything we do. Therefore if they are right, we are right with them, and if we are right they are wrong.

Bitouzy expounds on this rather interesting permutation of Pascal's famous wager by listing the five essential areas in which Catholics and Protestants disagree (the number of the sacraments, the legitimacy of confession, the real presence of Christ in the Eucharist, the existence of purgatory, and the intercession of the saints), and then demonstrating that on each of these topics the Catholic position offers "more security" than the reformed doctrine.[46] He ends his homily by admonishing his listeners, "A man that is wise and prudent must always take the most safe and the most secure way in everything."

All five of the issues mentioned by Bitouzy were real areas of disagreement between Rome and the churches of the Reformation, and quite often one of them would figure as the subject of an entire sermon.[47] One such topic was a defense of the legitimacy of the veneration of the saints, and John Bolton's homily on this subject illustrates the thoroughness with which the preachers could approach their task.[48] He begins by grounding the practice in Scripture, and then cites an opinion of an early church Father (in this case Saint Jerome). Next he explains the theological distinction between worship (*latria*) and veneration (*dulia*), and makes reference to the Council of Trent to verify his presentation. Finally, he attempts to clarify the various misunderstandings that can arise surrounding such practices, concluding that the reverencing of the saints is pointless for Christians, unless they "try to imitate their virtues, laying before...[them] their holy lives for a sample and pattern to copy after...."[49]

Though Bitouzy may have felt that he had managed to summarize the differences between the churches in five disputed points, there are some notable areas missing, not the least of which is the dispute over faith and works. One might have thought this issue too abstruse to serve as the topic for a homily, yet, on the contrary, three sermons confront this subject directly. Indeed, the controversy seems to have been quite pressing, as Henry Neale requests at the beginning of his discourse: "I beg you'll have patience to hear me out with a particular attention. It's a subject [that] deserves it at these times more than ever."[50]

The most exhaustive treatment of the topic is offered by Benet Neale, in a forty-five page manuscript most likely delivered over the course of two (or more) Sundays. He begins by examining the concept of faith, which he defines as: "A gift of God...a supernatural quality, a divine illustration or light infused by the Holy Ghost into our soul, by which we are inclined and enabled undoubtedly to believe, assent to, and judge infallibly true whatever God has revealed to us...."[51] Quoting Trent, Neale identifies this faith as being the beginning, root and foundation of salvation, while insisting that "it is manifest that a person is justified not by his own power, strength, or virtue, but purely for the merits of Jesus Christ." He discounts the term that "modern innovators" have given to this faith by calling it "historical"—thus dismissing it as insufficient for salvation—and he rhetorically questions their ability to ground this in Sacred Scripture.

As to what are commonly called "good works," Neale insists that all Christians are called to follow the commandments, and "To pretend then that Christ has fulfilled the law for us so as to except us from the obedience to the moral law is a damnable error of the antinomians...." He cites Matthew 25, wherein the divine judge sends the goats on his left off into punishment for ignoring his presence in the needy, as proof that Christ takes no notice of "their newfound special Calvinistical faith of assurance. He only condemns them for their neglect of good works...."

Neale further defends the ability of the faithful, aided by grace, to do good works, and condemns "the error of our modern sectaries, who hold all God's commandments impossible." He admits that the term "meritorious" can sound "very harsh to our brethren the Protestants of most, if not all persuasions" yet they fail to understand that: "It is his [God's] free goodness to give us that sanctifying grace, which confers all the value, all the merit of these good works. It is his free bounty to excite us by actual grace to the performance of them...."[52]

George Hunter points out that it is "not the name and open profession [that] makes the Christian, but a Christian life; and whence this is wanting there's no saving faith."[53] To drive his point home he notes that the earliest Christians were accustomed to use the witness of their lives in their apologetic treatises, thus proving "their faith from their manners. Learn, said they, our doctrine from our lives, learn the Gospel we preach from the lives we lead."

While Henry Neale asserts that good works are the "life and the soul of faith,"[54] he spends most of his sermon expounding on the necessity for faith to serve as the foundation of the Christian life. He makes it clear that "Actions, how moral, how great and heroical so ever they may be, if they are not performed in the spirit of faith, and if they are not dignified with the character of faith, avail nothing to salvation." Thus neither the Neales, nor George Hunter, present a view of Catholic doctrine that is skewed towards extreme reliance on works as many of their separated brethren would charge. All seek to describe the authentic teaching of the Church, which stresses the foundational character of faith, while not discounting the importance of charity in the Christian life.

One cannot help but perceive the sheer self-confidence in the Roman Catholic Church that the sermons exude, and the sincere inability of the priests to account for the existence of the churches of the Reformation. In a sermon on the Creed, using Matthew 18:17 and 16:18 as his text, John Williams observes:

The unerring authority of Christ's Church is so clearly established in these and sundry texts of Holy Scripture, that it seems surprising such as pretend to ground all their faith upon the written word of God should swerve from it in this fundamental article; and whilst they profess daily in their Creed to believe in the Holy Catholic Church refuse submission to its judgment in the most essential points....[55]

The most common reason assigned for this inability to realize the divine origin and nature of the Roman Catholic Church is not attributed primarily to malice, although such a charge is not absent in a few of the sermons.[56] It is not even seen as merely misunderstanding; rather, it is most often depicted as a willful spirit of innovation and novelty for its own sake. John Boone, for example, exclaims, "O my God! To what extravagant and monstrous length, will the pride, vanity, infidelity, and the itch of novelty carry themselves!"[57] Henry Neale speaks in the place of God and declares to those who have separated themselves from the Church:

You have abandoned the Church, which is my house, and made yourselves particular churches, every one according to his private fancy. You hear preachers and doctors that I have not authorized, and by a capricious, schismatical fickleness prefer their maxims and sentiments to the universal steady rule established by me.[58]

Even John Carroll professes to see something similar to this at work in the Reformation when he writes, of those who have rejected Confirmation as a sacrament:

In the face of such clear testimonies of Holy Writ and perpetual tradition, when a spirit of religious innovation set men at liberty some centuries ago, to coin for themselves new symbols of faith, they either rejected Confirmation altogether...or they...professed to receive it, not as a Sacrament, but an Apostolical ordinance....[59]

If the preachers believed so strongly in the rectitude of the Catholic position, and likewise assigned some degree of culpability to those who remained outside the fold of the Catholic Church, one might wonder how they viewed their non-Catholic neighbors' chances for salvation. An answer might be found in a remarkable sermon given by James Carroll on the occasion of a disruption in a Catholic congregation to which he had just arrived.[60] Carroll notes in his sermon that a schism "has depleted the congregation, and resulted in the neglect of the sacraments and an estrangement on the part of some of the faithful who believe they were too harshly dealt with by the last pastor." The cause of the "schism" would seem to have been an oath to which the congregation was asked to subscribe: "I am of the opinion that this great difference and disturbance which we have had concerning an oath required to be taken by all, proceeded from want of comprehending the sense of what was proposed." Though Carroll doubts that the oath "required by him [the pastor] differed in any substantial matter from the profession of faith proposed by the Church to all the faithful," he remarks:

I am willing to confess that the terms and expressions used on that occasion were not as mild as might have been used. *I am however far from thinking that my predecessor required of you to swear that everyone was damned who did not die a Catholic.* I am, I say, far from thinking him so severe for he knew that several are saved by ignorance, he knew that others might have received a particular grace at the moment of death...though during their lifetime they might have made no profession of their Catholic religion.[61]

Carroll continues by giving an interpretation of the Church's understanding of *extra ecclesiam nulla salus*, and stating: "The sense of this is that those can't be saved who make profession of a false religion either by neglecting to examine the true one, or refusing to embrace it after they have found the true one."

That the issue of the salvation of those outside the Church was a delicate one is surely no surprise, especially in Maryland where interfaith marriage was not uncommon, and where a number of Catholics refused (whether for political reasons or just sloth) to practice the religion of their birth.[62] If indeed the previous pastor had stirred up a hornet's nest by implying that those who died outside the Church were damned, Carroll is quick to note the broader way in which the *extra ecclesiam* teaching of the Church had always been understood. This interpretation allowed a degree of latitude to those who were invincibly ignorant of the Church, or who had received what Carroll terms a "particular grace" at death.

From this intriguing sermon one might venture to conclude that if the homilists were steadfast in stressing the distinctive nature and solid claims of the Catholic church to authenticity, at least some of their number—and those who supervised their pastoral assignments—were sensitive to the needs of the times in hesitating to erect (and then advertise) insurmountable barriers to salvation for those outside the visible Church.[63] It also offers us a glimpse of the independence which the Catholic laity brought to their individual congregations and an indication that, although they were attentive to the voice of their pastor, they were not always accepting of everything he had to say.

Before moving on to examine the attitude of the missioners toward those who they characterized as "libertines," the flaunters of all organized religion, it would be appropriate to say a brief word about the sermons' attitude toward another religious minority even smaller than their own—the Jewish people.

## Catholic Homiletics and the Jewish Religion

Although never numerous in the colonies, Jews had been included in the toleration that was granted by the Calverts in the early days of Maryland.[64] Though they are never spoken of in the present tense, the way in which the homilists refer to their role in history is illustrative.

The "Jews" are mentioned in at least forty-three sermons, and of those at least thirteen references can be considered to be neutral. They refer, for example, to the people to whom the Law was given, or to whom Jesus preached.[65] Another sixteen refer to the Jewish people as those who failed to recognize Jesus as the messiah, whether deliberately or not.[66] Two criticize the Jews for historical failures prior to the time of Christ,[67] while another nine berate them for their role in his death,[68] six of these rather intensely. John Lewis, for example, speaks of the "ungrateful and perfidious Jews who put him [Jesus] to death,"[69] and in another place calls them both "savage" and "wicked."[70]

Benet Neale writes of them as "bewitched."[71] The height of anti-Semitism is reached in Henry Pile's sermon on the Passion in which he speaks of the "hellish malice and cruelty of the Jews [which] fills you with horror" and declares "these savage murderers to be our mortal enemies" in their "brutish animosity."[72]

All these references seem to focus primarily on the people directly responsible for the death of Jesus (whom one might term the "leaders" of the people), and Pile does admit that "the Jews would never have crucified Jesus Christ, had not the sins of mankind doomed him to die." Yet it is difficult to imagine that the use of such vitriolic language does not reveal a level of underlying hostility to the Jewish people. Paradoxically, the only mention of them that could be possibly considered positive is also by Henry Pile, when he refers to the "Jews who followed him [Jesus]" into the Church, though of course by doing so they most likely ceased to be Jews in the eyes of the homilist.[73]

Though it is intriguing to examine such references in an attempt to glean information on the likely attitude that colonial Catholics had towards Jews, it must be admitted that few of them—the priests included—would have come into contact with a person of the Jewish faith on a regular basis, if ever. Such was not the case with those whom the priests style "libertines," and it is to an examination of the attitude expressed in the sermons toward these "scoffers" and "laxists" that we now turn.

## The Misuse of Liberty and Freedom

Though the Catholic community experienced hostility from many of the committed Protestants among whom they lived, a similar animosity was also directed towards them by those who scorned all religious belief. To such as these, Roman Catholics seemed egregious offenders against common sense. Many sermons make reference to being the object of such scorn; for example, Benet Neale drives home a point about the need for religious education by noting that at present:

To declare for an innocent and Christian life, is to incur the displeasure and satirical lampoons of many who are commonly distinguished by the name of free-thinkers, but [should] much more properly be styled a set of people without any sense or thought at all.[74]

In a similar tone Robert Harding laments that "we have the misfortune to live in an age, where the most sacred mysteries of the Christian religion are often times the subject of raillery and ridicule...."[75] Sylvester Boarman is more combative, when he condemns (as he says St. Paul would) those "modern infidels and deists, who are aiming constantly at the total destruction of the Christian religion."[76] Often times the attacks were more sharply honed, as when Louis Roels remarks that regular communicants are often subject to derision from "libertines and worldlings" who accuse them of being people who "often go to confession and communion...[but] have however as many faults as their neighbors."[77]

The response of the homilists to these attacks was twofold: on one hand they sought to point out the folly of those whom they commonly called "libertines," and on the other they cautioned against a one-sided glorification of reason and personal liberty.[78] As to those whom the priests styled "libertines," they are mentioned in over thirty-five extant sermons. Often they are presented as those concerned only with life's pleasures, as when Charles Sewall calls them:

Men void of faith, religion and morality; blind voluptuous men, bent only on the gratification of their sensual appetites: atheists, deists, philosophers, libertines. Libertines hardened in vice, men without faith and religion, may pronounce everything a blessing which gratifies their sensual appetites. With these it is vain to reason, these we exhort in vain.[79]

Some of the preachers did identify "libertinism" especially with sexual excess,[80] but it would seem that in general the term referred to those who, as the word implies, exalted human freedom, ignored the moral law, and thus—in the eyes of the ministers of the Church— sinned excessively. Ignatius Matthews provides a succinct portrayal when he describes a libertine as one "who values neither human or divine laws...and strives to laugh and ridicule religion and the precepts of the holy Church into utter contempt...."[81]

One should not assume that all "libertines" were outside the pale of the Catholic church, for one sermon makes it quite clear that the term could be leveled at errant Catholics. Robert Molyneaux bemoans the fact that:

The libertinism of opinions never runs higher than in the present age...these libertines have not religion enough at heart to expose themselves to the consequences of a visible schism. But though they remain in the communion of the Church, they do not nevertheless remain in its faith.[82]

Although libertines are most often depicted as those who entirely reject Church teaching and practice,[83] in a few cases the priests list specific tenets or doctrines that libertines are wont to reject: among them that a god could condescend to take on human flesh in the Incarnation, the idea of resurrection to eternal life, the existence of hell, and the teaching that Jesus is truly present in the Eucharist.[84] In the latter case Bernard Diderich notes that "libertines make a jest of...[the] real presence" and observes that many of the Protestant reformers, who similarly reject the Eucharist, do so because it is "contrary to their senses...."[85]

Indeed, priestly suspicion of over-reliance on human wisdom can be discerned in many of the sermons. Quite a number call attention to the dangers that await those who place all their trust in human reason, not the least of which is contempt for organized religion, and a descent into immoral behavior. For instance, John Boarman criticizes "superficial reasoners," who attempt to "resolve all piety into frenzy and enthusiasm,"[86] and James Ashby cites the "unreasonableness of some people who under the pretense of wit and caution refuse to believe some articles of faith till we give an evidence of demonstration...."[87] He insists that grace and revelation are necessary for an understanding of the mysteries of the faith and for leading a virtuous life as well. In so doing he refutes: "those men who would persuade themselves that religion is not necessary, and that to lead a moral life according to the dictates of reason is sufficient, without the practice of religion."

John Carroll, in a sermon on infidelity, reminds his hearers that people "in these our days" have "endeavored too successfully to introduce into the world principles and practices...repugnant to the maxims of the Gospel."[88] Though his reference is the French Revolution, he draws a conclusion relevant to his flock in America, stating he would like to make them

Sensible of the weakness and insufficiency of the human understanding alone, to discover all necessary truths, and lay down a correct system of morality; [furthermore] that we owe these blessings to divine revelation only....

Carroll is willing to admit that many of those who profess the primacy of reason in their lives are not like the scornful and insulting "libertines" and "atheists" who are so much excoriated in his confreres' homilies. Nevertheless, they have strayed from the Lord's flock, much to their own detriment:

Nothing is more common, in these days of pretended philosophy, than to hear men say: "We transgress not against the laws of God, we injure no man, we commit no violence, we wish well to every fellow creature, and assist the unfortunate to the extent of our faculties." But if we inquire farther, whether they perform other duties required by religion; whether they pay due respect to the commandments of the Church, with which Christ promised to remain forever...whether they ever appear at that sacred table, where the Savior of mankind offers himself to be the food for their souls; whether they exercise over their bodies, by fasting and abstinence, that useful and salutary self-denial, so essential to the spirit of Christianity; what my Dear Brethren, is the answer to many of these inquiries?[89]

Carroll answers his own question by affirming that they "form a religion for themselves, and circumscribe in obligations, not by the measure of the revealed will of God, but of their own defective and capricious understandings."

It must not be thought that in stressing the boundaries of human reason in a life of religion the homilists were dismissing it altogether in some manner of fideistic close-mindedness. On the contrary, as the excerpts cited above make clear, it was only a warped notion of an exalted reason which took precedence over all other considerations that the priests felt obliged to warn against. In actuality, a number of the sermons refer quite matter-of-factly to the necessity that the believer has of making use of reason. For example, Charles Sewall urges his congregation, when they: "hear the wicked exclaim against the rigor of the Evangelical laws...then call forth your reason, rouse your faith...[and] compare the advantages of complying with your spiritual duties with the dreadful consequences of their omission...."[90] In an earlier decade John Digges had instructed his flock that even philosophers agree that, "we are indispensably obliged to contradict the inclinations of our nature, whenever they are contrary to the dictates of reason...."[91] Indeed, reason is often seen as being a barrier to sin, as when James Ashby urges his listeners not to relinquish reason and give themselves over to their appetites.[92] Though it is sometimes stated that reason must submit to truths beyond its comprehension,[93] it is not uncommon for human understanding to be an aid to the acceptance of some Church teachings, as when Joseph Greaton considers that reason testifies to the existence of purgatory.[94]

Much of the foregoing discussion has revolved around the Catholic attitude toward those who profess other religions—or irreligion—and how they conceived of the nature of the Church in relation to these sects or opinions. Before concluding this chapter we should examine what the homilists had to say about that other perennial topic which has occupied human society: politics.

## Catholics and the State

For over seventy years, from the turn of the century till the advent of the War for Independence, Catholics in Maryland and Pennsylvania labored under a host of civil disabilities. These handicaps, while not threatening their lives or preventing them from amassing substantial fortunes in business, hampered their participation in the political life of the colonies, and prevented them from worshipping publicly (at least in Maryland).

We have already seen, in the treatment of the homilists' attitude towards the English Reformation, some evidence of their feelings about their civil condition. For example, Joseph Mosley was quite explicit about the disabilities that Catholics labored under, the "injuries, affronts, loss of estates, afflictions, tribulations, incapacity of public offices...," and placed the blame for these "calumnies and persecutions" on "our inveterate enemies."[95] An interesting sermon in this regard is one given by James Beadnall, on the text "Blessed are they who mourn." It speaks of the rewards of a virtuous life despite its attendant sorrows and in concluding Beadnall exclaims:

> For you seem to practice those virtues, you suffer persecution for justice sake! You're deprived of liberties! Debarred from high posts and offices, you're reviled (as I may say) but all for justice sake. Rejoice therefore and be glad for your reward is exceeding great in heaven.[96]

Though many of the homilists lament the sad state of Catholics in regard to their civil liberties and a few, like Mosley, berate their "enemies" for the persecution, most counsel patient acceptance of such disabilities as a way of growing in virtue. Peter Attwood is typical in this respect when he advises his flock that "we must equally kiss the hand that strikes as that which strokes us" and tells them to persevere even "when violent storms of persecution render it hard and difficult to avoid the rocks...."[97]

It had been hoped that the sermons would yield some telling insights on how the homilists viewed the War for Independence that the colonists waged against Great Britain, but not a single reference is to be found. A French visitor in Maryland at the time of the Stamp Act crisis reported that Roman Catholics were "cautious";[98] the clergy no doubt maintained this cautious stance throughout the conflict with Great Britain. Joseph Mosley reflected the resigned attitude of many of his confreres[99] when he wrote to his sister as the war loomed:

Times here look very gloomy and seem to threaten a stoppage of all intercourse with you. We must submit to the decrees of Providence, on whom must depend all events of war and even peace.... A clergyman's call has little to do with civil broils and troubled waters; the fisherman never chooses to fish in muddy or disturbed water.[100]

If the general disposition of a majority of the clergy was to endure the war in silence, in the years following the Treaty of Paris they reaped the benefits of religious freedom. Again, however, there is almost total silence on the newfound freedoms that were granted to Catholics in the wake of the war. Joseph Mosley may once more be cited as representative of the mind of the homilists when he wrote his sister, "The toleration here granted by the Bill of Rights has put all on the same footing, and has been of great service to us."[101]

The only one to speak at any length about these blessings was Bishop John Carroll, who used them to remind his flock of the great responsibility such freedom entailed. In a sermon commemorating American Independence, he declared: "God has visited you in particular by a signal instance of his mercy in removing those obstacles, which heretofore cramped the free exercise of our religious functions."[102] He continued by celebrating this wondrous event: "Now, agreeably to the dictates of our own consciences, we may sing canticles of praise to the Lord, in a country no longer foreign or unfriendly to us, but in a country now become our own, and taking us into her protection."

On another less auspicious occasion—during an excommunication in Philadelphia—he lamented the existence of disharmony in the Church, especially since it was occurring at a time when:

The fairest opportunity was offered to us...of extending our doctrine and the efficacy of good example, of unity and peace, the kingdom of Christ, the dominion of his holy faith; of that faith, which has been perpetuated through the ages, formerly so oppressed here, but now under the protection of righteous and equal laws.[103]

There is no reason to suppose that any of the other homilists would have disagreed with Carroll's evaluation of the political developments in America, even if they were not as willing to praise them openly in their sermons.

The comparative silence of the homilists relative to politics may be surprising to some, especially when compared with the loquacious defense of Catholicism they offered against the challenges from Protestantism and "libertinism." In actuality, such an approach is consistent with their constant efforts to support and nurture the Catholic community. That community faced an enduring challenge both from the proselytism and bigotry of the members of other denominations among whom they lived, and from those who rejected religion entirely. In this regard the preachers were strenuous in their defense of the integrity and beliefs of the Catholic church, especially when compared with those of its opponents. In this sphere, it would seem, they were fairly successful in keeping the community united in its faith and practice. With respect to the political arena, though, while it was not uncommon for the priests to lament the restrictions under which the community labored and to urge their flocks to persevere, in general it would seem they refrained from outright political commentary, especially in the tense years of the war with Great Britain. This approach would bear fruit for Catholics during the last decade of the century, when under the wise guidance of John Carroll they would prepare to enter an era of promise, in which the Church and its clergy would soon confront new challenges.

## NOTES

1    Patricia U. Bonomi, *Under the Cope of Heaven. Religion, Society and Politics in Colonial America* (New York: Oxford University Press, 1986), 73. On the other hand, Sally Schwartz notes that "Pennsylvanians seemed unclear about the theological differences that in Europe seriously divided Christians." Indeed, "most ministers recognized the tendency of Pennsylvanians to be undogmatic about their denominational affiliation, attend a variety of forms of worship, and form congregations consisting of a 'mixed multitude.'" *"A Mixed Multitude":*

*The Struggle for Toleration in Colonial Pennsylvania* (New York: New York University Press, 1987), 145, 263.

2    Mary Augustina Ray, B.V.M., *American Opinion of Roman Catholicism in the Eighteenth Century* (New York: Columbia University Press, 1936), 112-13. Ray's work is still unsurpassed in its treatment of the pervasive nature of anti-Catholicism in colonial America.

3    Witness the pervasive anti-Catholicism of colonial almanacs and periodicals (Ray, 165-212), and the bigotry enshrined in pedagogy; the latter extending from the *New England Primer*—with its woodcut of the pope as the "Man of Sin"—to the Dudleian lectures at Harvard dedicated to the "Errors of the Church of Rome." Ray, 119-23 and 126-36.

4    Michael James Graham, S.J., "Lord Baltimore's Pious Enterprise: Toleration and Community in Colonial Maryland" (Ph.D. diss. University of Michigan, 1983), 272-73.

5    ACSC, Bo-1. The same statement may be found in James Walton's sermon, which follows Boarman's closely, cf. Wa-4.

6    ACSC, Je-10, Bol-7. Henry Neale likewise speaks of the Fathers of the Church disputing with the "heretics of their times." Nea-4. For other examples cf. Boa-1, Neal-A.

7    ACSC, Je-20, Bol-11.

8    ACSC, Boo-3. John Lewis uses the moniker in a similar way when he comments that "No one can deny...heretics...have denied, ridiculed and made a jest of every article of the Christian faith...." Le-9, and Ignatius Matthews refers to those "Greek and Latin testaments, which are not corrupted by heretics...." Mat-3.

9    ACSC, Di-14, Boa-4.

10    ACSC, Dig-3. James Farrar, in the midst of a discussion on the forgiveness of sins, stresses the necessity of contrition for the worthy reception of the sacrament of Penance, and claims that this element "silences the cries and calumnies of heretics" who claim that absolution is automatic and unrelated to the disposition of the penitent (Fa-2).

11    ACSC, Nea-4, Ne-10, Bol-12. Sylvester Boarman also makes use of "sectary" as well as "heretic," here using it in reference to Turks and other non-Christian groups (Boa-11). "Sectary," however, also seems to highlight divisiveness and zealotry.

12    ACSC, Bol-11. Richard Molyneaux, early in the century, refers to the Protestants as "adversaries" (Mo-1).

13    ACSC, Se-12, Se-15.

14    "On Taking Possession of the Episcopal See of Baltimore," ACSC, Car-6; also JCP, 1:476-78. This is dated 12 December 1790.

15    ACSC, Car-20; also JCP, 3:389.

16    Not that Luther was the only Reformer found worthy of mention by name; Calvin is mentioned at least twice (Bo-4, Se-10) and even Wyclif is referred to, though this citation was later excised (Se-7).

17  ACSC, Be-4. Beadnall is here following Bourdaloue, *"Sermon sur la parfaite observation de la loi,"* in *Oeuvres de Bourdaloue*, vol. 1, (Paris: Chez Firmin Didot Frères Libraires, 1840), 315.

18  ACSC, Hu-2.

19  ACSC, Hu-3. This passage is crossed out in the manuscript, perhaps by Hunter himself, so it is uncertain whether he ever publically delivered himself of this opinion.

20  ACSC, Pi-5. This accusation of sensuality levelled against many of the reformers is quite common in the English recusant literature that was available to the colonial Catholics. For example, Robert Parsons, in his *A Treatise of Three Conversions*, describes the indulgence dispute as a pretense by Luther to obscure the fact that his theological questions were motivated by the desire to marry: "So did Luther, being a Fryar, and meaninge to marry, broke with the Sea of Rome vpon the very like cause, for that he and his order of Augustine Friars, were not permitted to be preachers of Indulgences in Germany...." (Aldershot: The Scolar Press, 1976), 118. Robert Manning in his popular treatise *The Shortest Way to End Disputes About Religion*, blames Luther's arrogance for God's allowing him to fall into "even the most scandalous irregularities in practice." Indeed "His marriage...betrayed a weakness of so scandalous a nature, as...will be an everlasting mark of dishonor to the reformation, and a convincing proof that God had no hand in it." (Dublin: R. Cross, 1795), 157. Finally, in John Heigham's *The Touchstone of the Reformed Gospel* it is noted that "we call all Religious that after marry (as Luther, Bucer, Peter Martyr, and the rest of that lascivious rabble) Apostates, God's adulterers, incestuous sacrilegious and the like." (n.p., 1634), 107. All three of these works appear on various booklists in the Maryland Provice Archives: 57,1 (a book order from 1716); 3,15 (Newtown Memoranda Book); 49,2 (Joseph Mosley's Accounts).

21  ACSC, Pi-5.

22  ACSC, Mo-1.

23  For background, see Timothy W. Bosworth, "Anti-Catholicism as a Political Tool in Mid-Eighteenth Century Maryland," *Catholic Historical Review* 61 (October, 1975): 539-63; Joseph J. Casino, "Anti-Popery in Colonial Pennsylvania," *Pennsylvania Magazine of History and Biography* 105 (July, 1981), 279-309; Beatriz Betancourt Hardy, "Papists in a Protestant Age: The Catholic Gentry and Community in Colonial Maryland, 1689-1776" (Ph.D. diss., University of Maryland, 1993), 254-310.

24  ACSC, Mos-1.

25  George Hunter makes a similar point when he confesses: "We have no tyrants at this time to try by fire and sword the firmness of our faith...." ACSC, Hu-3.

26  ACSC, Mos-1.

27  ACSC, Bol-12. For another author's treatment of the ecclesiology of the sermons, see Raymond J. Kupke, "Dearest Christians: A Study of Eighteenth Century Anglo-American Catholic Ecclesiology," in ACPP, 55-86.

28    ACSC, Bi-6.

29    ACSC, Wa-4; see also Bo-1 for an almost identical statement, indicating that either one sermon was based on the other, or that both have a common source.

30    ACSC, Boo-3.

31    ACSC, Di-20.

32    ACSC, Bi-9.

33    This emphasis on the infallibility of the Church and its relevance in ending disagreements between the Roman Catholic Church and the Protestant churches mirrors the thesis of Robert Manning's *The Shortest Way to End Disputes About Religion*, (Dublin: R. Cross, 1795), a work that, in an earlier edition, was popular among English Catholics and is known to have been available in America (e.g., Father Mosley records having lent it out in 1765. MPA 49,2). In it Manning states that "The shortest way to end disputes about religion is, to reduce them all to this one question, viz., whether the Church which Christ has established on earth, be infallible in deciding matters of Faith? For if it once be fully and clearly proved, that Christ has established such a Church, then all are bound to submit to her; and the decision of this one general point cuts off all particular disputes" (9).

34    ACSC, Ro-9.

35    Ibid.

36    This rather severe analysis seems to be challenged by a sermon given by the George Hunter, in which he welcomes a "new-born Christian being newly born to Christ by the Sacrament of Baptism" and congratulates him for "embracing our persuasion preferable to all others after having implored in a due manner...Providence to direct you to the right way...." This would seem to affirm the legitimacy of making an informed choice to become Catholic—albeit one influenced by God. ACSC, Hu-3.

37    One must not imagine that the missioners were only "preaching to the choir"; on the contrary, there is evidence they often addressed their message to audiences of Protestants and Catholics. Hardy describes debates between the Jesuits and the Rev. Giles Rainsford, an Anglican, in Prince Georges County, Maryland, 230. Tricia Pyne quotes a report from disgruntled Anglican ministers, lamenting the fact that Jesuits "publick (sic) preaching is so notorious and unreserved, that there are known Instances of their preaching to large, mixed Congregations in Port Tobacco Court House, in Charles County," "The Maryland Catholic Community, 1690-1775" (Ph.D. diss., The Catholic University of America, 1995), 53. The missioners' zeal manifested itself outside the pulpit as well, and took a more personal form. Maryland's Governor Seymour complained in 1704 that the priests "by their style and assiduous Endeavours (sic) to promote their superstition, run about the country to make Proselites (sic) and amuse dying persons with threats of Damnation." Hardy, 110. Even the flock were active evangelizers; e.g., two laywomen in Maryland in the 1690's were charged with proselytism. Hardy, 70-71.

38    ACSC, Di-18, Di-17. The practice of citing the testimony of these pillars of

the Church is very common, cf. Be-9, Nea-3, Mat-8, Mol-1, Ro-18, Wa-5, Bol-1, Je-12, Pi-12; often reference is made to church councils as well, as in Ma-1.

39    ACSC, Bo-7(a).

40    Ibid.

41    ACSC, Pi-5.

42    ACSC, Boo-3.

43    *A Mixed Multitude*, 144. Henry Melchior Muhlenberg (1711-87), a native of Hannover, Germany, arrived in Pennsylvania in 1742, and played a vital role in the establishment of the Lutheran Church in the colonies.

44    ACSC, Pi-5.

45    ACSC, Bi-7.

46    A typical example of his reasoning is as follows: as part of the belief in the real presence, Catholics, like Protestants, believe that the Eucharist is a commemoration; however, Catholics also believe Christ is really present in the sacred species through transubstantiation, so "the only thing that can be said against us is that we believe more than is requisite...."

47    That these topics were truly contentious may be seen from a sermon by Bernard Diderich on marriage, wherein he depicts a Protestant spouse taunting the Catholic partner in the following way: "Go and adore your wooden gods, angels and saints; believe that a man can forgive sins, and that a god gives his flesh to eat, and his blood to drink!" ACSC, Di-33.

48    ACSC, Bol-8.

49    Another example of a well composed sermon that focuses on one disputed issue and seeks to establish its legitimacy vis-à-vis the objections of the reformers is James Ashby's homily on Marian devotion (based on Bourdaloue), ACSC, As-4.

50    ACSC, Nea-4. He labored on the mission from 1741-48. A similar statement may be found in the homily of Benet Neale, who notes that the question of good works "has been often mentioned, and much harped upon of late," Ne-10.

51    ACSC, Ne-10.

52    The reference to the Protestants here as "brethren" is noteworthy, due to its rarity.

53    ACSC, Hu-3.

54    ACSC, Nea-4.

55    ACSC, Wi-3. John Williams, alias Mannington, was born in Flintshire. He served in Maryland from 1758-1768, after which he returned to England. He was the first priest to reside permanently at the Frederick mission. Thomas Hughes, S.J., *A History of the Society of Jesus in North America, Colonial and Federal: Text*, 2 (London: Longmans, Green and Company, 1917), 695; Geoffrey Holt, S.J., *St. Omers and Bruges Colleges, 1593-1773: A Biographical Dictionary* (London: Catholic Record Society, 1979), 289.

56    Cf. for example ACSC, Wa-4, Bo-1, Bo-4, which speak of the "malice of heretics."

57    ACSC, Boo-3.

58    ACSC, Nea-4. Oftentimes the reason for this capriciousness is given as a desire for laxity in doctrine, such as will be amenable to corrupt nature (the same charge often used against Luther, Henry VIII, et al.). John Boarman says that the "late Heresiarchs" have "expunged out all things, that were hard and austere in the Christian religion, consequently what they left agrees very well with our sensuality and natural inclinations." Bo-7(a); while John Bolton comments similarly that "innovators" have broached "new tenets more suitable to corrupt nature." Bol-12. John Williams notes that since "our poor unfortunate country fell from its mother Church" it is common that "for the generality, that religion most prevails, that suits best with everyone's interest, that gives their passions leave to live at large." (This section was later excised) Wi-1.

59    ACSC, Car-23; also in JCP, 3:420-24. Carroll sees the genesis of this change in a "spirit of innovation," though he does not assign a motivation for it.

60    ACSC, Ca-5. The sermon is undated, and the place of its delivery is not noted. It most likely was delivered sometime between 1749/50 and 1756 (when Father Carroll died at the age of 39), in one of the missions of Saint Thomas Manor and Newtown where he was stationed, but the exact location is unknown.

61    (Emphasis mine). Though Carroll defends the actions of the priest in question, and notes later that "he desired nothing more than to have sealed his faith by the loss of his blood [were people that discontented?]," he admits "it was prudently judged that nothing was more capable of allaying the tempests raised in the neighborhood than his absence."

62    One should note in regard to the latter Carroll's reference to those who made no profession of "their Catholic religion."

63    In fact many Protestants were attracted, or at least not repelled, by the Jesuits' preaching. One Anglican minister in Anne Arundel County, Maryland, reported in 1741 that when he was too ill to conduct services, some of his parishioners attended Mass at the homes of local Catholics. Hardy, 236-37.

64    Though they were excluded by legal statute—the Act of Toleration of 1649 excluded Jews and Unitarians—at least one case we know of suggests it was possible for a person of Jewish faith to live and carry on business in Maryland. Cf. the story of Jacob l'Ambrosos (or Lumbrozo) in J. Moss Ives, *The Ark and the Dove* (New York: Longmans, Green and Company, 1936), 245-46.

65    ACSC, Dig-3, Le-6, Ne-10, Di-8, Far-1, Ma-1, Mat-8, Bol-21, Bol-24, Bol-6, Se-12, Boa-6, Car-21.

66    ACSC, Le-10, Boo-3, Di-7, Ma-3, Mat-6, Mol-1, Mol-6, Ro-20, Wa-3, Je-16, Je-6, Neal-10(a), Neal-9, Pi-17, Xb-1, Xb-5.

67    ACSC, Se-2, Boa-7.

68    ACSC, At-2(d), Fa-1, Boa-3, Le-15, Le-19, Le-21, Ne-1, Bol-4, Pi-6.

69    ACSC, Le-15.

70    ACSC, Le-21.

71    ACSC, Ne-1.

72    ACSC, Pi-6. An earlier section stating, "The malice of the Jews must fill us with horror, and we consider their barbarity with an emotion of

indignation....," has been crossed out, but considering the vehemence of the sections which remain, one wonders why. A section from a sermon of Charles Sewall, upbraiding the congregation for being "more criminal than the Jews, more criminal than those heretics, whose sacrilegious profanations you look upon with horror," also bears signs of having been excised. Se-12.

73 ACSC, Pi-5.

74 ACSC, Ne-2. James Carroll offers sympathy to his flock when they are "censured at every tea table, or in every ale house by the invenomed tongues of worldlings." Ca-3.

75 ACSC, Ha-4.

76 ACSC, Boa-5.

77 ACSC, Ro-4. Charles Sewall notes a similar tendency in Se-6(b).

78 The term "libertine" was used very loosely by the homilists, leading the modern reader to puzzle over just what kind of behavior is being indicated. As Henri Daniel-Rops has remarked in connection with French "Libertines" (where the term referred to a defined group of people who challenged orthodox views, who in England often went under the name of "Deists"), "This word led to some confusion: the Libertines professed total freedom, but freedom of what kind—intellectual or moral? In the case of many, no doubt, both." Quite often the word pointed to a moral, not purely intellectual, stance. In numerous instances libertines "were only epicureans, who...sought to combine 'a purified scepticism with pious sentiments'...." *The Church in the Eighteenth Century*, trans. John Warrington (New York: E. P. Dutton, 1964), 8-9. In America the vast majority of those labled as "libertines" or "deists" were in fact Anglicans who professed a "rational piety," which, while not latitudinarian, stressed "moderation, comprehensiveness, liberality of doctrine, and stability of custom" (see Henry F. May's excellent analysis in his chapter "Slumbers and Dreams of the Church," in *The Enlightenment in America* [New York: Oxford University Press, 1976], 66-87, here 75).

79 ACSC, Se-13. In another sermon Sewall identifies the rich man who ignored the plight of Lazarus (Luke 16:22) as a libertine: "bent upon the gratification of his sensual appetites, and carried away with the spirit of pride and libertinism, he despised the poor and neglected the commanded duties of God." Se-16.

80 As when Digges notes that "the most debauched libertine will still choose the modest and virtuous woman if he design[s] to marry...." ACSC, Dig-1. Cf. also Se-1, Se-2, Se-13, Se-15, Bo-1, Wa-4, Boa-12.

81 ACSC, Mat-7. Cf. also Mat-9(a), Bol-12, Dig-3, Be-4, Hun-1, Pi-13, Le-8, Li-3, Ro-14(a), Wi-1.

82 ACSC, Mol-7. While the sermon is undated, it was most likely preached in Philadelphia, the cosmopolitan center of the colonies, and a prime venue for Catholics to come in contact with the views of "enlightened" Anglican "libertines." The Catholic "libertinism" referred to by Molyneaux can thus be assumed to be similar to that found in the Anglican church; that is,

characterized by a downplaying of spirituality and the sacraments, emphasizing repentance and hope, and lacking a rigorous moral code; cf. May, 67. To arrive at a balanced understanding of what constituted a lax, "libertine" morality, however, one should keep in mind that many American enlightenment "libertines" were respectful of conventional morality. At the same time, Molyneaux was known for his "elegant life and manners," and thus should not be thought of as a stern, puritanical moralist. Cf. Henry Steele Commager, "The Term Philosophe," in *The Empire of Reason* (Garden City, NY: Doubleday, 1977), 243; and Philip S. Hurley, S.J., quoting Father John Carroll, in "Father Robert Molyneaux, 1738-1808," *Woodstock Letters* 67 (October, 1938): 277.

83    ACSC, Le-9, Boo-5.

84    ACSC Ma-6; Nea-1, Se-8; Bol-7; Di-14.

85    ACSC, Di-14. One hears an echo of the Anglican divine John Tillotson (whose sermons were "enourmously popular among Englishmen at home and in the colonies"), who wrote that the Gospel "commanded us nothing...that is either unsuitable to our reason or prejudicial to our interest...nothing but what is easy to be understood, and as easy to be practiced by an honest and willing mind." In May, 17.

86    ACSC, Bo-1.

87    ACSC, As-7.

88    ACSC, Car-17; also in JCP, 3:383-386. He refers specifically to worship "due only to the living God, being transferred, sometimes to an imaginary deity, decorated with the name of reason; sometimes to licentiousness, miscalled liberty...." making the connection with the revolution in France quite clear.

89    ACSC, Car-47; also in JCP, 3:386.

90    ACSC, Se-13 (emphasis mine).

91    ACSC, Dig-3. This comment is made in reference to the discipline of fasting.

92    ACSC, As-5. Cf. Be-6 and As-2, where reason is seen as a defense against sin.

93    ACSC, Le-11, As-7.

94    ACSC, Gr-1.

95    ACSC, Mos-1.

96    ACSC, Be-10. Beadnall himself had been arrested by the sheriff of Queen Anne's County on 22 September 1756, charged with saying Mass in the homes of David Jones and Thomas Browning the preceding July—the sermon text records that it was preached at "Jones's" [*sic*]. His homily would therefore seem to reflect personal experience. For a treatment of the arrest and Beadnall's petition to the Proprietor, see Edward B. Carley, *The Origins and History of St. Peter's Church, Queenstown, Maryland, 1637-1976* (Baltimore, 1976), 23-24.

97    ACSC, At-3(d). It should not be thought that Attwood, since he counseled submission, was lukewarm in his hopes for freedom of religious practice. In 1720 he had written a treatise called "Liberty and Property, or the Beauty of Maryland displayed in a brief and candid search into her Charter, Fundamental Laws & Constitution" which claimed, in the words of Emmett Curran, that

"religious freedom was the fundamental right upon which rested the enjoyment of all other rights and privileges...." Robert Emmett Curran, S.J., *American Jesuit Spirituality, The Maryland Tradition, 1634-1900* (New York: Paulist Press, 1988), 13. See also Gerald P. Fogarty, S.J., "Property and Religious Liberty in Colonial Maryland Catholic Thought," *Catholic Historical Review* 72 (October, 1986): 573-600. A version of Attwood's treatise may be found in *United States Catholic Historical Magazine* 3 (1889-1890): 237-63.

98  Hardy, 371.

99  Mosley was later barred from preaching for almost two years due to his failure to take an oath of allegiance to the new government. Isolated as he was at the Eastern Shore mission of Tuckahoe, he was unable to canvass his fellow missioners for their opinions of the oath. Cf. Curran, 100; and Mosley's own notation in his *"Ordo Baptizatorum / Ordo in Matrimonis Conjunctorum"* on 12 August 1778: "No sermon, having not qualified by an oath to be taken by Law, by all that would preach, *Vide* Laws, that took place the 1st of March, 1778 for Independence of America." An entry for 12 September 1780 announces: "Sermon, having qualified by a private Act." MPA, 4,5. In Philadelphia, the representative of the French government had as his "avowed object...to win over all the Catholics to the side of the Revolution, by showing them that the French alliance would give them a guarantee of liberty." Fathers Harding and Molyneaux, resident in the city, did indeed declare their support for Independence in 1779. *Historical Sketches of the Catholic Churches and Institutions of Philadelphia* (Philadelphia: Daniel Mahony, 1895), 39, 34.

100  Letter of 16 August 1775, in MPA, Mosley Letters.

101  Letter of 4 October 1784 in MPA, Mosley Letters.

102  ACSC, Car-26; also in JCP, 3:460-61.

103  ACSC, Car-3; also in JCP, 2:13-20. The sermon was delivered 19 February, 1792. James Hennesey offers a concise evaluation of Carroll's political objectives when he observes: "Carroll's task was to work out the accomodation between American republicanism and monarchical forms inherited from the church's past. In pursuit of that goal his own genuine acceptance of concepts basic to the American experience helped: religious pluralism in a state religiously neutral, freedom of conscience and of the exercise of religion for all, sensitivity toward and toleration of religious divergence." In "An Eighteenth-Century Bishop: John Carroll of Baltimore," in *Patterns of Episcopal Leadership*, ed. Gerald P. Fogarty, S.J. (New York: Macmillan, 1989), 9.

# Conclusion

Peter Bayley has written: "Preaching is a *littérature engagée*: it aims to convince men of certain ideas and move them to act in accordance with certain principles. It is a record of temperament, taste, and conviction, and an especially valuable record at a time when church-going is widespread, and mass media unknown."[1] Certainly there are few groups in American History about whom as little is known than the Catholics of Anglo-colonial America. Truly the church there was an institution that by all rights ought never to have existed. As Catholicism was legally proscribed in every colony to some degree for most of the eighteenth century (even in tolerant Pennsylvania certain basic rights like the franchise and office-holding were restricted for Catholics), it should come as no surprise that the Catholic clergy maintained a low profile. What is astonishing is the extraordinary dedication of these ministers to the pursuit of their labors with what their separated brethren acknowledged was an extraordinary measure of commitment. A vital aspect of this apostolic ministration was their preaching; hopefully the preceding chapters have brought to life a number of characteristic elements that can be summarized here by way of a conclusion.

Perhaps the most important insight concerning colonial Catholic homiletics is its practical nature, both in form and content, and the way in which the clergy adapted their preaching to the needs of their scattered, dispersed flocks. We have seen that in the composition of their sermons the priests relied on a variety of printed sources—yet they rarely were content with copying from them directly. Indeed, it would seem that quite often a variety of sources, together with the author's own observations, were woven together to form a tapestry that was tailored to fit the needs of the preacher's congregation. The homilists were not at all reluctant to take their theme from one published source, add a point or two from another author, and conclude with a paragraph from a third. Along the way they not only changed examples which they felt were inappropriate for their "frontier" congregations, but also altered the essence of the spiritual advice offered by their sources if they felt it was in any way unsuited to their audience. Thus while the colonial clergy were not by and large an innovative band, they do seem to have shown a measure of concern to craft sermons which offered solid spiritual advice and were adapted to the needs of their congregations.

In terms of content, the homilies tended to be eminently practical, focusing on the immense challenge that the Catholic community faced as it confronted the world around it. Those familiar with Christian homiletics would argue that it has always relied on certain unchanging themes: the image of the believer's journey through life as an unremitting struggle, and the "world" as a force to be opposed. But, in fact, Catholics in eighteenth-century Anglo-America did face the ever-present hindrance of an often hostile, or at best indifferent social order, which sought to stifle the living out of their faith by legal statute, theological argument, and ridicule. Assimilation into the surrounding Protestant culture was another challenge to the community, which was only enhanced by the scarcity both of clergy and opportunities for corporate worship. With these distractions, if not outright obstacles, to the practice of Catholicism in mind, the homilists chose to recommend a variety of time-tested spiritual aids to their flocks. These included not only the vigorous promotion of the sacraments, but also the cultivation of an interior spiritual life through personal, familial and communal prayer both morning and night, spiritual reading and the examen. Such a "personal" spirituality was vital if a colonial

Catholic was to maintain his or her faith in the midst of a hectic and often tumultuous life (which for many included the arduous task of working their own, or another's, land).

The sermons delivered throughout the eighteenth century betray a certain static quality, changing little in either style or content. With the exception of Bishop John Carroll, whose refined, erudite, and irenic tone can be contrasted with that of his confreres, there is a surprising continuity between the spirituality and language of the fathers of the first half of the century (such as Peter Attwood), and those of the later years (like Sylvester Boarman). Even Carroll, notwithstanding his cosmopolitan manner, insisted strongly on the necessity of the sacramental life, the great worth of personal prayer and sanctity, and the importance of maintaining one's Catholic identity, elements which anchor him firmly in the tradition of his brethren.

Still, we might ask, how successful were the homilists in speaking to their congregations? They regularly addressed their hearers in stern and categorical language, and one wonders if such an approach was fruitful. Though we have seen that the community in Philadelphia expressed their satisfaction with their clergy at least once, it also happened that a congregation was so displeased by something a priest had preached that the poor missioner had to be retired post-haste. This suggests that the Catholic laity were neither impossible to please, nor were they unperturbable to the point of somnolence.

Certainly, the life and well-being of the community was the major concern of the preachers. It is hard to ignore the importance they placed on the communal dimension of the Catholic faith. While there is no lack of attention paid to individual spiritual and moral behavior, a surprising emphasis falls on the societal implications of the Christian faith, not only by highlighting such "social" sins as detraction, but also by stressing the obligations that each Catholic had to the rest of their community (e.g., charity and almsgiving). Considering the dispersed nature of the Catholic community—the fact that it was composed of numerous local "domestic churches"— and the numerous external pressures it labored under, maintaining the internal cohesion of the congregations would indeed have been a high priority of the missioners.

It is interesting to note the way in which the sermons shed a ray of light on the relatively murky realm of Catholic life in colonial America. Tantalizing comments exist which highlight aspects of domestic life, slavery, sacramental and devotional practice, social mores, and relations with other denominations and the civil authorities. One looks in vain, however, for a discussion of the War for Independence, though, considering the political climate of the times, and the caution that Catholics were routinely obliged to observe, this is not entirely unexpected.

The homilists were certainly not shy about commenting on the relationship between the churches, and here they tended (again with the possible exception of Bishop Carroll) to view the wider Christian community with emotions which could hardly be described as charitable. Protestant churches were regularly seen as "adversaries" at best, whose members were ever on the watch to entice unsuspecting Catholics away from the "true" Church, and into one of the "schismatic" denominations which were founded on the whim and stubbornness of individual reformers. Though these attitudes seemed to moderate somewhat as the century neared its close, the homilists were never shy about denouncing "error" wherever they found it. These perspectives, though, grew out of the lived experience of countless attacks on the church, and the source of such intemperance on the part of the preachers was doubtless an acute awareness of the very real nature of the challenges offered to the Catholic minority.

When all is said and done, the priests' concerns were primarily to instruct and influence their flocks, who were seeking to live out their faith on what was the "frontier" of the New World, both geographically and religiously. They sought, in essence, both to instruct their hearers in Catholic teaching, as well as influence them to live out this faith in an oft-times challenging cultural context. St. Paul, we might venture to conclude, would indeed have been proud.

## NOTES

1   Peter Bayley, *French Pulpit Oratory, 1598-1650* (Cambridge: Cambridge University Press, 1980), 4.

# BIBLIOGRAPHY

## *Manuscript Sources*

Special Collections, Lauinger Library, Georgetown University, Washington, DC
American Catholic Sermon Collection
Ashby, James, S.J.: 11 sermons
Attwood, Peter, S.J.: 10 sermons
Beadnall, James, S.J.: 11 sermons
Beeston, Francis, S.J.: 2 sermons
Bitouzy, Germain Barnabas: 9 sermons
Boarman, John, S.J.: 9 sermons
Boarman, Sylvester, S.J.: 16 sermons
Bolton, John, S.J.: 27 sermons
Boone, John, S.J.: 7 sermons
Carroll, James, S.J.: 5 sermons
Carroll, Archbishop John: 57 sermons
Diderich, Bernard, S.J.: 33 sermons
Digges, John, Jr., S.J.: 3 sermons
Farmer, Ferdinand, S.J.: 1 sermon
Farrar, James, S.J.: 3 sermons
Fleming, Francis A.: 1 sermon
Frambach, James, S.J.: 1 sermon
Gallagher, Simon Francis: 1 sermon
Gerard, Thomas, S.J.: 1 sermon
Greaton, Joseph, S.J.: 4 sermons
Harding, Robert, S.J.: 4 sermons
Hunter, George, S.J.: 7 sermons
Hunter, William, S.J.: 1 sermon
Jenkins, Augustine, S.J.: 26 sermons
Lewis, John, S.J.: 22 sermons

Livers, Arnold, S.J.: 4 sermons
Manners, Mathias, S.J.: 3 sermons
Maréchal, Archbishop Ambrose: 1 sermon
Matthews, Ignatius, S.J.: 11 sermons
Molyneux, Richard, S.J.: 1 sermon
Molyneux, Robert, S.J.: 10 sermons
Morris, Peter, S.J.: 1 sermon
Mosley, Joseph, S.J.: 10 sermons
Neale, Benet, S.J.: 10 sermons
Neale, Henry, S.J.: 4 sermons
Neale, Archbishop Leonard: 35 sermons
Pile, Henry, S.J.: 26 sermons
Plunkett, Robert, S.J.: 7 sermons
Poulton, Thomas, S.J.: 1 sermon
Roels, Benjamin Louis, S.J.: 32 sermons
Sewall, Charles, S.J.: 24 sermons
Walton, James, S.J.: 6 sermons
Williams, John, S.J.: 3 sermons
Anonymous: 7 sermons

Archives of the Maryland Province of the Society of Jesus
Catholic School Manuscripts Collection

Early Maryland Jesuits' Papers
Attwood, Peter
Digges, John Jr.
Mosley, Joseph
Thorold, George

Jesuit School Manuscripts Collection

Archives of the Episcopal Diocese of Maryland, Baltimore
Thomas Cradock Collection

Verticle File
Addison, Henry, Rev.
Chase, Thomas, Rev.
Gordon, John, Rev.
Goundril, George, Rev.
Read, Robert, Rev.

## Printed Sources

Agonito, Joseph A. "The Significance of Good Preaching: The Episcopacy of John Carroll." *American Ecclesiastical Review* 167 (December 1973): 697-704.

*American Sermons: The Pilgrims to Martin Luther King.* Edited by Michael Warner. New York: Library Classics, 1999.

Augustine, Saint. *Christian Instruction.* Translated by John J. Gavigan, O.S.A. Washington, D.C.: Catholic University of America Press, 1947.

Bangert, William V., S.J. *A History of the Society of Jesus.* St. Louis: Institute of Jesuit Sources, 1972.

———. *Jerome Nadal, S.J., 1507-1580.* Edited by Thomas M. McCoog, S.J. Chicago: Loyola University Press, 1992.

Bayley, Peter. *French Pulpit Oratory, 1598-1650.* Cambridge: Cambridge University Press, 1980.

Beitzell, Edwin Warfield. *The Jesuit Missions of St. Mary's County, Maryland.* Abell, Md.: Privately Printed, 1976.

Blampignon, Emile-Antoine. *Étude sur Bourdaloue.* Geneva: Slatkine Reprints, 1972.

Bonomi, Patricia U. *Under the Cope of Heaven: Religion, Society, and Politics in Colonial America.* New York: Oxford University Press, 1986.

Bonomi, Patricia U., and Peter R. Eisenstadt. "Church Adherence in the 18th Century British American Colonies." *William and Mary Quarterly* 39 (1982): 245-84.

Bosley, Harold A. "The Role of Preaching in American History." In *Preaching in American History*, edited by Dewitte Holland, 17-33. Nashville: Abingdon Press, 1969.

Bossuet, Jacques. *Chefs-d'Oeuvres de Bossuet.* Paris: Chez Lefèvre, 1844.

Bossy, John. *The English Catholic Community, 1570-1850.* London: Darton, Longman and Todd, 1975.

———. "Reluctant Colonists." In *Early Maryland in a Wider World*, edited by David B. Quinn. Detroit: Wayne State University Press, 1982.

Bosworth, Timothy W. "Anti-Catholicism as a Political Tool in Mid-Eighteenth-Century Maryland." *Catholic Historical Review* 61 (October 1975): 539-63.

Bourdaloue, Louis, S.J. *Oeuvres de Bourdaloue*. 3 vols. Paris: Chez Firmin Didot Frères Librairies, 1840.

Boyle, Patrick. *Instructions on Preaching*. New York: Benzinger, 1902.

Bremond, Henri. *Histoire Littéraire du Sentiment Religieux en France*. 11 vols. Paris: Librairie Bloud et Gay, 1916-33.

Burton, Edwin H. *The Life and Times of Bishop Challoner, 1691-1781*. 2 vols. London: Longmans, Green and Co., 1909.

*Canons and Decrees of the Council of Trent*. Translated by Henry J. Schroeder. St. Louis: Herder, 1941.

Carley, Edward. *The Origins and History of Saint Peter's Church, Queenstown, Maryland, 1637-1976*. Baltimore, 1976.

Carr, Lois Green. "Sources of Political Stability and Upheaval in Seventeenth-Century Maryland." *Maryland Historical Magazine* 79 (Spring 1984): 44-70.

Carroll, Anthony, S.J., trans. *Sermons and Moral Discourses on the Important Duties of Christianity*. Dublin: James Duffy, 1855.

Carroll, John. *The John Carroll Papers*. Edited by Thomas O'Brien Hanley, S.J. Notre Dame: University of Notre Dame Press, 1976.

Casino, Joseph J. "Anti-Popery in Colonial Pennsylvania." *Pennsylvania Magazine of History and Biography* 105 (October 1981): 279-309.

*The Catechism of the Council of Trent*. Translated by J. Donovan. Baltimore: James Myers, 1833.

Chadwick, Hubert, S.J. *St. Omers to Stonyhurst*. London: Burns and Oates, 1962.

Challoner, Richard. *The Garden of the Soul; or a Manual of Spiritual Exercises and Instructions*. Philadelphia: Joseph Cruikshank, [1774].

————. *Think Well On't; or Reflections on the Great Truths of the Christian Religion*. Philadelphia: Carey, Stewart and Company, 1791.

Cheminais, Timoléon, S.J. *Sermons du Père Cheminais*. 5 vols. Paris: Chez George et Louis Josse, 1694.

Chinnici, Joseph P., O.F.M. *Living Stones: The History and Structure of Catholic Spiritual Life in the United States.* New York: Macmillan, 1989.

Colombière, Claude la. *Oeuvres Complètes du Vénérable Père Claude de la Colombière.* 6 vols. Grenoble: Imprimerie du Patronage Catholique, 1900.

Commager, Henry Steele. *The Empire of Reason.* Garden City, NY: Doubleday, 1977.

Connors, Joseph M., S.V.D. "Catholic Homiletic Theory in Historical Perspective." Ph.D. diss., Northwestern University, 1962.

———. "The Vincentian Homiletic Tradition I, II, III." *American Ecclesiastical Review* 138 (October 1958): 217-27; (November 1958): 338-50; (December 1958): 391-406.

Curran, Robert Emmett, S.J. *American Jesuit Spirituality: the Maryland Tradition, 1634-1900.* New York: Paulist Press, 1988.

Daley, John M., S.J. *Georgetown University: Origin and Early Years.* Washington, D.C.: Georgetown University Press, 1957.

———. "Pioneer Missionary: Ferdinand Farmer, S.J., 1720-1786." *Woodstock Letters* 75 (June, October, December 1946): 103-15, 207-31, 313-21.

Daniel-Rops, Henri. *The Church in the Eighteenth Century.* Translated by John Warrington. New York: E. P. Dutton, 1964.

———. *The Church in the Seventeenth Century.* Translated by John Warrington. New York: E. P. Dutton, 1963.

Dargan, Edwin C. *A History of Preaching.* New York: Burt Franklin, 1968.

Darrell, William, S.J. *Moral Reflections on Select Passages of the New Testament.* 2 vols., London: W. Bickerton, 1736.

———. *Moral Reflections on the Epistles and Gospels for Every Sunday Throughout the Year.* 4 vols., London, 1711.

Davies, Horton. *Worship and Theology in England.* Princeton: Princeton University Press, 1962.

Davis, Cyprian, O.S.B. *The History of Black Catholics in the United States.* New York: Crossroad, 1990.

Davis, Richard Beale. *Intellectual Life in the Colonial South: 1585-1763.* 2 vols. Knoxville: University of Tennesee Press, 1978.

Devitt, Edward I., S.J. "History of the Maryland—New York Province: VI, Goshenhoppen (1741-1889)." *Woodstock Letters* 62 (February 1933): 3-15.

————. "History of the Maryland—New York Province: XI, Deer Creek." *Woodstock Letters* 63 (October 1934): 400-405.

————. "History of the Maryland—New York Province: X, Saint Joseph's Church, Willing's Alley." *Woodstock Letters* 63 (April 1934): 213-30.

————. "History of the Maryland—New York Province: IX, Bohemia." *Woodstock Letters* 63 (January 1934): 1-38.

Dolan, Jay P. *Catholic Revivalism: The American Experience.* Notre Dame: University of Notre Dame Press, 1978.

————. *The Immigrant Church.* Baltimore: Johns Hopkins University Press, 1975.

Duffy, Eamon, ed. *Challoner and His Church: A Catholic Bishop in Georgian England.* London: Darton, Longman and Todd, 1981.

Durkin, Joseph T., S.J. "The Mission and the New Nation, 1773-1800." In *The Maryland Jesuits, 1634-1833*, edited by Robert Emmett Curran, S.J., 29-45. Baltimore: Corporation of Roman Catholic Clergymen, 1976.

Ellis, John Tracy. *Catholics in Colonial America.* Benedictine Studies, no. 8. Baltimore: Helicon, 1965.

————. "A Venerable Church of Maryland." *Woodstock Letters* 78 (May 1949): 133-39.

————, ed. *Documents of American Catholic History.* Milwaukee: Bruce Publishing Company, 1962.

Everstine, Carl N. "Maryland's Toleraion Act: An Appraisal." *Maryland Historical Magazine* 79 (Summer 1984): 99-116.

Fogarty, Gerald P., S.J. "The Origins of the Mission, 1634-1773." In *The Maryland Jesuits, 1634-1833*, edited by Robert Emmett Curran, S.J., 9-27. Baltimore: Corporation of Roman Catholic Clergymen, 1976.

————. "Property and Religious Liberty in Colonial Maryland Catholic Thought." *Catholic Historical Review* 72 (October 1986): 573-600.

Ganss, George E., S.J., ed., trans. *The Constitutions of the Society of Jesus.* The Institute of Jesuit Sources. Chicago: Loyola University Press, 1970.

Gillow, Joseph. *Biographical Dictionary of the English Catholics.* 5 vols. London: Burns and Oates, 1885-1903.

Gisbert, Blaise, S.J. *Christian Eloquence in Theory and Practice.* Translated by Samuel D'Oyley. London: H. Clements, 1718.

Gleis, Paul G. "German Jesuit Missionaries in 18th Century Maryland." *Woodstock Letters* 75 (October 1946): 199-206.

Gleissner, Richard A. "Religious Causes of the Glorious Revolution in Maryland." *Maryland Historical Magazine* 64 (Winter 1969): 327-41.

Gother, John. *Spiritual Works of John Gother.* Newcastle: F. Coates, 1792.

Graham, Michael James, S.J. "Lord Baltimore's Pious Enterprise: Toleration and Community in Colonial Maryland." Ph.D. diss., University of Michigan, 1983.

————. "Meetinghouse and Chapel: Religion and Community in Seventeenth Century Maryland." In *Colonial Chesapeake Society*, edited by Lois Green Carr, Philip D. Morgan, and Jean B. Russo, 242-74. Chapel Hill: University of North Carolina Press, 1988.

————. "Popish Plots: Protestant Fears in Early Colonial Maryland, 1676-1689." *Catholic Historical Review* 79 (April 1993): 197-216.

Guibert, Joseph de., S.J. *The Jesuits: Their Spiritual Doctrine and Practice.* Translated by William J. Young, S.J. Edited by George E. Ganss, S.J. The Institute of Jesuit Sources. Chicago: Loyola University Press, 1964.

Guilday, Peter. *The Life and Times of John Carroll.* 2 vols. New York: The Encyclopedia Press, 1922.

————. *The Life and Times of John England, First Bishop of Charleston (1786-1842).* 2 vols. New York: America Press, 1927.

————. "The Priesthood of Colonial Maryland." *Woodstock Letters* 43 (June 1934): 169-90.

Hanley, Thomas O'Brien, S.J. *Charles Carroll of Carrollton: The Making of a Revolutionary Gentleman.* Washington, D.C.: Catholic University of America Press, 1970.

Hardy, Beatriz Betancourt. "Papists in a Protestant Age: The Catholic Gentry and Community in Colonial Maryland, 1689-1776." Ph.D. diss., University of Maryland, 1993.

Heigham, John. *The Touchstone of the Reformed Gospel.* 1634.

Hennesey, James J., S.J. "An Eighteenth-Century Bishop: John Carroll of Baltimore." In *Patterns of Episcopal Leadership,* edited by Gerald P. Fogarty, S.J., 5-34. New York: Macmillan, 1989.

———. "Several Youth Sent from Here: Native-born Priests and Religious of English America, 1634-1776." In *Studies in Catholic History in Honor of John Tracy Ellis,* edited by Nelson Minnich, Robert Eno, S.S., and Robert Trisco, 1-26. Wilmington, De.: Michael Glazier, 1985.

Hilton, J. A. "'The Science of the Saints': The Spirituality of Butler's *Lives of the Saints.*" *Recusant History* 15 (May 1980): 189-93.

*Historical Sketches of the Catholic Churches and Institutions of Philadelphia.* Philadelphia: Daniel Mahoney, 1895.

Holt, Geoffrey, S.J. *The English Jesuits, 1650-1829: A Biographical Dictionary.* London: Catholic Record Society, 1984.

———. *St. Omers and Bruges Colleges, 1593-1773: A Biographical Dictionary.* London: Catholic Record Society, 1979.

Honrnyhold, Joseph. *The Commandments Explained in Thirty-Two Discourses.* Baltimore: Fielding Lucas, n.d.

Hughes, Thomas, S.J. *A History of the Society of Jesus in North America, Colonial and Federal: Text.* 2 vols. London: Longmans, Green and Company, 1917.

Hurley, Philip S., S.J. "Father Robert Molyneaux, 1738-1808." *Woodstock Letters* 67 (October 1938): 271-92.

Ives, J. Moss. *The Ark and the Dove: The Beginning of Civil and Religious Liberties in America.* London: Longmans, Green and Company, 1936.

Jedin, Hubert. *A History of the Council of Trent.* Translated by Ernest Graf. 2 vols. St. Louis: Herder, 1961.

Joerndt, Clarence V. *St. Ignatius, Hickory, and Its Missions.* Baltimore: Publication Press, 1972.

*The John Carroll Papers*, Edited by Thomas O'Brien Hanley, S.J. 3 vols. Notre Dame: University of Notre Dame Press, 1976.

Jordan, David W. "'The Miracle of This Age': Maryland's Experiment in Religious Toleration, 1649-1689." *The Historian* 47 (May 1985): 338-59.

Kelly, Ellin, and Annabelle Melville, eds. *Elizabeth Seton: Selected Writings.* New York: Paulist Press, 1987.

Kennedy, George A. *Classical Rhetoric and Its Christian and Secular Tradition From Ancient to Modern Times.* Chapel Hill: University of North Carolina Press, 1980.

Kirlin, Joseph L. *Catholicity in Philadelphia from the Earliest Missionaries Down to the Present Time.* Philadelphia: John Joseph McVey, 1909.

Krugler, John D. "Lord Baltimore, Roman Catholics, and Toleration: Religious Policy in Maryland during the Early Catholic Years, 1634-1649." *Catholic Historical Review* 65 (January 1979): 49-75.

————. "'With Promise of Liberty in Religion': The Catholic Lords Baltimore and Toleration in Seventeenth-Century Maryland, 1634-1692." *Maryland Historical Magazine* 79 (Spring 1984): 21-43.

Kupke, Raymond J. "Dearest Christians: A Study of Eighteenth Century Anglo-American Catholic Ecclesiology." In *American Catholic Preaching and Piety in the Time of John Carroll,* edited by Raymond Kupke, 55-86. Melville Studies in Church History. Lanham, Md.: University Press of America, 1991.

LaFarge, John, S.J. "Our Pioneer Adorers of the Blessed Sacrament." *Emmanuel* 35 (July 1929): 176-79.

Lewis, Clifford M., S.J., and Albert J. Loomie, S.J. *The Spanish Jesuit Mission in Virginia, 1570-72.* Chapel Hill: University of North Carolina Press, 1953.

Linck, Joseph C. "The Eucharist as Presented in the Corpus Christi Sermons of Colonial Anglo-America." In *American Catholic Preaching and Piety in the Time of John Carroll,* edited by Raymond Kupke, 27-53. Melville Studies in Church History. Lanham, Md.: University Press of America, 1991.

Luckett, Richard. "Bishop Challoner: The Devotionary Writer." In *Challoner and His Church: A Catholic Bishop in Georgian England,* edited by Eamon Duffy, 77-87. London: Darton, Longman, and Todd, 1981.

Luria, Keith P. "The Counter-Reformation and Popular Spirituality." In *Christian Spirituality: Post-Reformation and Modern*, edited by Louis Dupré and Don E. Saliers, 93-120. New York: Crossroad Publishers, 1989.

Lurie, Maxine N. "Theory and Practice of Religious Tolertaion in the Seventeenth Century: The Proprietary Colonies as a Case Study." *Maryland Historical Magazine* 79 (Summer 1984): 117-25.

McAdams, E.D. "Jesuit Missionaries at Elkridge, MD." *Woodstock Letters* 74 (March 1945): 30-34.

McGrain, John W., Jr. "Priest Neale, His Mass House, and His Successors." *Maryland Historical Magazine* 62 (September 1967): 254-84.

McNamara, Robert F. *Catholic Sunday Preaching: The American Guidelines, 1791-1975.* Washington, D.C.: Word of God Institute, 1975.

————. "John Carroll and Interfaith Marriages: The Case of the Belle Vue Carrolls." In *Studies in Honor of John Tracy Ellis*, edited by Nelson Minnich, Robert Eno, S.S., and Robert Trisco, 27-59. Wilmington, De.: Michael Glazier, 1985.

Manning, Robert. *Moral Entertainments on the Most Important Practical Truths of the Christian Religion.* Dublin: Richard Grace, 1839.

————. *The Shortest Way to End Disputes About Religion.* Dublin: R. Cross, 1795.

Massillon, Jean-Baptiste. *Oeuvres de Massillon.* 2 vols. Paris: Chez Firmin Didot Frères Librairies, 1853.

————. *Sermons by Jean-Baptiste Massillon.* Translated by William Dickson. Brooklyn: T. Kirk, 1803.

Mattingly, John, S.J. "Documents." *Catholic Historical Review* 2 (October 1916): 316-19.

May, Henry F. *The Enlightenment in America.* New York: Oxford University Press, 1976.

Melville, Annabelle M. *John Carroll of Baltimore.* New York: Charles Scribner's Sons, 1955.

————. *Louis William DuBourg: Bishop of Louisiana and the Floridas, Bishop of Montauban, and the Archbishop of Besançon, 1766-1833.* 2 vols. Chicago: Loyola University Press, 1986.

Metzger, Charles H., S.J. *Catholics and the American Revolution*. Chicago: Loyola University Press, 1986.

Norman, Sister Marion, I.V.B.M. "John Gother and the English Way of Spirituality." *Recusant History* 11 (October 1972): 306-19.

O'Neill, Charles Edwards, S.J. "John Carroll, the 'Catholic Enlightenment' and Rome." In *American Catholic Preaching and Piety in the Time of John Carroll*, edited by Raymond Kupke, 1-26. Melville Studies in Church History. Lanham, Md.: University Press of America, 1991.

Parsons, Robert, S.J. *A Treatise of Three Conversions*. Aldershot: The Scolar Press, 1976.

Peay, Bede S., O.S.B. "Change in the Theology and Practice of Preaching in the Roman Catholic Church in the United States, 1935-1983." Ph.D. diss., Saint Louis University, 1990.

Perry, William S., ed. *Historical Collections Relating to the American Colonial Church*. New York: AMS Press, 1969.

Pyne, Tricia T. "The Maryland Catholic Community, 1690-1775." Ph.D. diss., The Catholic University of America, 1995.

Quigley, Robert Edward. "Catholic Beginnings in the Delaware Valley." In *A History of the Archdiocese of Philadelphia*, edited by James F. Connelly, 1-62. Philadelphia: Archdiocese of Philadelphia, 1976.

Quinter, Edward H., and Charles L. Allwein. *Most Blessed Sacrament Church, Bally, Pennsylvania*. Bally, Pa.: By the authors, 1976.

Ray, Sister Mary Augustina, B.V.M. *American Opinion of Roman Catholicism in the Eighteenth Century*. New York: Columbia University Press, 1936.

Repetti, W. C., S.J. "Catholic Schools in Colonial Maryland." *Woodstock Letters* 81 (May 1952): 123-34.

Reville, John. *Herald of Christ, Louis Bourdaloue, S.J.* New York: Schwartz, Kirwin, and Fauss, 1922.

*The Roman Catholic Prayer Book: or Devout Christian's Vade Mecum*. Baltimore: William Warner, 1814.

Russell, William T. *Maryland: the Land of Sanctuary.* Baltimore: J. H. Furst Company, 1907.

Schwartz, Sally. *"A Mixed Multitude": The Struggle for Toleration in Colonial Pennsylvania.* New York: New York University Press, 1987.

Skaggs, David C. "Thomas Cradock Sermons." *Maryland Historical Magazine* 67 (1972): 179-80.

————, ed. *The Poetic Writings of Thomas Cradock, 1718-1770.* Newark: University of Delaware Press, 1983.

Skaggs, David C., and Gerald E. Hartdagen. "Sinners and Saints: Anglican Clerical Conduct in Colonial Maryland." *Historical Magazine of the Protestant Episcopal Church* 47 (1978): 177-95.

Smith, Donald George. "Eighteenth Century American Preaching: A Historical Survey." Ph. D. diss, Northern Baptist Theological Seminary, 1956.

Sommerfeldt, John R. *The Spiritual Teachings of Bernard of Clairvaux.* Kalamazoo: Cistercian Publications, 1991.

Spalding, Thomas W., C.F.X. "Frontier Catholicism." *Catholic Historical Review* 77 (July 1991): 470-484.

————. "The Maryland Tradition." *U.S. Catholic Historian* 8 (Fall 1989): 31-58.

————. *The Premier See: A History of the Archdiocese of Baltimore, 1789-1989.* Baltimore: Johns Hopkins University Press, 1989.

Van Voorst, Carol L. "The Anglican Clergy in Maryland, 1692-1776." Ph.D. diss., Princeton University, 1978.

# Index